From Zion to Atlanta

Memoirs

Walker L. Knight

© 2013

Published in the United States by Nurturing Faith Inc., Macon GA

www.nurturingfaith.net

Library of Congress Cataloging-in-Publication Data is available.

ISBN 978-93-8514-16-6

To

Daddy's
Memory

Mother's
Love

and

Oakhurst's
Faithfulness

Contents

FOREWORD

By Marv Knox

Walker Knight gripped the controls of his small airplane. Trusting God, the plane and his own skill, he flew on when a storm blew up the Mississippi River from the Gulf of Mexico.

That was years ago, when several staff members at the Southern Baptist Home Mission Board held pilot's licenses and flew—partly to save money, but also to enjoy the adventure—across the United States on assignment. Everett Hullum, Walker's longtime associate editor for the board's *Home Missions* magazine, recalled:

> Walker was flying us from St. Louis to New Orleans on a story coverage when we ran smack into a semi-hurricane coming out of the Gulf. It was dark. Walker was on instruments. Lightning was flashing on all sides, and the fury of the winds was tossing us up and down, hundreds of feet at a time. I was hanging on for dear life to everything that wasn't bolted down in the cockpit.
>
> Suddenly the thunder clapped, the lightning seared the sky, and we whooshed downward—the nose of the plane pointed straight at Mother Earth.
>
> I'd been growing more and more anxious, but Walker had remained calm and imperturbable, as is his way. This sudden downward plunge must have gotten to him, too. He was pulling back on the wheel with all his might when I heard him say, "Whoa, whoa!"

Knight, recipient of the 2002 William H. Whitsitt Courage Award, kept his composure, fought off the downdraft, steered through the storm, and landed his plane. And Hullum, of course, lived to tell about it.

Friends and associates, as well as close observers of Southern Baptist history during the last half of the twentieth century, could agree that plane ride characterized the life and ministry of Knight, who has served God in religious journalism with Baptists for five decades.

They talk about Walker's purpose and wisdom, his insight and integrity, his faith and courage. As a Baptist journalist, he calmly articulated a message of missions ministry that focused on grace, compassion, inclusion, and reconciliation, even when storms of protest threatened to blow those ideals out of the sky. His vision took flight and carried others with him to destinations previously unimagined.

Walker scarcely could have imagined them himself while he was growing up in the home of a newspaper editor—who taught him the journalism trade and provided one of his earliest influences, at once positive and negative.

Walker's early involvement in journalism and his developing spiritual sensitivity set off competing desires. Eventually, however, he discovered through learning and experience a ministry of seeking justice through journalism.

When he saw racism and other troubling issues at play in Baptist life, he addressed them.

"I felt journalists' lights should be shed on these," he said. "It wouldn't be done through preaching, but through reporting."

Walker set a new standard for denominational journalism by repeatedly devoting entire editions of *Home Missions* magazine to specific issues that impacted the context for missions. He gained a reputation for cultivating talented associate editors. He nurtured their skills and passion, blessed them to do their jobs and took the heat their stories generated.

Walker advanced civil rights without belligerence, said his friend and colleague Dallas Lee. "He was not confrontational, but he was faithful to his instinct of faith. He tried to drive the issue forward, but in a very sensitive manner."

Through the magazine, Walker continually held up a mirror to Baptists, forcing them to face issues that shaped society and impacted the church, Hullum added.

"Not only did Baptists find themselves confronting the truth about race, but also being challenged on such varied fronts as the death of the family farm, the problems of migrant workers, the psychological problems of the pastorate," Hullum recalled.

Strong criticism came from near and far.

"Walker became the lightning rod for every racist, bigot, crackpot, and shallow thinker" in the Southern Baptist Convention, Hullum said. "He never flinched, as far as I know."

Walker left the magazine's editorship to start an independent national news journal in 1983, during the battle for control of the SBC.

"My desire was to see a national publication for Baptists, to let both sides argue it out," said Walker, who insisted that the newspaper abide by his high standards for journalistic fairness and openness.

His friend and former pastor at Oakhurst Baptist Church in Decatur, Georgia, John Nichol, has spoken of Walker's consistency throughout his life and ministry: "He is one of those Christians who is in it for the long haul. No matter how long it takes, he'll be right there."

NOTE: This foreword is adapted from an article written by Marv Knox, editor of *The Baptist Standard*, for *The Whitsitt Journal* on the occasion of Walker Knight receiving the William H. Whitsitt Courage Award from the Whitsitt Baptist Heritage Society in 2002. It is used with permission.

PREFACE

When I was told in 1992 that there would be a fourth grandchild, I thought chances were slim that I would see my grandchildren reach adulthood. For even in fifteen more years I would be eighty-three, and in the Knight family that is a long time. Even in Mother's Henderson family, with Granddad living into his nineties, most everyone else died in their seventies.

With that depressing thought in mind, I determined I would consider writing my memoirs, but I actually undertook an abbreviated autobiography. My grandchildren, I thought, should know what it was like to grow up in the 1930s in Henderson County, Kentucky. How wonderful it would have been to have had a first-person account from any of my parents or grandparents—to read events from their perspective, not just from the history books.

One day I sat down before my computer (maybe if there had been computers we would have more memoirs) just to get a feel of how it might go. Once I started I couldn't easily stop. Nell went off to visit her mother for a week in Tyler, Texas, and I spent almost every hour—when I wasn't working at *SBC Today/ Baptists Today* or playing golf—writing, sometimes six- and eight-hour days and finishing a version of this book in less than a month.

I worried at first that I might not remember much and that not in detail. Memory seemed to be keyed to emotions. Almost every strong memory was associated with a feeling that had seated the memory in my mind, like a spanking, a fear, an injury, joy, or depression. Once back in time these memories had associations, and those triggered other associations.

Some nights I would lie in bed remembering, spending almost the entire night in light sleep, almost wallowing in memories. One night the names of many persons I had not been able to recall just came to me, like John Bennett and Everett Hooper.

Writing of these early periods was like therapy must be for some people. In fact, therapy probably would be good preparation for the writing of memoirs. I know that some painful periods took more than the usual willpower to stay at the task of writing, and when I finished chapter six, "War," I was in tears, almost sobbing.

Even as I write this, I tear up. I had trouble remembering in that period some things and their sequences, probably because they were so painful to live through.

I know that my early life profoundly affected my adult life: For one thing, children of alcoholics gravitate to the Christian ministry, and they have, according to studies, grandiose plans of making everything right and tend to be perfectionists. Well, two out of three hit home.

Also, my parents either were not around or were extremely busy with other children, so not a lot of affection was openly expressed. Mother and I did more of this in our letters while I was in the military than we ever did in each other's presence. My own children, especially sons Walker and Ken, helped me to be more demonstrative after they became adults. It was easier for me to relate to my daughters Nelda and Jill, but even then I was not as demonstrative as I might have been.

Another thing, being the oldest of nine gave me such a sense of responsibility that I have to hold back in groups to keep from seeking to take charge. We Knights appear to all have some of that characteristic, however, and we have an above-average sense of competitiveness whatever our endeavor, at work or at play.

If we can't compete with someone else, we will compete with each other. I can't discover from whence came the competitiveness, for it seems to have been with me from my earliest memories. Maybe it was just part of the culture, and not just being in a large family or being small, although these would no doubt contribute.

On a visit to Coral Gables in Miami to see Walker and his partner, Jud McDonald, we stopped at a bookstore and I found a number of helpful volumes. But two—*Inventing the Truth*, a book on writing memoirs, and *Children of Alcoholism*, a survivor's manual—have been very helpful.

I have read extensively of others who wrote memoirs and autobiographies: Buechner, Wakefield, Nouwen, Jung, Shaw, Thoreau. All were helpful, but especially Buechner's three books—*Journey, Now & Then,* and *Telling Secrets.* I enjoyed "wallowing" in my memories. Frederick Buechner, in *Telling Secrets,* wrote an appropriate word:

> But I talk about my life anyway because if, on the one hand, hardly anything could be less important, on the other hand, hardly anything could be more important. My story is important not because it is mine, God knows, but because if I tell it anything like right, the chances are you will recognize that in many ways it is also yours. Maybe nothing is more important than that we keep track, you and I, of these stories of who we are and where we have come from and the people we have met along the way because it is precisely through these stories in all their particularity, as I have long believed and often said, that God makes himself known to each of us most powerfully and personally. If this is true, it means that to lose track of our stories is to be profoundly impoverished not only humanly but also spiritually.

And in *Now & Then* Buechner added, "If we really had our eyes open, we would see that all moments are key moments."

Acknowledgments

Acknowledgments must start with the most recent, and then travel backwards. First, to my dear friend Dallas Lee who not only assisted with editing and direction in my writing but also aided in the gift of perspective about my life.

An amazing new friend is ninety-six-year-old poet Margaret Clark Sargent who read an early version of my manuscript. She had worked as a proofreader at the Nuremberg trials in Germany and graciously reread my writing for punctuation and other changes.

Thanks also must be extended to John Pierce, editor of *Baptists Today* and publisher of Nurturing Faith books, for additional editing and insights and to Jackie Riley for copyediting the manuscript.

Thanks go to my extended and scattered family for corrections, going through albums, dusty drawers, and yearbooks for pictures and recalling stories I had forgotten.

I apologize for a twenty-four-plus-year section for failing to name an amazing group of cohorts who shared my journey as writers, photo-graphers, designers, artists, and office helpers while at the Baptist Home Mission Board in Atlanta. Any achievement this group and I accomplished was possible because of the graciousness of President Arthur B. Rutledge who led the agency during its most profound and comprehensive accomplishments in history.

I did not name these scores of friends because of my memory and the fact that my bound volumes have been sent to Mercer University with the promise of other materials later. The same is true for ten years at the *Baptist Standard* in Dallas.

One reason for not saving more of my written memories is that I did not expect to live into my late eighties, especially to outlive Nell, my wife of sixty-five years who died in 2008 from the ravages of Alzheimer's disease with Bell's palsy.

Everett Hullum, an unselfish high achiever in many areas, captured the strengths in my prose poem, "The Peacemaker," and has written the introduction for its printing in this book. Its continuing journey still amazes me.

First, in 1972, this poem was five opening devotionals delivered at Carolyn Weatherford's request for a meeting in Florida. Then Everett, over my reluctance, placed it on twenty-two pages of the December issue of our magazine, *Home Missions*.

Then Bob Burroughs created it as a musical, but it was never published. However, the Oakhurst Baptist Church choir thought I should hear it once and performed it under Mike Weaver's direction.

Oakhurst pastor John Nichol used portions of the poem in a sermon heard by Robert Maddox and one of President Jimmy Carter's sons. Maddox wrote it into President Carter's remarks at the 1979 Israeli-Egyptian Peace Treaty signing.

Widespread publicity called it to the attention of the Baptist Peace Fellowship, and it has been republished a number of times, especially the phrase "Peace like war is waged"—showing up on banners and even a small magnet.

The last complete printing added the subtitle "A Psalm of Peace." May this poem continue to bless lives.

Chapter 1

"Bunk"

The day I was born must have been very similar to the Februarys I experienced after 1924—overcast and cold. The air had a smell about it, a taste even, as the thick, low clouds held the smoke from the coal fires close to the earth and the smoke left its mark everywhere. The dominant smell in winter was always the smoke.

The virgin snows, which covered the land with their purity, were violated by the soot, and within a day or two after falling the snow turned into a dirty gray, as did the carefully washed clothes and even the window panes of our houses.

No stories were told about 1924 being especially difficult in Kentucky. As I would read about the times later, only a few years past World War I, the economy was on the upswing. Most people who wanted work labored in the mines, the farms of Henderson County, and in the stores or the few manufacturing plants that had located in or near the town of Henderson.

The city was a smaller twin city to the larger Evansville, Indiana, just across the long bridge spanning the Ohio River at the point where Kentucky's Green River emptied into the larger stream.

The streets of Henderson were so broad, cars could park not only on the sides but also in the middle, and the streets crisscrossed the high bank beside the Ohio River like a grid of asphalt laid to keep the earth and rock from sliding into the deep, muddy water.

The river provided the reason for the city. Its power and transportation were free for the harnessing. The river also had played another, less spectacular role in shaping the character of the people who had settled Henderson County. While the river was an unobstructed highway for the traveler going southwest or laboring up to the northeast, it was a barrier north and south, and many years passed before a bridge spanned the nearly mile-wide rush of water.

The people on each side of the Ohio developed independently and consequently in unique ways. On the Indiana and Illinois side, hardy Germans and Dutch had moved out of northeastern states such as Pennsylvania to farm the countryside, but into Kentucky and Tennessee came the Scotch, the Irish, and the English from Virginia and North Carolina following Daniel Boone's trailblazing expeditions into and across the Appalachian hills.

Boone was largely financed by Colonel Richard Henderson of Virginia, who had dreamed of founding the nation of Transylvania in the territory. Henderson, a judge for England, had formed the Transylvania Company with himself as president, and in 1775 the company had paid three Cherokee chiefs 10,000 English pounds for an area as big as Virginia itself.

Colonel Henderson died in North Carolina in 1785, but in 1797 the company's surveyors followed the Green River to its mouth and there laid out the city in neat squares and wide streets, incorporating the small settlement of Red Banks. Henderson's nephew, also named Richard Henderson, settled in the county and named the city for his famous uncle.

Henderson is known as the only town on the Ohio River that has never been in it, a tribute to the surveyors who picked the high ground. The ancestors of my grandfather, Tandy Henderson, have been traced to Scotland in the sixteenth century, as have the ancestors of my grandmother, Mariah Griffin, but neither line crossed that of Colonel Henderson.

The area was graced not only by the dominant rivers, but an even greater wealth lay hidden beneath the rich farm lands of Henderson County—coal, bituminous coal. It was the southern end of one of the largest deposits in the nation. In 1924 that black stone formed from long-decayed vegetation heated the homes, powered the industry, and warmed the work force.

While my life has taken me to all the continents, save South America, and I have lived in Georgia longer than I did in Kentucky, the geography seared upon my soul has two deep rivers, waving fields of tasseled corn, and a landscape marred by the ugly corrugated steeples of coal mines. At Henderson the Ohio River stretches as wide as most of the Mississippi into which it empties not many miles southwest, and wherever I was to gaze upon a river, it was always compared to the picture I carried in my soul.

The Yangtze in China had steeper banks, but it was not as wide. The Brazos in Texas was little more than a creek by comparison, and the Chattahoochee in Georgia might serve canoes, but not a paddle-wheeled steamboat. Henderson had its wide streets and high banks, and Henderson County in my mind was deep, wide rivers; rich, fertile farms and black, rusty mines; and the memory of these features marked all of us who were born and raised there.

On that February 6 in 1924 I entered the world as the child of Cooksey Bennett Knight, twenty-two, and Rowena Henderson Knight, then nineteen. Both had come from the small village of Zion, and it would be to that village where our hearts would always be drawn.

Bennett, whom friends called Ben, had found employment as a reporter for the twice-daily *Gleaner & Journal* newspaper, despite having only an eighth-grade education. Businesses seldom checked educational qualifications at the time. The questions publisher Leigh Harris had probably asked were, "Can you type? Can you spell? Can you write?"

Given his nature, I'm sure Daddy's answer to all three was a forceful "Yes." He was probably bluffing on the typing, but he would quickly develop a hunt-and-peck system using three fingers from each hand, and he had "Anna," as he called Mother, to help with the spelling. She had graduated from high school.

Besides, Daddy was tired of farming; he hated working at the coal mines, and he was bored with the only other work he had tried—barbering in Zion. In fact, Daddy had closed his barbershop to take the position with the *Gleaner & Journal*.

Over and over I heard family members relate how Frank Reid, the Zion barber, had pushed Daddy into barbering one day when Daddy had ridden his young horse, Trevor, to the barbershop to show off a new western saddle.

The men loafing at the shop had all come outside to inspect the saddle when Daddy had mentioned it, and Frank had started needling Ben about what he would take for the outfit—horse, bridle, and saddle.

3

"You don't have enough money!" Daddy had quipped, probably wanting to appear older and wiser, especially since the group included the man he was named after—Cooksey Bennett, a well-to-do farmer with whom my grandfather, Homer Hiram Knight, was close friends.

"Surely, you've got some idea," Frank insisted. "Come on, now. What'll you take? I may need a good horse."

Daddy had looked around at the small barbershop with its swivel chair; the row of clippers, combs, razors, and mugs; the coal stove, cabinets, and cane-bottomed chairs lined against the walls for waiting customers and visitors.

Finally, he said, "I'll trade even for your dad-blamed shop!"

The crowd gasped slightly and quieted, looking now at the barber. They sensed the joking had stopped. Frank walked back to the door of his shop, as though to appraise its contents and then walked around the horse.

He stopped in front of Ben and loudly announced, "It's a deal. I'll trade even-Steven. I been want'n to go to Lou'ville and wondered what I'd do with this here shop."

Frank stuck out his hand, and Daddy looked down at it for a long moment before taking it to shake on the deal. Thus Daddy had become a barber, and while we boys loved the story, we would always hate having our hair cut by the old dull clippers he never gave up.

After officially handing Trevor's reins to Frank, Daddy had walked up the slack-covered road to home and soon returned with his father in tow. With Frank supervising, he cut Papa Knight's hair. Ben's older brothers—George and Homer—were lucky they were farming, but Belle—Momma Knight to us—had come a few minutes later to witness the historic occasion.

However, the economics that had forced Frank to leave Zion did the same for Daddy. After a year, he sold most of the equipment and took the job as a reporter in Henderson.

Walker's paternal grandparents, Belle and Homer Knight, in the 1920s. Papa Knight died in 1929, and Momma Knight went to live with her daughters.

4

I was not the first child born to Ben and Anna. Mother became pregnant the first year of their marriage, but near the end of her term the child was stillborn. They buried the boy in a tiny box near the gooseberry bushes beside Granddad Tandy Henderson's white frame house in Zion. Maybe that was the way stillbirths were handled in those days, but after I learned the story, that area of the house and yard was hallowed.

Granddad Henderson was named William Tandy, and he had married Mariah Griffin. Anna was the second of their four children; Mary Bernice was the oldest. After Mother came William Douglas (Doot) and finally Daniel Shacklett (Shack).

Granddaddy had probably heard that I was to be named Walker Leigh, Walker from Walker Smith, the business manager at the *Gleaner*, and Leigh from Leigh Harris, the owner. But Granddaddy had other plans. He thought everyone but himself had to have a nickname.

Maybe Tandy sounded enough like a nickname so that no one had bothered giving him another one. He had a nickname picked out for me, however—"Bunk."

A close friend of his was Bunk Chaney. And Bunk it was until I entered the Army in 1943, where I became known simply as Knight and only later would friends and acquaintances call me Walker.

I never held it against Granddaddy, though. In fact, I never thought much about it. My cousins were Russ and Coonk, or Buck and Peeny. Two of my brothers became Buddy and Bubba, the latter a child's version of brother.

My earliest memory when we were living in Zion is associated with the pain of a spanking by my mother, quite possibly my first—at least it was the first to register on my psyche as well as my bottom. At the time we were living in a small house next door to Granny and Granddad Henderson in Zion. I must have been somewhere between two and four years old.

A bright coal fire burned in the fireplace, casting light and shadows around the dimly lit room. A large circular, brown rug covered most of the floor, and I played on the rug with a fuzzy puppy. I was encouraging the tiny dog to act inappropriately when mother suddenly entered the room. The spanking followed, and the puppy and I were separated.

I don't know where Buddy was during this episode, but I am sure he was somewhere in the house, probably still in an infant bed. He was born the twelfth of August the second year following my birth, and was promptly named Cooksey Bennett Knight Jr. I never learned why my parents had not named me after my father, for it was the custom to so name a firstborn son.

It could have been they had intended to name the stillborn boy Junior, and grief or the fear of casting some spell upon my life had led them to choose Walker Leigh instead. Or there was the possibility that Daddy was seeking favor from the executives at the newspaper. By the time Buddy came along my parents had probably forgotten these reasons, and the baby received the blessing or the curse of being named after Daddy.

Of course, our newest addition had to have a nickname, so he was called Buddy for no reason that I ever learned. Only eighteen months separated us, providing the grounds for a rather intense sibling rivalry in which I always had the upper hand by virtue of size and age. At times his frustration would become so intense he would resort to attacking me with sticks or stones.

Once, when he had complained in tears for the umpteenth time to a rather distraught mother, she had blurted out, "Well, hit him with something." But most of the time we played well together, and everyone knew us as "Bunk 'n Buddy." We were seldom separated.

By the time I was five we were living in a white, frame "shotgun" house on First Street in Henderson. It was 1929, the first year of the Great Depression, but Daddy still held his job with the newspaper.

Our house got its name from its length: four rooms deep, one behind the other, with a hallway running the entire length of the left side. The narrow front was spanned by a porch that began at the sidewalk. The purpose of the construction was to place the most house on the smallest of lots, and our house was one of four identical structures, side by side, separated by about eight feet of bare yard. A small backyard provided room for a clothes line, which mother always had filled.

By this time our family also included two girls: Betty Jean (born July 16, 1927) and newborn Dorothy Rose (born December 2, 1928). Girls didn't get nicknames for some reason, although Dorothy did get hers shortened to Dot later.

Mother, however, didn't always shorten our names or use the nicknames. Quite frequently she called each of us by our full name, especially when she was "put out" with one of us. When I heard her say, "Walker Leigh!" I jumped.

I do not remember seeing much of Daddy during those days. The burden of the four children, all of us under six years of age, fell entirely upon Mother. She was a small, attractive woman with slightly curled auburn hair, a quick smile and an even quicker mind.

Mother had a zest for living that attracted everyone to her. She seemed always able to find a bright side to the most difficult situation. And she was willing to put aside other tasks to organize the family for a picnic or some other outing.

Because Tandy and Mariah had insisted, Mother had graduated from high school, topping Daddy's education by four years. Daddy was only five feet six inches tall, but he was trim and handsome, with dark, slightly waved hair, heavy eyebrows and a native intelligence that made everything come easy for him. When he was a cub reporter, however, he had depended on Anna for his English and spelling.

Now he was working long hours, as the paper had cut back on its staff, and he quite frequently fought off the fatigue with a few bottles of beer. Leigh Harris, with the help of his wife, Jane, was still producing both newspapers, the *Gleaner* in the morning and the *Journal* in the afternoon; however, they were basically editions of the same paper.

The latest news would be placed into whichever edition was available. No Kentucky paper provided much competition, but the large Evansville daily maintained an office in Henderson and bled off significant advertising and circulation.

The most exciting moments of my early life were those when Daddy took me downtown to the paper on Elm Street, housed in a beautiful colonial building.

Once, Publisher Leigh Harris, a tall, imposing man with baggy eyes and lined face, approached me with the question, "Son, what's your name?"

I knew that he knew, but I quickly answered, "Walker Leigh Knight," stressing the Leigh. He handed me a dime, saying, "Get yourself something with this dime, but if your name had been Leigh Walker, I would have given you a dollar."

I immediately ran to Daddy with the request to have my name changed, but I should have gone across to the business side and told the short, heavyset, cigar-smoking Walker Smith about the offer, to see if he would at least have matched it.

The busy back shop attracted me because of the varied activity. The odor of ink, paper, and hot metal mingled with the smoke from cigars and cigarettes, and the noise of the machines made conversation difficult. I would stand as long as allowed beside my favorite Linotype operator, watching him hit the keyboard to drop the matrixes and the space bars into the line arm. When filled it would be raised to form a mold for the line of type cast with hot lead.

Then the matrixes and space bars would be redistributed to their slots in the large magazine, and the slug of type would drop into its place on the right side of the operator. More than once I would be handed a hot slug with my name on it. At other times I would follow the type to the stone slab where the page would be made up inside a large metal frame the size of a single page, the larger headline type having been set by hand or on another machine.

Photographs, or cuts, had been etched into dots on zinc plates and mounted on blocks that made them type high. These pages were placed on the flatbed Mehle Press in the basement and run out four pages to a side. Other men operated small job presses for calling cards, stationery, or circulars.

I was also fascinated by the daily task Daddy had of receiving the news from the Associated Press office in Louisville. For this he placed a headset over his ears and used a telephone at the end of a flexible extension attached to the wall.

Daddy, with coat off, tie open, and an unlit cigar in his mouth, sat at his typewriter pounding away while someone in Louisville read to him the latest news. Daddy had learned to type well with no formal instruction, and he used three fingers on each hand to beat with a steady and rapid rhythm heavily upon the well-used Underwood.

I could not wait until I was old enough and smart enough to work at the newspaper in any capacity.

Chapter 2

HOUSES AND SCHOOLS

My formal education started in the first grade of the grammar school at the corner of Center and Green Streets in Henderson, known as the Center Street School. I had spent half a year in the kindergarten, however, housed in a small separate building at the same location. Kindergarten was an exciting half-day's play with blocks and sand and books and crayons.

I probably got the half year of kindergarten because my birthday came in the middle of the school year, and I'm sure Mother welcomed having one less child at home for the morning. Three others filled the house: Buddy, Bettye, and Dorothy—with another child on the way.

I walked the four blocks to school in fair weather, enjoying the time with others and feeling grown up. With three other children at home, Mother could not accompany me. Daddy, now promoted to managing editor at the newspaper, most often had worked late at night on the *Gleaner's* morning edition, so he would be in bed when I left for school. But if it were raining, he would get up and drive me in our Model A Ford—an inexpensive car owned by half the population.

The school's silver fire escape fascinated all the students who saw it as an exciting ride, as one made circles on the descent. The metal structure clung tightly to the right side of the three-story, imposing red brick building capped by a white cupola.

The white slide looked as though someone had attached a misplaced silo in which to store the grains of truth the school was feeding to the children. However, for us it was a fantasy express, and we explored it at every opportunity during school hours and afterwards if we found the doors open. The slide did not go directly down, but circled round and round inside the container.

The metal slide had a tendency to rust, but we found that if we took waxed bread wrappers to sit upon we could happily grease the ride and clear up the rust. Thus prepared, we would descend with exhilarating speed through the darkness, getting a glimpse of where we were when we passed the window light of the second and then the first floor before being dumped out unceremoniously into the gravel yard.

I have often wondered how safe such fire escapes were. Would they jam with students in an actual fire and would they become dangerously heated because of their all-metal construction? Thankfully, this one was never tested in an actual fire, and was not duplicated anywhere else to my knowledge.

Daddy soon moved the family to a two-story brick house on Ingram Street, even closer to the grade school. We children loved the spacious stairway near the front door of the house, for the railing was one more free ride. We also had more room and even a small front yard. Daddy was becoming better known in the city; and he and Mother widened their circle of friends, including the county sheriff and his wife.

Daddy often sang in a barbershop quartet composed of friends. He loved to sing such songs as "Sweet Adeline," "Bicycle Built for Two," and "My Gal, Sal."

One Sunday, Mother and Daddy were entertaining guests in the living room and the conversation was animated and gay. All of the children old enough to walk had been sent outside to play. I was told to watch the younger children, but they were playing safely in the backyard, so I had found a special place between the shrubs under the large window on the front. From my hiding place I could overhear the adult conversation through the slightly opened window.

Daddy was telling one of his latest racial jokes: "This Negro family had gone blackberry picking with another family, and when they got to the field where the bushes grew, the teenagers had separated from the adults. After some time had passed, the mother of the teenage boy called out, 'Son, you getting any?' and the boy had replied, 'Uh huh, black-berries, too.'"

While I didn't fully understand the joke at the time, I remembered it and told it to older boys who explained it very clearly and graphically.

That the joke was told at the expense of black people was part of the racism of that day. Blacks lived in another section of town, went to their own schools, and we children usually saw them only where they worked or shopped.

When the music teacher, who visited our class on certain days of the week, came to lead the second grade in singing, I participated with all the sound my small voice could produce, thinking I could sing like my Daddy. While I sang, however, the teacher moved closer in order to hear me more clearly. I poured it on.

When we had finished the song she came to my desk and said, "Walker, please do not sing. You are getting the entire class out of tune." It was my first time to discover I could not carry a tune, and I never enjoyed singing after that day.

For some reason we did not stay long on Ingram Street, moving to a house on Cherry Street at the west end of town only a few blocks from Leigh Harris's mansion, which could have influenced the move. It meant Buddy and I would attend another school. The house provided one compensation. It was but a few blocks from open fields with exciting areas for us to explore, and explore we did.

We spent as much time as possible out of the house, as mother was busy with the newest of our clan: William Griffin, born June 5, 1931 on Daddy's twenty-ninth birthday and, of course, he had a nickname— Bubba. In the fields we played hide-and-seek, discovered reed-like plants strong enough to make kites or bow and arrows, and we found one plant we thought resembled tobacco, so we rolled our own and smoked the weed.

The brown frame house had been built on a small hillside, with a three-foot-high retaining wall holding back the small yard in the front, but the back yard was spacious and included a two-room shed with one room usually filled with coal. One day I undertook to create a parachute by taking an old bicycle tire and attaching a large blanket.

Holding it over my head I tested my parachute by jumping from the restraining wall, but this was not high enough to allow the air to inflate the blanket. Next I climbed on the porch railing and jumped over the shrubbery, again not high enough. Finally, I went to the coalhouse, climbed to the roof and jumped. I severely sprained my ankle and walked for weeks with a crutch and a bandaged foot.

The neighborhood included a number of teenagers, and one boy in particular paid more than usual interest to our group of youngsters.

After a few days of playing with us outside, telling us wild stories about his experiences, he invited us to visit with him inside the house when his parents were gone. He led us small, wide-eyed boys to the bedroom where he lay on the bed, pulled down his pants and revealed the largest, angry private any of us had ever seen. When he invited us to stroke it, we all turned and fled, leaving him literally with his pants down. We avoided him completely after that.

One morning at breakfast—it must have been Sunday, as Daddy was eating with us—we heard a popping noise coming from the nearest room of the shed. Suddenly Daddy jumped up, shouting, "Oh, my God!" as he ran to the shed with all of us following, wondering what had excited him. When he threw open the shed door the popping sound was louder, accompanied by a hissing.

An entire batch of newly bottled beer had not been mixed properly and had exploded. He lost the lot. These were the years of prohibition, and most drinkers brewed their own—Daddy not excepted. I'm sure we could ill afford the expense of replacement, but Daddy had to have his beer.

We lived on Cherry Street for less than a year before moving to another "shotgun" house on Third Street, not many blocks from the houses where we had lived on First and Ingram Streets. We children never knew why we moved so often, but it must have had some connection to Daddy's drinking, the deepening depression, and our growing family.

I remember the Third Street house because of two events. Once we were playing softball beside the house in a game that included Dot and Bettye. Since the girls were too small to bat, I was hitting for Bettye, and she stood behind me waiting to run. Buddy pitched the ball. I swung and missed. But in coming around I hit Bettye on the forehead with the bat, knocking her down and raising a knot nearly half the size of the ball. She was rushed to the doctor's office but was found to be only slightly the worse for the severe blow.

The other event was a Christmas gift for all the children from our parents: a complete twenty-four-volume set of Junior Classic Books. I was overjoyed. One half of the set was age graded, starting with a collection of the world's nursery rhymes and proceeding through excerpts and essays of the best of literature.

My favorite section included the stories of King Arthur and the Knights of the Round Table. I read them again and again. Our games from that time on took a turn toward making wooden swords and shields. And why not? Were we not already Knights?

The other half of the set of books consisted of complete novels, such as *Little Men, Little Women, David Copperfield,* and *Treasure Island.* I soon devoured them all, for I had discovered the wonderful world of books. I would never again experience a dull moment that could not be escaped into the pages of a well-written book.

Within months Daddy found a better house a block away on Fourth Street, but it was beside the L & N (Louisville and Nashville) railroad line. Trains with their angry steam engines and constant smoke were not pleasant to live beside. In a way we were not so much beside the railroad as below it, for the railroad at this point began a long climb to the bridge that crossed the Ohio River. A few blocks north of our house the railroad tracks were high enough to cross above the streets.

Our move to this house, coming so quickly after all the other moves, was very unsettling to me. While the house itself—the usual frame dwelling with a spacious porch—was better than the shotgun at the other corner of the block, at nine years of age I felt the status of living next to the railroad was demeaning, and I was now old enough to be sensitive to such things. Besides, we found it difficult at first to sleep through the night as the passing trains shook the house while chugging their way up the grade. But people usually can adapt to most anything, and later we were not even conscious of the trains at night.

Also the family had grown again with the birth of Mary Ruth on March 9, 1933, and the sexes were now even at three each. Mother was now caring for six of us—nine years and younger. It seemed she constantly had two in diapers. Our back yard was always filled with these fluttering white flags, and for the longest time Mother did all her washing by hand on a scrub board.

Except for the house on Cherry Street, we seemed always to be living within walking distance of Immanuel Baptist Church. At times we were but two blocks away. Almost as early as I can remember I occasionally attended a Sunday school class in the basement of Immanuel's large, imposing building on Second Street. The entrance to the sanctuary stood twenty steps above the sidewalk, guarded by the huge, white colonial pillars that seemed to grace every building I liked.

I remember the sanctuary as a dark, spacious but inviting area with light from stained glass windows casting interesting patterns around the room. Mother and Daddy almost never attended the church, but they did encourage any of us who wanted to go to attend Sunday school and/ or worship services. Both of my parents had grown up attending Zion Baptist Church. The only pastor of Immanuel that I remember was Truett Miller Sr., a pleasant, rather large man who had a soft-spoken way with children.

The move to this side of town made it mandatory that we attend a new school, my third in four years. Bettye, now six years old, had joined Buddy and me (at eight and nine) in this insistent search for education. My unhappiness with the family's move and my confusion with events I did not understand manifested itself in discipline problems at school. Once I was sent to the principal's office for disobedience and talking when a student was in charge of the class while the teacher was out.

I received a lecture and was told to bend across a chair while I was spanked—a very humiliating experience. At home that night I received an even harder spanking when Daddy read the note I was forced to take home. As he whipped me with his belt, he said, "Remember this, Walker Leigh: you will always receive more and harsher punishment at home any time you are disciplined at school."

Once was enough. I never received another spanking at school.

Walker (right) at age 10 with his siblings in Zion in 1934 before moving to Henderson: Buddy (9), Dot (5), Bettye (7).

Buddy and I began to make the best of our situation. We explored the world of the railroad and the switching yard across the tracks. We would climb the huge parked boxcars, search through the empty ones, and on top run the length of the walkways, jumping the space from one car to the next when they were close enough. Other boys joined us, and we fashioned new versions of hide-and-seek, cops and robbers, or cowboys and Indians in and out and around the yards. Workmen would often run us off, but we would return as soon as they were out of sight.

When these games grew tame, we found more dangerous amusement. Trains moving north up the long grade to the bridge were forced to slow their speed, especially if they had stopped to drop off or pick up boxcars in Henderson. We would run alongside the slow-moving train, grab the metal ladder of a boxcar and swing ourselves upon the step to ride for a block or more before dropping off at a safe place. If the train was especially long, we could take more than one ride.

Almost all of my earliest childhood memories relate to events that took place outside of the house. Things inside the house were probably hectic, or we were constantly admonished to be quiet: "The baby's asleep" or "Your daddy's sleeping" or "Do your playing outside where you have room for all that."

I spent a big part of the winter months inside reading, sprawled on the floor or bed or in some corner out of the way. In the summer I read outside, usually lying in the swing with my head on a pillow and one foot pushing slightly on the chain to give a gentle movement to the swing.

During summer months country relatives would often give Mother some relief by having one of us spend weeks and even a month or more with them. My favorite at this time was to stay in Zion with Granny and Granddad (Tandy and Mariah) Henderson. They had moved to Zion when newlyweds from Hopkinsville, Kentucky, but both had relatives in Henderson County. Granny was a Griffin, and there was a large number of Griffins throughout the county.

Everyone thought of Hopkinsville as the site of the insane asylum, and if we thought someone was acting strangely we would say, "You ought to be sent to Hopkinsville." In fact, Granny and Granddad did rent their home in Zion for a couple of years in the early 1930s to take work at the asylum, Granny as an orderly and Granddad as a carpenter. One of his duties was to build coffins. Everyone was thrilled when they returned to Zion.

When staying in Zion I could play with cousins Russ and Coonkie Nichols. Russ was nearly three years my senior and Coonk only a year older, both big enough to dominate the decision of what we would play and who did what, a change in roles for me. Both Russ and Coonk had quick tempers, but they were interesting playmates who could be counted on for new ways to spend summer days.

15

A favorite pastime was to construct rabbit boxes using Granddad's tools and lumber, for he was a carpenter and contractor. His constant reminder was, "Put the tools back where you found them."

The rabbit boxes were a little larger than a shoebox, just big enough for a good-sized rabbit to enter. In the back third of the top we bored a hole in which we inserted a stick with a notch at the end to hold the stick from coming out. Another long stick was attached by leather to this and draped across a Y-shaped stick planted firmly in the top, and at the other end of the long stick was the trap door, also attached by leather.

The door was held within a groove above the opening by the first stick. We placed carrots or other rabbit food inside at the back of the trap, so when the rabbit entered to eat he brushed against the notched stick and the door dropped. We made three or four of these traps, carried them to the fields where we found rabbit trails, and then left them there for the unsuspecting prey.

Once caught, we would either eat the rabbits or sell them. They were especially treasured by two black families in Zion. If we ate them, we tanned the skins by stretching them fur side in on boards, and when soft and pliable we used the pelts for hats or mittens.

We also made slingshots ("nigger killers" we said in our unknowing prejudiced ways). These were Y-shaped sticks with rubber strips from automobile inner tubes tied to each end of the fork and then attached to leather squares, which would hold the rock. From hours of practice we became rather expert in shooting these stones at bottles, cans, or birds, and even at each other.

We found another use for the inner tubes by cutting across the tube to make a large rubber band, and we took a board about two inches high and eighteen inches long to which we attached a clothespin at one end. The clothespin would hold one end of the rubber band while it was stretched to the other end.

These became our guns, and by opening the clothespin to release the rubber band we could shoot each other without inflicting much pain. We devised many variations of this gun, making them longer by tying rubber bands together or creating better release mechanisms.

Also, we spent hours shooting marbles. For this game we established a line and about three feet away drew a circle into which each player placed an equal number of marbles. We would take turns shooting with our taws at the marbles. Taws were either larger marbles or agates made from hard stone, not the cut glass that often shattered.

Any marbles that we knocked out of the circle became ours if the game was "keeps." But if we had not decided on "keeps" at the start, we returned the marbles to each other and decided a winner by the number of marbles.

A variation on this game was to draw a six-foot circle, place our marbles in the center, and shoot one at a time from anywhere on the circumference. We looked for "suckers," that is, unskilled youth, with a bag full of new marbles, whom we could talk into a game of "keeps."

Granddad's two-acre yard and garden area was a magical land to be explored time and time again. As I entered the driveway I passed two stately pear trees on the left, like sentinels against unwanted visitors. Next I approached a low-spreading plum tree inviting me to partake of its large bright purple fruit. If I continued along the fence, instead of turning right toward the house and the side porch, I came to the small, three-hole privy walled within a high wooden stockade.

Granddad often moved the privy, then planted tomatoes where the old one had been. They were some of the largest tomatoes anyone in the county grew, but almost no one would eat them if they knew their origin.

The stable, with its huge loft, stood to the right of the privy and for the longest time housed a cow and buggy but later became the garage. As I continued along the back fence separating Granddad's place from Newman's Auto Garage business, I found two apple trees, each of a different variety, but these trees did not produce summer fruit and held little attraction for me. To their right was a three-room shed: washroom, tool room, and coal room. These rooms seemed to personify my grandparents' industry.

Granny and Granddad never seemed to stop working. Granny was so neat she swept the bare ground in front of the washroom around the huge, black wash pot. Each Monday, Granddad filled the pot from the cistern and built a roaring fire that eventually had the water boiling. Then Granny threw in the lye soap she had made and dumped in the clothes, stirring the lot with a huge ladle. The clothes would be rinsed in a big, number ten washtub beside a hand-cranked wringer through which the clothes were passed to press the water out before they were hung on the line.

If I continued around the yard, I came to the cherry tree—my favorite of all the fruit growing in the yard. It was planted close to the fence where the Newman Pruits lived, and they shared in the fruit. Out from the cherry tree and near the house were two Damson plum trees, which never seemed to grow very large, and whose dark fruit dared me to eat them before they were fully ripe. If I did, my mouth would pucker up so much I could hardly spit.

Finally, I came to the garden, always without weeds and well tended. Running along the side nearest the house was a magnificent grape arbor, a most welcome place to build roads for toy cars, all the while eating my fill of the juicy fruit that dangled above me.

Beside the house were the gooseberry bushes, a place of reverence for those of us who knew that our stillborn brother had been buried near there. On the other side of the house we could slip into the dark, damp cellar that always seemed to have some water in it. The cellar was filled with Granny's canned goods, potatoes, apples, and the little wine that Granddad made from the grapes, for most of the grapes ended up in Granny's grape jelly. We found the wine very sweet to the taste when we snitched a sip from one of the jars.

We loved Granny's interesting and inviting house. Chimneys, like huge brick bookends, rose on each side, while a flue served the kitchen and dining room. A low porch spanned the entire front of the house, and it held a swing and rockers. The large back porch contained the mysterious cistern, a wide deep hole lined with bricks then covered with mortar to hold the water drained off the roof. The cistern was covered with a wooden frame topped by a wide-mouthed hand pump.

A drainpipe from the roof held a lever at the fork of a Y so that when it began raining, Granddad allowed the first few minutes for the water to cleanse the roof, before turning the liquid into the cistern. Also, if the cistern was nearly full, he did not add more water. In dry spells water had to be hauled to fill the cistern, which stored not only the drinking water but also water for washing clothes and bathing.

Inside the kitchen, Granny presided over a handsome black stove trimmed in chrome with a warming area about head high. The stove burned wood and coal, and the surface was large enough for many dishes to be cooking at the same time. The oven produced treats that could drive a hungry boy wild, for Granny had a well-earned reputation as one of the best cooks in Henderson County.

Her coconut cakes were three layers high and surrounded with big flakes of freshly ground coconut. Her oyster dressing at Thanksgiving was as heavenly in its own way as the coconut cake, and her biscuits melted in my mouth. She made a corn pudding that tasted like dessert. We never had to be called to a meal at Granny's. We were usually there waiting.

Granny and Granddad's bedroom was just off the kitchen in the dead center of the house in a small, windowless room. With two other bedrooms available and more spacious, I never knew why they chose this smaller room. Maybe they wanted the room because it was the closest one to the stove and to the back door. The room held a brass bedstead on which Granny piled a soft, rolling mound of a feather mattress in which we children could get lost.

Granny once complained of Tandy being hard to sleep with and a grandchild suggested she might use one of the other beds. "I didn't marry Tandy Henderson to sleep in another bed," she snapped and the subject didn't come up again.

Both grandparents were affectionate, but Granddad especially liked to hold us and tease. When I was small, he would sit me on his knees and give me a bumpy ride while he half sang:

Ride a little horsey, up and down;
Ride a little horsey, all around.
Ride a little horsey, up and down;
Ride a little horsey, don't fall down!

Then he would spread his legs and allow me to fall gently to the floor. Almost every time he held me he asked if he could chew my ear. When I protested, he would offer a nickel. And if I still refused, he would act as though he was chewing my ears anyway, tickling me to no end. Afterwards he usually gave me a nickel.

Granddad had a reputation as a hard worker and a stern employer. Once when Cager Hatfield (the nickname came from a former job of managing the cage at the mine that carried the men deep into the mines) was working as a carpenter for Granddad to construct a barn, Granddad had him climb a tall pole in order to nail a board at the top. Cager scaled the pole and was hanging on with all his strength to his slippery perch, trying his best to hold the board, hammer, and pole with his two hands. Granddad shouted from the ground (probably joking), "Cager, I'm paying you to work with both hands!"

On another occasion when Granddad was converting an old store near Cousin Ed's blacksmith shop into a house for Aunt Mary and her family, he enlisted all of the children big enough to work. The old store had once housed a grocery, a post office, and a barbershop, but for years it had stood empty or was used for storage. Granddad stripped it down to its shell and rebuilt it into a three-bedroom house.

This day Russ, Coonk, and I were helping roof the structure, and we were hammering away. Coonk, like the others of us, was new at the task, and he was choking the hammer by holding it near the head, getting no leverage to strengthen his blows. Granddad watched him for a while, then yelled for Coonk to throw him the hammer, which Coonk carefully did.

Granddad took his handsaw and proceeded to cut off six inches of the handle. He threw the sawed-off hammer back to Coonk with the words, "Here, I was afraid you'd hurt yourself." None of us ever choked up on a hammer again.

Newman's Garage was located behind Granddad's stable and operated by Newman Pruitt. Boys were not encouraged to hang around the garage, but a few men often gathered there. Newman, tall and lanky, smoked a pipe continuously while he worked or when sitting propped back in his chair. He talked the least of any man I ever knew. Customers bringing in their cars for repairs would tell him the trouble and he would just nod his head, or if he had to, ask a terse question.

If he said something otherwise, you almost jumped in surprise. His only child, a son we called John N., was a couple of years younger than I and not much fun to play with. Being an only child, he did not have good interpersonal skills and was clingy, getting mad if we left to go play somewhere else when his mother refused to let him leave the yard. We felt sorry for him because of her overprotectiveness, but we weren't about to stay confined to that yard.

Next to Mother, Granny was the person I most loved. I begged to be allowed to visit Zion and to stay with her, not only because of her excellent meals and the chance to play in the yard and with my cousins, but also because of the special attention she paid to me and the love she expressed. Hers was a quiet and gentle affection that was never confining or demanding but that nevertheless held an expected discipline. Granny's love was a constant in a time of moving and uncertainty, and Granddad was a figure of strength and power, someone to look up to and depend upon.

Granny and Granddad were active members of the Zion Baptist Church, a congregation founded before the Civil War. The Baptists worshipped in a long, white frame building whose sides were graced with clear, deep windows. The interior was heated by two pot-bellied stoves, one on each side about halfway down the inside of the auditorium.

The oak pews were serviceable but hard to sit on for long periods of time. Overhead wires crisscrossed the ceiling, providing paths for the curtains that divided the single room into many smaller ones for Sunday school classes. The pulpit and choir area was raised about a foot higher than the rest of the room and was surrounded by a railing, which I figured was either to fence the choir in or us out.

I loved to hear the congregation sing, "We're marching to Zion, beautiful, beautiful Zion. We're marching upward to Zion, the beautiful city of God." I thought someone had written the song especially for those of us in Zion, Kentucky, for it expressed my sentiments about the small town exactly.

Granddad was treasurer for the congregation, and after the offering was taken he would dump the coins and bills from the plates into a large cloth bag, carry it home, and drop it into the storage area of the seat on their oak hall tree in the foyer. Later, when he had time, he would take the sack out, count the money, and deposit it in the bank. I enjoyed helping him count the stacks of coins.

Zion Baptist almost always found its pastors from the Southern Baptist Theological Seminary in Louisville, usually among the graduate students. The pastors would drive down on Friday and back on Monday. Two who became nationally well-known among Southern Baptists were A. C. Miller, later head of the Christian Life Commission, and Davis Wooley, who would lead the Historical Commission, both located in Nashville, Tenn.

When I was nine the pastor was Clyde Hanks, who later became a missionary in Africa. He was preaching a revival for the church, and Granny was taking me to every service. She had started asking me questions about whether I believed Jesus was the son of God and did I feel "lost." I tried to answer as I thought she wanted, and one night when Hanks was giving the invitation for people to come to the front to make a profession of faith in Christ, Granny nudged me ever so slightly.

I slid out to go take the pastor's hand. I found that I had made everyone happy with the decision, but since I lived in town I was not expected to join the church or to be baptized there. I did not say anything about it at Immanuel Baptist Church. But who can deny that God could use a grandmother's concern to start a small youth upon the path of service to God?

The basement of the Zion grade school provided—despite the fact that it sloped toward the front stage area—a room big enough for community folk dancing. Van Byrne would bring his fiddle and Cager Hatfield his guitar, while other musicians would add their talents on occasion. At least fifty people would attend, taking turns with square dancing or the Virginia Reel.

The reel was so easy. Most of us were allowed to dance a set or two when men and women lined up across from each other, with couples taking turns moving to the center and do-si-do'ing around each other, grabbing hands and skipping down the line and back, while someone called out the steps. At one point all the couples would hold their clasped hands high and the dancers would go under their arched arms. I loved the music, the dancing, and the close community feeling of such occasions, hoping Zion would have a community dance every visit I made to Granny's.

Our extended family included not only the Hendersons but also Daddy's parents, Homer Hiram and Belle Staples Knight, who also lived on the edge of Zion behind Cousin Ed Henderson's blacksmith shop. We called them Mama and Papa Knight. Each was an orphan, raised by families in the country, and no one knew any previous history. They seemed older than Granny and Granddad, and we seldom spent the night there. Papa Knight farmed land just outside Zion, but he died in 1931 at the age of seventy-two. He seldom joked or kidded us.

I remember him as a small, quiet man, whiteheaded with a bushy white mustache. When I visited he prayed long, solemn prayers at meals, at times so long Mama Knight would interrupt saying, "Homer, say the blessing now and your prayers at night."

Mama Knight continued to live alone for many years after his death, and she always had a huge jar of tea cookies. Even when I stayed with my other grandparents, I would run up to Mama Knight's to raid her cookie jar.

We had uncles, aunts, and cousins all over the county. Mother's sister, Mary Bernice, had married Johnny Nichols (he was called Johnny Nick or just Nick). Daddy's sisters, Mary Lou and Ninny, had married Johnny's brothers Peck (Fredrick Young) and Touie (Robert Louis). (It was years later before I knew their legal names.)

Because we touched the Nichols from three marriages, we felt we were kin to that whole clan. Having close relatives, especially loving grandparents, filled an emotional void in my life left by Daddy's heavy work schedule and increased drinking. Granddad Henderson especially provided me with a positive role model.

I search my memory for tender, loving moments with my parents, especially my mother whom I loved dearly, but those moments were not strong enough to have been seared into my memory. I realize that other than the first eighteen months of my life, there was always a new, helpless baby demanding Mother's almost constant attention within the enlarging family. Now I wonder how she even found the time to keep us fed and clothed, much less meet our increasing emotional needs. And she had the burden almost entirely to herself, for Daddy was either at work or somewhere drinking with friends.

It is possible that Daddy's drinking and Mother's repeated pregnancies placed dampers upon my spirit, and it was not the practice of either the Hendersons or the Knights to demonstrate affection by hugging and verbalizing one's emotion. I never felt unloved or rejected, just emotionally cast adrift to fend for myself, "to be the oldest," to be responsible for the others, to be the one in charge, thus to grow up fast.

Daddy would still take me to his office where I would fill the time learning to type and also running errands for him and the other workers. And if I was sent to buy Cokes, I was always treated. Daddy on these occasions, especially riding back and forth, would often talk to me about his dreams of working for other newspapers, but he realized it would be very difficult to move with such a large and young family.

Chapter 3

DATES AND TROUTLINES

S ome stability came into our nomadic life with a move to Center Street, about eight blocks from the grade school where I had attended kindergarten and the first grade and to which I now returned for the sixth grade. Our house was a spacious brick of two stories, with a porch across the wide front and another in the back. A broad stairway at the front entrance led to the upper floor's two rooms and the ample landing area at the head of the stairs.

Daddy was able to rent out the upper floor for a while to a gentle and gracious widow who did not seem to mind the racket created by our family of eight.

Daddy was now managing editor of the *Gleaner & Journal*, but the paper was not doing well financially. In fact, Leigh Harris was finding it difficult to meet the payroll. However, he raised chickens on his farm and sold eggs whenever there was a market for them. On more than one occasion he partially paid Daddy with a case of eggs.

Mother, who was pregnant again, became very creative in preparing the eggs for the family. We not only had them scrambled, fried, or boiled for breakfast—or any other meal, for that matter—but she also made eggs a' la' goldenrod; that is, the eggs were boiled and the whites cut up in a thick gravy that was poured over toast and topped with the grated yellows.

She made egg salad, put eggs in potato salad, deviled them, made egg custard, put them raw in milk, and was liberal with them in cooking any other dish. I came to the place where I could not stand to look at an egg—no matter how it was disguised—and for more than five years I would not eat one.

I was now nearing eleven years of age and old enough to work. Of course, the first place I turned was to the *Gleaner & Journal* where I was allowed to sell the *Journal* in the afternoons on Main Street, between First and Second Streets. I would pick up my bundle of carefully counted papers from the basement of the newspaper building and carry them to my area of town, leaving most of them secure under a brick in the door-way of a seldom-used building.

I would walk the streets, yelling out: "Journal, get your journal, five cents!" Sometimes I would call out something about the news. I received three cents for each paper I sold, plus any tips. On a big day I would sell twenty papers, but most of the time I sold an average of ten.

Soon I was saving my money to buy a Boy Scout uniform. I eventually had enough for the purchase of a maroon and gray scarf, the colors of our troop that met in the basement of Immanuel Baptist Church on Second Street. I had become close friends with John Wilkerson, who lived only three blocks west of our house. John had invited me to go to church with him and then to join the Boy Scout Troop when we were both twelve years old.

I loved scouting, and John and I studied the manual, learned to drill and to tie knots for which we never found a practical use other than the square, granny, and noose or slip knots—which we knew anyway. We both eventually advanced to become first class scouts, and I saved enough money to buy the treasured hat like those worn by Canadian Mounted Police and a shirt.

The pants were too expensive for me, but I finally bought a pair sec-ondhand, hardly noticing that they were lighter than my newer shirt, but no one wore the uniform with more pride. The event of the year was to go for an overnight hike into the woods around Audubon State Park, just recently built by the Civilian Conservation Corps (CCC).

At the park we learned that Henderson had had a world-famous citizen in John James Audubon, the artist and naturalist. He had lived in Henderson in 1811 and ran a successful store.

In 1816 Audubon and his brother built a steam mill in Henderson on the bank of the Ohio River. But the mill failed, leaving him bankrupt. He returned to Louisville, but while living in our area he had painted many of the birds of Kentucky: among them the bluebird, the blue jay, the wild turkey, and the Kentucky cardinal.

Now we knew why the southwest section of Henderson was called Audubon, an area where he built the first house, and we were told that the CCC was still at work constructing a huge museum to house a collection of Audubon's paintings and drawings. But we Boy Scouts were much more interested in experiencing the out-of-doors by ourselves.

My favorite uncle was Mother's youngest brother, Shack. He graduated from Western Kentucky State Teachers College at Bowling Green, and when no work was available he joined the CCC to serve out west somewhere. Returning to Zion, he had married Martina Byrnes, the daughter of the superintendent of the Zion Coal Mine, Van Byrnes. Martina was vivacious and extremely attractive.

All the Byrnes had tightly curled, brown hair, and they were the only Catholic family in Zion. Besides that bit of strangeness, Martina's brothers, Irvin and Charles, didn't have nicknames. Well, they almost didn't. We did call Charles, "Charlie." Martina and Shack for some time had but one daughter, Annette, and everyone agreed that for Shack's sake she should have been a boy.

Shack, who had found employment by teaching school, was seen as a man's man. He hunted, fished, golfed, gambled, and attracted other men and boys to himself like a pied piper. All of the boys were allowed to call him Shack, and he treated us like adults, giving us permission to do things—like steering his pickup, smoking, and cussing—and getting from us more responsibility and loyalty than we would give anyone.

He had a rough exterior, cussing with every sentence, but they were usually only the milder words, like "Hell, damn, damn it, and shit." Unlike most men, he cussed in front of everyone, male or female, sometimes even in front of Granny. While he sounded rough, inside he was as tender as a baby's butt, as he might say.

Birthdays were events to be celebrated, and for most of his adult life Shack celebrated his in style. He would throw a party for his friends, and he had more friends than anyone in the county. But there would have been a crowd if only the relatives had come. For the occasion Shack killed a goat and barbequed it over an open pit. He and close friends spent the night making burgoo, a Kentucky stew first made by pioneers using a huge, cast iron wash pot.

Into the pot would be thrown various quantities of tomatoes, corn, okra, potatoes, and two or three kinds of meat—chicken, pig heads, and ox tails. Everyone in the county had a favorite recipe for burgoo, but one of the more famous belonged to John Cunningham. He would come help you, but he would not give the recipe away.

On the day of his birthday, Shack dished out the food and drinks. While the women sat and talked, the men spent the hours shooting skeet, pitching horseshoes or washers, or playing softball. The skeet shooting was the most exciting event of the day, and usually reserved as one of the last. Of course, Shack was one of the best shots, and the men bet on the number of clay pigeons they would shatter with the shotgun blasts. We younger boys collected the spent shells or recovered the pigeons that were missed so they could be thrown again.

Scouting had given me a taste of camping, but Shack took us all on the real thing. He would fill his pickup with boys, most of them his nephews: Russ and Coonk, Charlie and Irvin, Buddy and I, and anyone else who had caught Shack's fancy and whose parents would allow them to make the three-or four-day trip to the Green River up past Hebbardsville. Our main assignment on the trip was to run "troutlines" across the river for the purpose of mostly catching catfish.

When we got to the camping site, Shack organized us for the varied tasks and instructed us how to make our beds. We didn't have tents, so we prayed it wouldn't rain. The beds of blankets and old tarps were laid in a wide circle around the large campfire, with depressions dug where our buttocks fit. It was rough and hard, but after the first night we slept rather well.

Making the troutline took an afternoon. The line consisted of a heavy cord long enough to stretch across the river, tied around a tree on each side. Every three or four feet along the heavy line we would tie thinner cords of about two feet in length to which hooks had been attached. Once the troutline was placed in the water we would use the small fishing boat Shack kept at this location all year, retracing our way along the line, baiting the hooks with worms or with a concoction of dough.

The line usually hung many feet deep into the river, for the catfish lived close to the bottom. We took turns all during the night and day, usually at about four-hour intervals, "running the line"; that is, one of us would work at the front of the boat pulling in the line and taking off the fish then re-baiting it while another maneuvered the boat.

We caught a lot of fish, and we ate many of them during our meals at the camp. The rest we kept alive on strings in the river until we took them home for the families to enjoy. Green River was famous for its catfish, and

I saw some that were more than fifty pounds in weight. The biggest we usually caught were two- or three-pounders.

When we were not running the troutline, we fished with poles or went swimming, diving from the low-hanging tree limbs stretched out over the water. At night around the campfire we told ghost stories that had us all on edge and ever watchful. When not playing, we had tasks we were expected to do: cooking, keeping the fire going, washing dishes, cleaning the camp, or running errands for Shack.

Once Russ, who was one of the older boys, refused to take his turn at cooking.

"Damn it, you will cook on your turn," Shack told him.

"No, I won't. You can't make me. You're not my boss," Russ shouted back.

"The hell I'm not," Shack said. "Get your butt over there and cook or you will not eat."

"Then I'll not eat the shitty stuff," Russ answered and walked off.

He kept to his refusal for what seemed to be a long time and the tension was felt by all in camp, but Shack also kept to his refusal of food. Hunger, finally, won the day.

In Zion we boys often gathered at the coal mine, fascinated with the industry. Small ponies were used inside the mines to pull the coal cars. We would gather at the corral when the men were not around and catch one of the ponies to ride, but they were trained for pulling the coal cars, not for riding by small boys. It was always a contest to see who could stay on the small wiry animals the longest.

I was fascinated by the tipple—the huge corrugated tin structure that rose by tiers scores of feet into the air. When the men were working in the mine, they would send up the carloads of coal to the top of the tipple. Once there the coal would be dumped, and as it made its way down inside the sloping building it would pass over grating or screens with holes of varying sizes.

The smallest pieces of coal would drop first, and only the largest pieces reached the bottom at the farthest point. Thus was the coal graded for size, and different sizes had different uses. The pea coal, with nuggets about the size of my fist, was the choice for home use. If we got big pieces for use at home, I had to bust it up with a sledgehammer. The slack was used for industry or for covering our roads. Piles of the slack stood all around the mine yard, and we often climbed them to play king of the hill, much to Mother's disapproval.

The men used carbide lamps attached to hard hats for their light in the mine. Carbide, a form of carbon, created a gas when mixed with a small amount of water. The burning of this gas provided the light, and the flame burned at the center of a reflector about three inches wide. The lamps attracted us boys, and whenever we could find one unattended, we would light it, wear the hats and play at being miners. I'm sure this flame was dangerous in the mines because coal dust was highly combustible, but I do not remember any disasters at the Zion mine.

Uncle Johnny Nick worked the mine for years and paid the price with congested lungs. We didn't hear much about "black lung" in those days, and everyone who had work was grateful to have it.

Our favorite gathering place at the mine, especially during cold months, was the steamy washroom, which stood vacant most of the day while the men were in the mine or out on runs hauling the coal to the rail yards, factories, businesses, or homes. In the wash house we were undisturbed by adults and so tried our hand at smoking, telling smutty jokes, looking at pornographic comic books, and letting our imagination run wild.

In Henderson, John Wilkerson and I became inseparable friends—together at school, at church, at scouting, and at play. He had a slightly older brother, Shirley, but no other siblings, and I often spent the night at their house. He didn't stay at my house often. Guess there was nowhere for him to sleep.

Breakfast at the Wilkersons' always surprised me, for it invariably consisted of toast with peanut butter dipped into coffee, which had been heavily diluted with milk or cream. I much preferred the oatmeal, biscuits, and gravy that were Mother's usual fare, spiced lately with Leigh Harris's eggs. Children at our house were seldom given coffee. It was milk, water, or hot chocolate on rare occasions.

John and I both had skates, and on them we could travel the length and breadth of Henderson, especially in the early summer months. The skates had straps that fit over the ankles and clamps that tightened on the shoe soles at the front. One pair of skates would fit anyone by loosening a nut underneath and extending the body. With heavy wear, all of these eventually would become undone, so we carried wrenches and skate keys to keep everything tight to avoid accidents.

Skates had to be oiled frequently to insure longer life, but we were constantly buying new wheels or new skates. The best skates had a hard rubber bushing on the front wheels, making turns easier.

We spent hours on the skates, wearing blisters that eventually became calluses. We learned to do tricks, skate backwards, make long jumps, and play a form of street hockey with sticks and cans. Henderson's streets were paved with asphalt and provided a much smoother surface than the sidewalks of concrete, for the metal wheels did not wear well upon rough surfaces. However, in the hottest summer months the asphalt became soft and we abandoned the skates in favor of bicycles.

My first bicycle was a small used one with big balloon tires and inner tubes. The tires and inner tubes were old, and I was forever fixing flats. I carried a pump and patching materials with me, prepared at a moment's notice to handle an emergency.

Later I got a bigger bike with smaller tires requiring no inner tubes, and these could be patched by loading rubber bands on a needle-like device that I would insert into the leak. I could release the bands, leaving them in the tire when I withdrew the needle. Then I would strike a match to fuse the rubber to the tire.

In Henderson we had weeks and weeks of snow in the winter, and we dressed as warmly as possible for we would play for hours in it. One winter I had a favorite pair of boots reaching nearly to my knees. The boots laced up part of the way, then there were small hooks to catch the rawhide laces the rest of the way to the top.

We always had sleds, some better than others. The best ones were long with front crosspiece handles by which we could turn the runners. We would carry the sled high in our arms, run hard down the street, and then flop upon the sled to slide until it stopped. We sought out the steepest hills and slick, refrozen streets for the best rides.

In the wintertime in Zion we would find a pond or small lake and ice skate, building a fire on the bank. We would skate until nearly frozen ourselves and then rush to the fire to warm before going out again. I knew of no sight more beautiful than Zion covered in snow and bathed by moonlight with the scene sparkling from the light of "coal-oil" lamps in the days before the county areas had electricity.

When a new snow covered the ground, Mother would gather a large pan of the freshly fallen flakes and make us snow ice cream by sprinkling it with sugar and vanilla flavoring. Another special treat was popcorn and hot chocolate. Henderson expected the snow in winter, and our schools seldom closed. Everyone had metal chains for their cars, and there were still horses around if we got stuck.

I remember one year the cold weather stayed around so long that the Ohio River froze over, and that river was about a mile wide near Henderson. Some fools even drove a team of horses across from Kentucky to Indiana. What we hated about cold weather was the slush when it thawed. Our shoes got wet, the sleds wouldn't work, and it was messy everywhere.

When we had the money and were hungry, John and I would patronize one of the few small restaurants, usually only a counter with six or eight stools. We invariably bought either a large bowl of chili with beans or a big hamburger. Each of these would cost five cents. We heard, but didn't care, that the blue plate dinner special at the Kingdom Hotel was 35 cents.

Sometimes we would spend our nickel for a candy bar: Mars, Milky Way, Butterfinger, Three Musketeers (each of the three sections would have a different colored center), Baby Ruth, or Payday. They were all so large we could hardly eat any one of them without stopping, but Payday was the largest. RC Cola was our choice for pop because it was twice as large as a Coke, which came only in the six-ounce bottle.

If we had an extra penny, we would buy a handful of peanuts and pour them into the pop. Maybe, if we had been working and had another nickel, we might buy the huge, round MoonPie—two layers of chocolate on graham cracker-like crusts with a creamy center between the layers. If we had but one or two pennies we had a choice of peppermint or licorice sticks, bubble gum (for a nickel you could get a sheet of it with a baseball trading card), or jawbreakers. The candy was held behind large glass counters in bins tilted towards the customer, and clerks were always getting impatient with us: "Come on now, I don't have all day to wait on you to spend that penny."

Like most of our friends, John and I began to smoke, mostly rolling our own cigarettes from the sacks of Golden Grain or Bull Durham that we purchased for a nickel each. At times I would snitch a few tailor-made cigarettes from Mother's pack of Lucky Strikes on the bedroom dresser. We would try to hide the fact we were smoking, but Mother would often smell the smoke on our clothes or even find our "makings." Her admonition was to wait until you are old enough, meaning late teen years.

The Ohio River both fascinated and frightened us, according to its moods. Sometimes in dry weather and on clear days there was a gentleness to the smooth surface as it ran silently toward its destiny with the Mississippi. At other times it was muddy and angry, overflowing its banks and churning its way downstream. The worst flood came in 1937, when much of the county was under water and those living in low places came to the schools and churches for shelter and food. I remember helping set up cots in the basement of Immanuel Baptist Church.

The Ohio River at Henderson, just below where the Green River had joined it, was said to be a mile wide, and it took five large steel spans and many other pillars on each side to cross the stream. John and I spent many an afternoon on the river's banks.

A special attraction would be the rare coming of the lumbering showboats, driven by their paddle wheels and announcing their presence by a raucous playing of their calliopes, which sounded like a cross between an organ and a steam whistle. We could hear them over half the town, and if we were in earshot we took off for the river landing at the end of Second Street.

To me the showboats looked like they had taken a two-story shotgun house and placed walkways around each level. They were a vanishing form of entertainment and no longer carried the famous entertainers and performers who once had paraded down Henderson's streets. Now the showboats were mostly for dining, dancing, and excursions to Evansville. To John and me they were just for looking at or for listening to the loud calliope; we didn't have the funds or the permission to go on board.

At the river in summer we eventually dared to venture into the waters as we learned to swim. However, the river was treacherous, at times seducing us with its calm but swift current while at other times warning us to stay away with its darkened surface. A favorite swimming area was under the train trestles, for the bank was not quite so steep there as in other areas, and we were usually not alone when swimming as other boys (no girls; we swam naked) gathered there also.

One hot day when many of us were swimming and wading near the bank, three boys dared each other to swim out to the enormous pillar that held the first span of the railroad bridge. Some older boys yelled warnings to them that the current was very swift out there, but they continued swimming anyway. Suddenly someone on shore hollered, "Hey, that colored boy's doing tricks. He's swimming under the water some."

"Those are not tricks," another answered. "I think he's drowning!"

We all began to watch in fascinated horror, and sure enough we saw him come to the surface, try to yell and feebly wave his hands. Then he disappeared, not to resurface. Some of the older boys jumped into the water to try to find him, and others ran for adults. We stayed there for two hours, but the body was not recovered until the next day. It was a searing experience to view death first hand. From then on, John and I decided to do our swimming in safer areas, and for the first time we began to wonder what it meant to die.

One day at grade school I was at recess when Pastor Miller from Immanuel Baptist Church found me on the busy playground and asked that I come sit and talk with him for a while.

"Brother Hanks of Zion called me the other day," he said, after we had found a place away from the other children. "He said you had made a profession of faith in Jesus during their revival while you were staying with your grandmother. Is that correct?"

I nodded my head and quietly said, "Yes." I was more than a little overwhelmed that he had made the effort to come to talk with me, and I was a little embarrassed that I had not minded Granny and had told no one at Immanuel about the decision I had made at Zion.

"Do you believe that Jesus is the Son of God?" he asked. And again I nodded, pushing any doubts I had aside.

"Jesus asks that those who believe in him indicate that by being baptized. Would you like to be baptized at Immanuel and be a member of our church?" he continued.

Again I nodded.

"Well, next Sunday at the end of the service, you come down the aisle when I extend the invitation. I'll talk with one of your parents."

"Okay," I said.

Later that week I told John about the visit and the conversation. I was surprised at his happiness over my decision. I knew he was already a member at Immanuel, but we had never talked about my joining. Mother informed me that Pastor Miller had told her about our conversation, and she was pleased I was going to join the church.

Sunday morning during worship, John sat beside me, and when Brother Miller finished his sermon and gave the invitation John stepped out in the aisle nudging me ahead. He walked down the aisle with me, I guess sensing my shyness and aloneness.

Afterwards I felt I had been pushed into the decision somewhat, first by Granny, then by Pastor Miller and John. I never regretted my action, but I often wondered how much of the decision was theirs and how much of it was mine. There had been no emotion involved in the decision, depriving me of some depth to my commitment. Even then I had some doubts about what had happened, but I kept the doubts to myself and enjoyed the affirmation that came from everyone.

My first date came during my year in seventh grade, housed in the middle school just across the street from Barrett High. Middle school included both the seventh and eighth grades at that time in Henderson, and classes were held in a box-like, two-story brick building with a plain, no-frills front.

At the time I had the beginnings of acne, and I worried about the pimples on my face. I just knew none of the girls would date me, so it was a major achievement when I finally had the nerve to ask a favorite girl— I don't remember her name—to be my date to the school dance. She surprised me by saying, "Yes, I'd be happy to go with you."

"I'll come by for you at 7:30," I replied, backing away from her all the while.

At home we prepared for this date for weeks. The dance had been scheduled since the opening of school, and Mother and Daddy both had decided that it would be my first date. I know they got more pleasure out of the occasion than I did.

From somewhere out of our need they had bought for me a new, white dress shirt, a splendid and colorful tie, new shoes, and a dress coat. Even though the new clothes and shoes felt stiff and awkward at the first wearing, I was enormously proud and grateful, knowing some sacrificing on my parents' part had been necessary to outfit me in such splendor.

Daddy gave me a haircut early in the week. He cut all of the boys' hair, using old clippers he had kept from the time he owned the barber shop in Zion. Only now, some of the teeth in the hand clippers were missing, causing the clippers to pull our hair. We hated to have our hair cut because of the pain, and when Daddy announced, usually on Saturday, that he was going to cut hair we all scattered, hiding as long as possible under beds, under the porch or house or running off down the street.

Daddy would start with the youngest, for they could be easily captured. He would sit us on a high stool on the back porch, drape us with an old shirt of his, and start the cutting. Daddy would be saying, "Sit still!" and we would be crying or complaining with, "Ouch! That hurts." I submitted readily to the weekly haircut for my date, hardly complaining at all.

Mother, with occasional help from Daddy, began to rehearse me in how I would act during the evening of my date. She went over how I would address my "girlfriend" and her parents when I got to their house, and on return what I would say in leaving. Mother also told me how to act during the evening, but I knew that once out of sight of adults I would be alright.

Daddy had agreed to be my chauffeur, escort, companion, etc.—anything, I thought, but "Daddy." My date lived only three blocks toward downtown on Center Street, but we drove nevertheless. Her house sat far back from the street, "a mile" I thought when I got out of the car and made the trek to the front door.

With nervous bravery I knocked, made my introductions to her parents as they politely smiled at this rite of passage into teenage misery, and willingly turned over to me their daughter who was also on her first, formal date. At the car I went through the introductions with Daddy, and thus passed the test of being "a polite boy." We sat in the back seat of the Ford, and Daddy drove us to the dance while we giggled out our nervousness. He let us out at the building and told me what time he would return.

Once delivered and inside at the dance, I didn't know what to do. I had never learned to dance! The rage then was jitter bugging or the slow two-step, and there hadn't been enough time for Mother or Daddy, both good dancers, to teach me. My date and I got sodas, listened to the music and stood around talking to other couples, who may not have known how to dance either.

I should have learned to dance listening to the music on the radio, for the radio was an exciting part of our life. We all had our favorite programs, and the entire family would gather around the large console when programs such as *Amos 'n' Andy, Burns & Allen, Jack Benny, Fibber McGee & Molly, Firestone Theater*, or other favorites played.

When Daddy returned after the dance and we had taken my date to her home, I experienced a sense of relief that this first formal date was over. I wasn't sure I wanted to continue dating if it required this much preparation and logistics. I would give my time and energy to other pursuits.

When the carnival came to town and set up its pavilions, rides, and sideshows on an empty field west of town, we made plans to attend. To finance a visit we found odd jobs, dug into piggybanks, sold pop bottles, and begged for an extra nickel or dime or two from any relative we thought would respond. I eventually had an entire fifty cents to spend at the exciting rides and shows, and my major choices would reflect my growing interests at the time: education and sex.

Once on the grounds I first made my way slowly and leisurely around the entire carnival, stopping outside to hear the barker's spiel at the freak shows with midgets, giants, two-headed snakes, and other of nature's strangeness; watching the teasing display of flesh by the exotic belly dancers, or wondering what was in store at the show that promised acrobats and drama. But all of these seemed too expensive for me; they usually wanted a quarter.

One side show, however, was only a dime, and the banner outside promised "the lesson of your life." The barker elaborated on the banner: "See this show and get a lesson you will remember all your life," he shouted. "Only ten cents, one dime."

I stood around for a long time, watching the people go in and come out smiling. Finally, my thirst for such eternal knowledge at a peak and pleased to find a show I could afford, I gave the man my dime and went through the tent flaps.

There were a few chairs placed before a small stage, and I took one along with two or three other viewers. We did not have long to wait. A man carrying a cane-bottom chair walked out from the wings, stopped at center stage, and sat down. Then we noticed he was carrying a small piece of wood. He pulled a large knife from his pocket, opened the blade, and began to whittle. As he whittled he repeated these words, matching the words with his motions: "Always cut from you, and you will never cut yourself. Always cut from you, and you will never cut yourself."

We sat there for the longest, but nothing else happened. "Always cut from you and you will never cut yourself," he continued to say as he whittled. People turned to each other and asked, "Is that all?" The man on the stage kept up his monologue: "Always cut from you, and you will never cut yourself."

Realizing we had seen the entire show and had learned our lesson, we all trailed out. But the barker was right, it was a lesson I never forgot, and there's no telling how many cuts I have avoided with that ten-cent lesson.

I had ridden the rollercoaster, and a chance meeting with a relative had gotten me some cotton candy. I still had money for another side show. The one that fascinated me the most was the exotic dancers, including a striptease artist.

The barker promised that the artist would "take it all off." I had never seen a naked woman. The closest I had come had been the drawings in the smutty comic books we boys had passed around, so I decided this was my chance.

When I went to buy my ticket, the barker looked down at me. "How old are you, son?"

"I'm thirteen. I'm just small for my age," I lied—about my age, not about being small.

He winked at another worker and took my money. Inside, the area was larger, the crowd bigger than the show with the "lesson," and the seats were almost all taken. I went as close to the front as possible because I didn't want to miss anything.

Three dancers in thin costumes of beads and bangles came out to wiggle and sway and make lewd suggestive movements to the music from an accordion. The barker doubled as the emcee and stand-up comic, but I didn't get all the jokes.

Finally, the striptease artist appeared and began to take off all she wore, and she did strip to "all-together." Her big breasts were amazingly large and her hips were constantly moving, and her private area was all covered with hair. It was disgusting.

"I've been cheated again," I told myself as I left. "What's all the excitement about?" The dancers had been more interesting than the naked woman. I told my family about the lesson on whittling, but I didn't tell them about the naked lady.

Later I would take dates to the movies, the main weekend attraction for most of us. Henderson had three movie houses during my childhood, but usually only two were open at the same period. The first movie I remember seeing was *Ben Hur* in the late 1920s. Advertisers often gave Daddy passes, and we could get into the theater for a nickel and a pass. Most likely the nickel covered the taxes.

We paid no attention to when a movie was scheduled to start. We went when we were ready, and if we came in at the middle of a show we simply stayed until it came around to that part again. We would say, "Well, this is where we came in. Let's go." Or, we would stay to see it through to the end, even to see it entirely a second time.

Most theaters showed a cartoon, an episode of a serial such as Buck Rogers, and the featured attraction or even a double feature. My favorite western star was Ken Maynard. I thought Roy Rogers was sissy looking. On Saturdays we would be at the theater when it opened at ten o'clock in the morning and stay until four or five in the afternoon.

I was prone to have migraine headaches. We called them "sick headaches." On many occasions I would come home sick from having watched the movies without eating anything but a candy bar. The headache would be only a nagging pain in the back of my eyes at first, but by the time I got home it would be so severe I would be vomiting. I could not shake the headache without going to sleep, but once asleep I would awaken without it, only weak from the ordeal. I finally learned that if I took an aspirin just when I felt the headache approaching, I had a chance of avoiding it. Otherwise, I went to bed.

My smallness of stature, light complexion, a propensity to tonsillitis, and tendency to have "sick headaches" gave me the reputation of being a frail child. I was also allergic to poison ivy, which grew all over the county, and at times much of my entire body would be covered with the rash and blisters. On those occasions I would be confined to the house, able to wear only a nightgown—for my hands had spread the rash to my genitals.

I would cover the rash with a homemade paste to stop or contain the itching, but there were times when I would scratch sores on my body. The attacks of tonsillitis at times would be so severe I could barely swallow, but we seldom visited a doctor. Mother and Daddy used what home remedies seemed appropriate.

I usually did not mind the confinement to the house, for it gave me opportunity to curl up with a book. As a young teenager I lost myself in Zane Grey's western novels and in the series about Tarzan of the Apes. A forerunner to paperbacks, called Big Little Books, hit the stores with short versions of classics and other novels. These books were about three inches square and very thick with a heavy, cardboard cover. They never lasted long because the size and the thickness made it difficult for the publishers to create a strong binding.

Robert Hiram was born on July 14, 1935. It was an exciting event, as we all took part in naming our newest brother. Daddy wanted to honor his father by naming this child Hiram, and Mother had agreed.

"But that's so old-fashioned," some of us complained.

"Well, we don't have to call him that. What's a first name we can use?"

Eventually we settled upon Robert, mainly because we could use "Bob" as a nickname and it had a nice sound when coupled with Hiram. So Robert Hiram it was, and all of us boys would now have nicknames starting with "B": Bunk, Buddy, Bubba, and Bob or Bobby. However, it was never to be. Hiram was so unusual, everyone started calling him only that and we couldn't make Bob stick.

An accident at home was to change our family forever. Mother had prepared her wash water the usual way one morning; that is, she heated the water in a large pot on the stove then poured it into the tub. This day she had set the tub on the floor near the stove to make the transfer easier, and most of the hot water had been added.

Before some of us older boys could move the tub, two-year-old Hiram came toddling toward it and fell forward into the hot water. He screamed and Mother quickly pulled him out, but not before he was burned over the entire surface of his arms. They were bandaged with light gauze, and for weeks he would look like a mummy about to be freed from his wrappings.

Within a week or so of this accident, on January 22, 1938, Jane Harris was born. She was named after Mrs. Leigh (Jane) Harris, and may have been Daddy's way of currying some favor with his boss, but we all had an affection for this strong-willed and caring woman whom her children called "Momajane." Now we had four boys and four girls, and I had not quite reached my fourteenth birthday.

Aunt Ninnie and Uncle Touie Nichols, when they heard of the difficulty our family was having, offered to take the three older girls—Bettye, Dot, and Mary Ruth—to live with them until Mother could get on her feet and manage things. Mary Ruth was nearly five years old at the time, and had stayed with Ninnie and Touie on other occasions.

Ninnie and Touie were childless, and both had literally fallen in love with Mary Ruth. Bettye and Dot were ten and twelve at the time, and both were anxious to get back home. But Mary Ruth stayed, since she could not take care of herself as well as the older girls. One month became two, and one year became two. They asked if they could start her in school, and they finally were given permission to adopt her.

Mary Ruth went from being a young child on one of the bottom rungs of a large family ladder to having the top rung all to herself, being loved and cared for as only childless adults could. They gave her everything she wanted and more.

On her side, Mary Ruth never lost her identity as one of the Knights, but she became a Nichols nevertheless. She sensed that she was fortunate to have escaped the type of living-on-the-edge existence we experienced, and she never exhibited any of the "spoiled" characteristics of the child who is given everything.

She seemed never to expect anything and was always grateful for all that came her way. Everyone sensed that she was "gift and grace" to Ninnie and Touie, and they to her. While theirs was a family created in adversity, it was one also created in heaven.

I made another close friend in an older teenager, Walter Farley, who lived three doors down Center Street with his older sister, Edna, and his Aunt Rosalee. Walter was gifted, handsome, and intelligent. He played the violin, excelled at school, and was well mannered and well liked. He became my first older friend and met some intellectual needs I had not known I had. Walter seemed goodness personified. Edna was wildness personified.

A few years before we moved to the area, Edna and Walter's parents had abandoned them, leaving the two to live with their Aunt Rosalee, a small, stooped woman in her late forties. She seemed literally to be pouring her life out for the sake of these two young adults.

Her primary income came from quilting, and from morning until night she bent over the huge frame on which was stretched each new pattern. She answered her door with needle and thread in her hand, and seemed always trying to straighten up. The second finger on her right hand was marred with a large callus from pushing the needle into the layers of cloth, and the second finger of her left hand had another large callus from stopping the needle. Of course, she had thimbles, but she worked faster without them and cared not for the ugliness of the calluses.

Edna, older than Walter and a beautiful redhead, was continuously sought after by suitors. She loved to party. On occasion she would join us on a late evening when Walter would buy a pint of ice cream and we would sit outside to talk about some of the deepest feelings of our hearts.

I think it was on one of these nights when I first told Walter that I had the impression I might become a minister. I have no idea where the idea came from, only that I had sensed it for some time. It could have been that Granny planted the thought on one of my visits with her. Wherever it came from, it stuck.

Walter, Edna, and I talked about any and everything. On one occasion Edna began to relate her sexual experiences with boyfriends, one in particular. She seemed to have kept count about the number of times they had intercourse and where and when each encounter took place. It was the most titillating thing I had ever experienced or imagined, and all of it being told by one of the most beautiful girls I had ever seen.

I never knew how much of this she had actually experienced and how much was fantasy for mine and Walter's sake, but even then I could sense she was desperately grasping to fill strong, unmet needs in her life. In fact, more than once I saw Aunt Rosalee leave the house in her bare feet to go searching for Edna up and down the streets.

One morning when I was walking to middle school, I was on one side of the street and a black youth was walking on the other. He was probably on his way to Douglas High School for Negroes some blocks away. No Negroes lived near our house, so he must have walked quite a few blocks.

We did not exchange words, but the next day we were again on the same block at the same time. He yelled at me, "Quit looking at me that way!" Then he threw a rock that hit me in the back of the head, opening up a gash. I grabbed my head and turned around, heading back for home moaning with the pain. He became frightened and ran toward his school.

At home, Mother took one look at the gash and called Daddy. He hurried home from work in the Ford to take me to the doctor who stitched the cut. Next, Daddy took me to the Negro school, where he talked with the principal. The three of us then went from one class to another until I saw the boy and pointed him out. The principal said he would take over from there, so Daddy and I left.

I never knew what the discipline was for the black youth. Daddy had questioned me at some length about what had happened between us. Had I done anything to provoke the other boy? I said I had done nothing but look at him, and told Daddy that the other boy had yelled that I should quit looking at him that way. But I didn't know in what manner I was looking. I pondered on this episode for months, but I never understood what had provoked him to throw a rock at me.

At the time I was very naive about race relations. I was aware that blacks had their own school, lived in their section of town, and were disliked by many whites. No hatred of blacks was expressed in our home or at Granny's and Granddad's, and there was little contact with them. I did sense from the rock throwing that there was some tension between blacks and whites, but I had taken the injury as personal, not racial.

Chapter 4

HARD WORK

I found an evening job at the bowling alley located on the second floor of a garage on Second Street, near the center of town. Five alleys with the larger pins served most adults and hard throwers, and one with smaller pins—about a third as large as the bigger ones—served children and some women. Pins had to be picked up by hand and placed in their exact spot.

To insure that each pin was placed correctly, I stepped on a pedal that raised metal spikes up through the lane. Each pin had a hole on the bottom, and I slid the pins over the spikes. My job also was to clear the alley of downed pins after the first ball was rolled and to reset all the pins after the second ball. Each boy (no girls allowed) could work two alleys when be became proficient at setting the pins.

We all hated to set the small pins. When men or large, older boys bowled the small pins, they would throw the ball so hard it would scatter the pins in every direction, including up and out of the lane. We were constantly dodging those flying pins. A metal bar hung across the back of the alley, and we would grab the bar, pulling our feet as high as possible to avoid being hit. We must have looked like monkeys.

Some of the bowlers even tried to throw the balls in ways to scatter us, making us part of their game. At times we were hit, but suffered no serious injury. At the end of the night I was paid by the number of games I had worked in the often hot, closed quarters of the pin area. It was usually ten o'clock at night or later when I rode my bicycle home exhausted.

One of the other pinsetters, by some chance of fate, was the African-American youth who had hit me with the rock that day when I was on my way to school. He was a veteran at setting pins, and I found he was slightly older and larger than I.

I discovered no rancor over our previous encounter, and he even taught me some of the tricks of the trade, like picking up the pins at the small neck in such a way that I could hold two at a time in each hand and immediately set them in place. The faster I worked, the more games customers played and the more money I earned.

We became friends, and from him I gained insights into the prejudices of our culture. I sensed that he had seen more in my white face and long stare toward him on the street that day than I had intended. We did not discuss the incident after the first day, and I don't remember his ever telling me why he threw the rock.

I had seldom been around black people. The two families in Zion were the only ones with whom I had associated. One of the fathers held the record in my book of being the most frugal person of anyone I knew. John Taylor was his name, a lanky man of very dark color who did a lot of hauling off junk. He would often allow us boys to ride with him around Zion in his mule-drawn wagon as he picked up trash and items he could sell.

John Taylor (everyone referred to him by both names, for some reason) liked to smoke cigars, an expensive habit for a junkman, but John Taylor had found an inexpensive way to meet the demands of his habit.

John Taylor bought King Edward cigars, two for a nickel. When he took the wrapper off one, he cut the cigar in two equal lengths—I guess as a way to ration them. He would smoke the half cigar as long as he could, finally extinguishing it and cutting off the ash end. What was left he chewed. When this no longer pleased him, he took it out of his mouth and laid it somewhere to dry. Finally, he smoked the dried tobacco in his pipe. The cigar had been reduced to smoke and ashes.

I experienced an entirely new form of work when Daddy employed me on Friday nights at the *Gleaner & Journal* to answer the phone when fans called to ask the score of the high school football or basketball games. At times the phone would ring as soon as I replaced the receiver, especially right after the game was scheduled to end.

Most of the time, however, I was not too busy and would read the "funnies" for a month ahead, leafing through the stack of asbestos matrixes the back shop would use to cast the strip in lead for printing.

At other times I would practice typing on the upright Underwood, which sat silent after the reporters had gone for the day.

One day the miraculous Teletype was installed to bring us the daily Associated Press wire, thus freeing Daddy from hours of dictation on the phone. I would stand over the clattering machine and read page after page of the news. Sometimes Daddy would let me tear it off and sort it according to news categories. At other times I drifted to the back shop to watch the men at work and to take some of their good-natured teasing.

Daddy would often leave the office and cross the street to the American Legion Hall for a beer. The entire county was not only open for beer and liquor sales now that prohibition had failed to pass again, but the county was also wide open for gambling. When Daddy did not come home after the paper closed, Mother frequently sent me to the pool halls to find him. He was rather skilled at pool and liked to play.

If he was not at the pool tables, I would always look in the back room where men gambled around large, circular, felt-covered tables lighted by a low-hanging light. Gambling became so pervasive in Henderson County that one could find slot machines at the gas or "filling" stations, and there were no restrictions on who could play the machines. I dropped many a nickel into the slots hoping to hit the jackpot, but being grateful if I hit the frequently rolled two cherries and a plum that paid back 15 cents.

The really big-time gambling and nightclubs were located across the Ohio River near Evansville. The river had changed course at one time, cutting into the Kentucky side and leaving a few hundred acres of the Bluegrass state on the Indiana side. This became a no-man's land in a way, as the Henderson County law enforcement officials did not police the area. Gamblers made the most of it.

The Dade Park Race Track was built there, as were a number of large, famous nightclubs. The most famous was the Trocadero, an enormous two-story frame building whose back nudged the river. The "Troc" attracted such a large and free-spending clientele, the owners were able to book nationally known bands like Tommy Dorsey and Glenn Miller. Senior classes of the high schools often held their graduation parties at the Troc, using only the first floor and avoiding the gambling upstairs.

Every community, no matter how small, had a roadhouse where liquor and beer were sold, slot machines were displayed, and a juke box blared away for dancing to such tunes as "Chattanooga Choo Choo," "Stardust," "I'll Be Loving You Always," "Blue Moon," "Deep Purple," or "I Got You Under My Skin."

Zion had DUMMY'S, located less than a mile south toward Hebbardsville. Robert Bennett, one of the sons of Cooksey Bennett for whom Daddy was named, was deaf. The term used by the community was "deaf and dumb," and his wife was also deaf, but their children were not.

Dummy could read lips rather well, and he could talk in the loud, monotone one associates with many deaf persons. Close friends could understand him, but I never could. There were no age restrictions on places such as DUMMY'S, and most of us went to these "joints" from our early teenage years on, usually without our parents' knowledge.

However, I would never drink beer or whiskey for fear that I might become an alcoholic like Daddy. I feared that Daddy's drinking might be a curse, a family flaw, so I would not even drink small amounts of alcohol. Of course, what I feared turned out to be no bogeyman but in reality a curse that would work its way through the generations. At the time I felt he was doing enough drinking for us all.

On occasion, when Daddy was feeling the effects of his drinking, he would talk to me about what was going on in the county. "I could blow this town wide open," he would say. "All I would have to do is publish how these illegal businesses operate. You wouldn't believe what I know."

He never named names, but I assumed that friends were on the take from the gambling. Everyone in power was turning a blind eye to the problem. I sensed that Daddy was in conflict between what he saw as his responsibility as an editor and blowing the whistle on friends.

Daddy's increased drinking was making things difficult at home, not only because we could not afford the expense or that he would fail to come home some nights, but also because it was the primary cause of severe arguments between him and Mother. Before I started to school I remember Mother and Daddy going to or hosting parties. Mother seemed to enjoy them as much as Daddy did. They moved in a circle that included the county's sheriff and other up-and-coming young business persons.

But as our family grew and Daddy's drinking increased, Mother dropped out of the partying almost entirely. Her anger at his drinking and frustration at not being able to meet the needs of her children would erupt when Daddy would stagger in after a day of drinking beer during work and a night of partying. Their fights usually came late in the night, and the shouting coming from their bedroom would awaken us.

On occasion Daddy would strike Mother, and I would rush to her defense, yelling, "You can't hit my mother! You can't hit my mother!" I would grab him by the legs or waist and try to make him stop, which he had usually done anyway, for he never seemed to strike her more than once or twice. Once sober he was always very repentant, and they would make up.

More than once, Mother would send me downtown to find Daddy. She knew no one at any of his haunts would tell her the truth about whether he was there or not, so telephoning was out of the question. I would first search the three pool halls, both in the front where he played nine ball, then in the back where he might be gambling or watching others gamble. Next I checked the American Legion. If the doors were closely guarded, I would have to ask someone I knew to check for me. Then I made my way to the downtown saloons.

This search for my father became almost a ritual, and even as a preteen I realized I was losing my Daddy. We were all losing contact with him as the drinking took over. He seemed to need his beer all through the day, staying just drunk enough that it would ease whatever pain bothered him. Maybe he had adopted this style of drinking so he could continue functioning at the newspaper, but he never became angry or mean, only testy and short of temper.

During the summer when I was in middle school I was allowed to visit the farm operated by Uncle Peck and Aunt Mary Lou Nichols. One of their sons, Elbert Sawyer (nicknamed Tom), was only a month or so older than I. We looked so much alike that Tom's friends were often confused. On more than one occasion I would ride a horse into the village of Geneva, and Tom's friends would accuse him of being a "high hat" because he had not spoken to them.

The land in Henderson County was fertile, especially where the Ohio and Green rivers would flood. Such areas were called "bottom land," I guess because they were sometimes the bottom of a river. When they were flooded, the rivers left rich deposits of topsoil washed in from upstream.

The entire county, however, produced above-average crops of corn and wheat. Before the day of chemical fertilizers and more scientific methods, the land would produce more than 100 bushels of corn to the acre—a goal prized by all farmers. I remember the darkness of the earth and the richness exhibited by the number of earthworms when it was turned over by the plows being pulled by two straining mules or one of the new tractors the big farmers were beginning to buy from John Deere or Ford or International Harvester.

Uncle Peck and Uncle Touie jointly farmed hundreds of acres of rich bottom land owned by one of the county banks, and they employed a number of hands in addition to Tom and his two brothers, Penny and Buck. That summer I found a new definition for work. We started early and we quit late.

No matter what age you were, you did not escape a full day's work in the summer. Anytime we stopped working I could go immediately to sleep, under a shade tree, in the barn, or on the porch. I graded work in three stages: the farm the hardest, next Granddad's carpentry, and then Daddy's desk work at the paper.

I learned to harness rawboned mules and to hitch them to a cultivator or wagon. Each mule had a name: like Jim, Red, Blue, or Jake—almost always one-syllable words—and each mule had a distinct personality. They were matched as teams. That is, mules would be placed together that worked at the same pace and that tolerated one another. Some worked better on one side than the other. Some were slow and lazy, others cantankerous and mean, ready to bite you if you turned your back or to kick at you.

I soon learned which mules to be careful around, but they usually gave me the slower and older ones because I was still learning. Each driver would have a favorite team to work. We "cultivated" the corn, one row at a time, letting the sharp disks cut away the weeds and at the same time throw some dirt against the small stalks. On other occasions the weeds would be so thick, we were told to take hoes and chop them out from between the corn stalks and at the same time to thin the stalks so that the ones allowed to live would be strong and healthy.

In addition to farming, the Nicholses raised cattle, which frequently had to be moved from one field to another. Their big Kentucky horses were not trained for this task, so from Texas they bought a small western horse named Billy. I was allowed to ride Billy whenever I wanted to help move the cattle. The first time I saddled Billy they were all watching, and, of course, they didn't give me any warnings.

Billy had a mind of his own. When a cow moved out of line, he immediately turned to head it back without any directions from his rider. That was his job, and he did it well. The first time he made the maneuver with me, it was grab the saddle horn and hold on for dear life. And if you were running Billy and drew back on the reins for him to stop, he spread his legs stiffly out in front and stopped! I nearly went over his head that first time, but we eventually became good friends.

He was hardy and responded to the slightest indication from his rider. If I moved the reins to one side, he went that way. If I applied pressure with my knee, he responded. If I leaned in one direction, he turned. He was trained to allow his rider to use his hands for other tasks, such as throwing a rope.

Billy and I had a special job when the Nicholses threshed their wheat. For the threshing a contractor brought in a huge steam engine. The device looked much like a train engine, with its large boiler, smoke stack, and massive wheels. The steam turned another mammoth wheel on the side of the engine around which a leather belt, nearly a foot wide and twenty feet long, was looped and extended to the thresher.

The thresher was located central to the wheat fields. Out in the fields a mower had cut the wheat and men bound it in sheaves. Other men were busy stacking until a wagon came along to carry the wheat to the thresher. From the wagon it was tossed into the thresher and the grain separated from the stalk and chaff.

My job was to take fresh water around to the men in the fields, for they were constantly moving and stayed thirsty from the dust and heat of the summer. I carried two one-gallon jugs slung across the saddle near the horn. The first day it was fun, but the second day it hurt. I had worn my inside thighs raw from moving in the saddle, and I was the brunt of a lot of jokes when I insisted on walking straddle-legged. For the next few days I carried a small sack of flour or cornstarch to dust myself throughout the day. Eventually I welcomed the calluses that formed, and the problem disappeared.

Threshing sometimes took as long as a week, and the Nicholses hired fifteen or more extra hands or neighbors swapped time. The women spent the mornings cooking lunch (we called it "dinner") for the entire crew, which would be eaten on makeshift tables beside the house. The food was not exotic, but plain and plentiful: fried chicken and country ham, corn on the cob, creamed potatoes, green beans, black-eyed peas, and light (yeast) rolls or corn bread. Dessert was cobbler or pie. We drank milk, buttermilk, iced tea, or water. Food never tasted as good as it did following a hard morning's labor, and the dinner break was a welcome time to rest a minute.

One job I hated was working tobacco. It was such a labor-intensive crop that most farmers planted only one or two acres, almost never more than five. The county had once been a world leader in the raising of dark tobacco. That was in the 1820s before Great Britain had placed a restrictive tax on the product and the market had sharply declined.

We started our crop with the preparation of a plant bed, burning timber over a small patch of ground to destroy any weeds. When the ground was ready, we planted the seeds and then placed over the bed a gauze-like cover to keep birds out and protect the tiny plants from overexposure to the weather. When the plants were about six inches high, we plowed the field. Then using a hoe, we made a mound for each plant that was placed in a hole made with a tobacco stake. We would usually water each mound. During early growth time we kept weeds out by hoeing.

When the plants were two or three feet high, they had a tendency to start new growth. This growth was called "suckers," and came at the point where the leaf joined the stalk. We would walk through the field checking each leaf and breaking off each sucker to allow the early leaf to get as large as possible.

At the same time we would turn the leaf over and check for tobacco worms—large, soft, chartreuse caterpillars that we killed by pulling their heads off or by stomping them into the ground. Some leaves would be entirely destroyed by the worms.

The gum from the sticky leaves would get all over our hands and clothes, and after a day or two of wearing the same jeans we could almost stand them up. Late in the season the top of the plant was broken off, or "topped," to stop additional growth. But if the plant was to provide seed for next year's crop, then we allowed it to flower and go to seed. The worming and suckering had to be done two or three times a year before pesticides came along to do much of the worming work.

When the plant reached full growth, we took sharp, hook-nosed knives and cut it near the ground, then forced it at the thickest point over a tobacco stick on which we had placed a sharply pointed steel end. Each stick would hold eight plants, and these were tossed on a wagon to be carried to the tobacco barn where they were hung in tiers for curing, sometimes with smoke.

After some weeks the tobacco was taken down, stripped from the stalk, and sorted into grades. Then the stalk was taken to the market housed in long, corrugated tin buildings where the tobacco was spread on the floor and an auctioneer walked through selling it to buyers who followed him. By this time the farmer was only a month or two away from starting a plant bed again.

Tobacco brought good money, but it was hard-earned money. Soybeans were a new crop I heard the men talking about. They said Henry Ford had been able to make a steering wheel for his cars out of the beans, and scientists were finding other uses for it. Besides it was good for the soil, they said, and easy to grow.

I had often heard men cuss, and we boys tried out all the new words at one time or another when we were not around adults. On the Nichols farm, cussing reached a new height. All the words I had ever heard were strung together at such length and in such creative ways, I was constantly amazed. Most of it was directed at the animals, as they were encouraged to keep up a steady, hard pace or to make some difficult maneuver. I tried my best, but I never seemed to get my heart into cussing like Tom could.

We would occasionally have an afternoon off to play, and we would saddle horses to ride to a pond for swimming or fishing or just checking things out. I remember one place where Peck Nichols lived had the remains of an old icehouse in which we sometimes played. The icehouse consisted of a large hole in the ground that had been thickly lined with bricks and over this had been erected a shed to protect it from the sun.

When it was used, ice was cut from the river or lake and stacked in the icehouse with straw separating the large blocks. In this manner, ice could be saved into the hot summer months. One month I had the job of taking those old bricks and others from an abandoned house and cleaning them, that is, knocking the mortar off so they could be reused.

I had a new BB gun one year, and late in the summer Tom and I got into a playful fight in a field where the corn had been cut and stacked. Hiding behind the stacks, Tom would throw ears of corn at me and I would shoot the BB gun at him. Neither of us could hit the other, but once when he stuck his head from behind a stack I fired from the hip and hit him in the forehead.

A huge knot immediately arose and he bled. We were both frightened at how close the BB came to his eyes, for he could have been blinded. And the adults never let me forget that either. I was severely chastised, and the gun was taken from me for the rest of my stay. I had learned another hard lesson.

On the farm I got a new introduction to the facts of life. When the heifers were calving, one invariably needed help, and the men would reach into the cow's vagina to straighten the calf or to help pull out the newborn. On occasion the birth was so difficult that both cow and calf would die, and Uncle Peck would really cuss then.

I made more than one trip to another farm to witness the breeding of a mare in heat to make another mule. For this, the mare would be mated to a jackass, always much smaller of body but usually with a penis that just barely cleared the ground when excited. I never understood why this mating of jackass and horse produced a mule, which in turn could not reproduce its kind.

Reality was to teach me more about human sexuality. Granny and Granddad's oldest son, William Douglas (nicknamed Doot) graduated from Western Kentucky State Teachers College at Bowling Green and began teaching in Henderson County. His constant companion was William Evans Bennett, another son of Cooksey Bennett. Both Doot and William Evans were teachers at Audubon High, the section of Henderson named to honor John James Audubon.

Wherever you saw Doot you would find William Evans, who was always called by his full name. They took their vacations together, usually traveling to some distant area of the United States. I remember all of Zion was impressed in 1936 when they bought matching Chevrolet coupes with rumble seats, that is, a seat opened out of what I thought would be the trunk. It was an open seat and could only be used in good weather, but it made a statement about going in style. For their vacation that year they took one of the cars to tour much of the West.

Both Doot and William Evans lived with their parents, and everyone considered them above average in intelligence. I remember Doot as one who read widely, held strong opinions, and was quick to be offended. I was embarrassed by his sharpness with Granny and Granddad, and when he was around I tried to get out of the way. He sometimes worked as a carpenter with Granddad during his summer vacations, and he helped Granny around the house. The family considered him a better cook with desserts than most of the women.

Doot and William Evans were rumored to be lovers, and boys called them "homos" or "queers." Tragedy struck their lives one school term when they were both arrested and charged with molesting some of their young pupils. They were not held in jail long and never served a prison term, but neither one was ever to teach again.

The extended family was divided on whether they were guilty or not, but I came to believe they were when I was once molested by William Evans when he had given me a ride home. I never told anyone and managed never to be alone with him again. I never understood why they stayed in Zion after they lost their teaching jobs and faced virtual exile by the community. William Evans worked at several odd jobs after that, and Doot worked as a carpenter with Granddad.

I learned to drive one summer while staying with Granny in Zion. My teacher was Johnny Nick, the father of Coonk and Russ, and his brothers were Uncle Peck and Touie. Johnny Nick had a Model A roadster with a huge steering wheel and a choke and throttle located on the shaft of the wheel. In my early teens I constantly begged to be allowed to steer, first from his lap and then by myself.

He started my driving, but it was Coonk who let me drive enough that I learned to synchronize the clutch and the gears without problems. Kentucky at the time did not require driving tests and licenses. Learning to drive in the country was much safer than in the city, and when I proved to Daddy that I had really learned, he let me drive our car some.

Johnny Nick was one of the most profane men I knew: foul-mouthed, loud, and blunt. You always knew where you stood with Johnny Nick. Like his brothers, Peck and Touie, he had been cussing all his life. At first I was somewhat frightened of him, but I soon learned that this was just his way. The rough words actually had little meaning except as an outlet for frustration or to emphasize a point, and he had a lot of points.

The large Nichols family had once owned hundreds of acres of land between Zion and Henderson, and we passed the old, deteriorating Nichols mansion each trip to and from the city. Because the Nicholses had married Hendersons, Knights, and Bennetts, I was always confused about my kin. I knew if anyone had lived in the county long, there had to be some blood connection somewhere.

Johnny Nick had left farming to work in the Zion coal mine. The work was hard but steady, and it never rained or snowed in the mine. It was the same day in and day out. The miners only stopped working when they had dug more coal than they could sell.

Johnny Nick married Mother's older sister, Mary Bernice, who countered Johnny Nick's profanity with her strong character that more than matched his profanity—she was never cowed.

She was heavyset and had a voice that could be heard all over Zion when she called her children for meals or bedtime. And she loved to sing, while working at home or as a soloist at the Baptist church. My all-time favorite was to hear her sing, "His Eye Is on the Sparrow."

Johnny Nick never went to church; for that matter, neither did Peck or Touie until Mary Ruth went to live with Ninnie and Touie. When Mary Ruth joined the church so did Touie, and Uncle Peck's family became very involved in the Baptist church. Their daughter, Maggie, even married a preacher, Everett Hooper.

In my later teens I got part-time work at the Red Front Grocery on Green Street on the west end of Henderson, actually not too far from the house on Cherry Street where we lived briefly when I was in the second grade. Customers would hand me their list for groceries, and I would scurry all over the store gathering what they wanted. If they did not have a list, they would stand at the counter calling out what they wanted while I picked it up.

During each weekend the manager would have us "push" one item, such as two-pound boxes of Velveeta Cheese, and he would have a large display of the item in the center of the store. The manager would organize contests to see who might sell the most of that product, and I was surprised at how much we could move by simply calling an item to the customer's attention. I also remember receiving a box of the cheese as the prize for one weekend, that is, for Friday and Saturday as the store was not open on Sunday.

Daddy's drinking became so bad that it drastically affected his work and our lives. He would cross the street to the American Legion Hall hourly, and by the end of the workday he would have consumed eight to ten bottles of beer. He would then stop somewhere on the way home to continue drinking, imbibing as much as twenty bottles in a twenty-four-hour period. Of course, it impaired his driving as well as his work, but he had only minor accidents.

One day our world crashed. Daddy was fired! The dismissal had come after repeated warnings, but he seemed powerless to stop drinking. He was an alcoholic.

We had no savings. We were behind in the rent. The nine of us would have to find new housing almost immediately, and no relative had room for all of us.

Chapter 5

ZION

When faced with one of the most serious difficulties of their lives, Daddy and Mother turned to their roots—the Kentucky village of Zion. Granny and Granddad still lived there, as did Uncle Johnny and Aunt Mary, Mother's sister, and their four children. Besides, we thought half of the 200-plus population of Zion was kin to us. Unlike the urban areas of the state, at Zion one knew all of the families, the names and ages of the children, and even the names of the dogs.

Zion was only six miles east of Henderson, my birthplace. Zion was established in the early 1800s when well-to-do farmers clustered their homes on its two hills. The tipple of the Zion Coal Mine appeared to stand guard like a steel-clad sentinel at the entrance to the village, while the Zion Baptist Church, three quarters of a mile away, watched over the exit.

It was as though the mine guarded our economic welfare and the church watched over the spiritual. One kept us from starving and the other from sinning, and both were only moderately successful.

I sometimes felt the church was more creative than the mine, for the church kept finding sins under every newly functioning gland. Not only were we not to "drink, cuss, or chew or go with girls that do," we were not to play tennis, softball, baseball, or other active games on Sunday. We were not to go to movies at all.

I never understood why all movies were banned when all books were not. We also were not to dance or visit the honkytonks (small night clubs). Thank heaven our elders had not heard of, or if they had they had rejected, the ban imposed by Baptists in Texas against "mixed bathing"; that is, boys and girls were not to swim in the same pool at the same time.

The homes in Zion on the average were more attractive, the lawns better kept, and the look of the village more prosperous than almost any of the county's numerous other small towns. Many of the homes seemed to be hiding behind huge oaks scattered about their spacious lawns, while other homes proudly revealed their inviting porches and gabled roofs.

At the dip of Zion's first hill, where a narrow road zigzagged across the highway, stood Crafton's General Store. To the left the side road ran past a few homes on its way to farmland, but to the right it sauntered to an abandoned coal mine whose tipple had been razed but whose threatening shaft worried many an anxious mother when her children played on the slack mounds around it.

Houses, smaller and less pretentious than those on the highway, were scattered along other "streets" around the old mine, like faded monuments to a bygone industry.

Near the top of the second hill out on the Henderson highway another slack-covered road turned off to the right, and there stood Cinnamon's Store—one of the first constructed in Zion—commanding a view of most of the village. Across the side road, Frank Reid had reopened his barbershop in the tack room of a former funeral home. Up this side road about the equivalent of two normal city blocks, at the intersection of another small highway that curved into Zion, Cousin Ed Henderson operated his blacksmith shop.

Residents of Zion ranged from tottering oldsters who minded everyone's business to prosperous farmers and business persons and finally to the swarming army of teenagers and children who made up more than the expected percentage in a village of 200. But families liked to raise their children in Zion because everyone helped to mind them.

"You better quit that or I'll call your mother!" or "Does your mama know where you are?" were admonitions yelled at every child in Zion at one time or another.

I loved being at Zion. The businesses of the small town provided me, and any other boy who wanted it, contact with adults, a chance to hear them talking at leisure about their world, especially at Cinnamon's Store, Frank Reid's Barber Shop, Cousin Ed Henderson's Blacksmith Shop, and the Zion Baptist Church.

Politics and Philosophy

At Cinnamon's a sprawling front porch connected the dry goods side with the grocery side, and a single gas pump stood guard over the narrow driveway running parallel with the highway. The gas pump was operated by gravity. Mr. Cinnamon would operate a lever that pumped the gasoline into a ten-gallon glass tank. Lines on the tank marked the gallons as they were released into the vehicle.

Over the years at Cinnamon's I informally studied politics and philosophy in classes in the huge, white frame building. W. E. Cinnamon was called "Spud" by all the men, while most women and children called him Mr. Cinnamon. Everyone referred to his wife as Mrs. Cinnamon.

Spud was a small, thin man in his sixties who carried a dignity and reserve that set him apart. He seemed a little stiff, though, maybe a carryover from the time he was a school teacher—or it could have been because of those high, firm collars he always wore.

Most customers charged their groceries, paying by the week or month or with some farmers paying when the crops were taken to market. Spud never charged interest. Each family had a book, actually a receipt book. Using a common piece of carbon paper, Spud gave a copy of each day's purchases to the customer. Mother left specific instructions with Mr. Cinnamon about what we children could charge when she sent us to the store.

The women and the girls didn't stay inside long after their shopping. They either went home or visited on the front porch, probably because of the spitting. My class in politics and philosophy met on the grocery side around the huge potbellied stove. The men sat in a tight circle on nail kegs or full bean and feed sacks or in the two cane-bottomed chairs. We boys flopped on the floor or hung around in the background. No one sat in Mr. Cinnamon's small rocker.

Everyone but Mr. Cinnamon used tobacco, one of the county's big money crops. The men smoked, dipped, or chewed; the chewing was most interesting. Some of the men were experts at spitting. They could hurl a huge stream accurately toward its target—usually one of the red spots on the stove—where the spittle would sizzle into steam. Others were rather sloppy, and some so inadequate they had to get up and spit into the dusty ashes in the box at the front of the stove.

After politics and gossip, checkers was a favorite pastime. The men made a checkerboard by drawing or painting the squares on a large board or piece of cardboard, and used soda bottle tops for checkers. One player turned them up, and the other turned them down. Some of the men were very good, but one of the best was Cager Hatfield.

Cager usually played at the other store in town but would drift up to Spud's for a new challenge. On more than one occasion he taught me some of his strategy and traps.

My courses in politics leaned heavily for or against FDR's New Deal, and there was a strong-enough mixture of Democrats and Republicans to keep everybody honest. There was a lot of concern at the time about the depression we were going through and mixed opinion about Roosevelt's policies. Many of us, including high schoolers, were employed by the WPA.

Philosophy came mostly in parables, taught by the older men, who loved to tell some stories so often we learned them by heart. But we seldom tired of listening, because the stories were about crisis times in their lives, and they told them with feeling. They remembered fires, floods, and diseases that killed families and friends and when times were much better than presently.

Yarns could be told at length, for it was an unhurried time. Children were not allowed to enter into the conversation, but the men seemed to know this was school for us.

They allowed questions now and then, and, if the discussion wasn't too heated or too involved, some occasionally explained certain points. We paid our tuition by running errands, like going to tell their wives something, or we caught the brunt of some adult joke.

Health, Hygiene, and Sociology

I studied health, hygiene, and sociology at another school just across the road from Spud Cinnamon's Store: Reid's Barber Shop. By simply crossing the road I entered another world. It was a man's world, never invaded or disturbed by women.

Here men (and boys) had the freedom to be their male selves without being heard by a woman, much less being contradicted, chided, or corrected by her. Consequently, the talk centered on women—women as sex objects, as the butt of jokes, or, on the plus side, as an idol to be worshipped and marveled about.

The barbershop was operated by the same Frank Reid who had traded his previously owned shop for Daddy's horse, saddle, and bridle, giving Daddy his first job. His first customer was my grandfather Homer Hiram Knight. At that time Frank had left Zion to barber in Louisville, where he was moderately successful until stricken with palsy—a career-threatening illness for a barber. He had returned to Zion where he was known and trusted. You have to trust a man before you allow his shaking hand to come at your face with a straight razor.

The barbershop occupied the harness room of the former carriage house of a funeral home, long since a victim to newer forms of trans-portation. Old tack still hung from pegs in the room, and the smell of hair tonic and soap competed with the odor of leather and staleness. Inside the huge, dark interior of the barn—a spooky place for us "young-uns"—were the last remains of the funeral home: two magnificent horse-drawn hearses.

They stood ready to be hauled out on yet another trip to the cem-etery, resplendent in their red velvet interiors, cut glass sides, and black frames. They had waited in the semi-darkness for years, ever since the new automobiles became the way to rush the dead to their graves. Now such time and splendor were reserved only for presidents. The funeral parlor, a separate structure, had become home for Frank and his invalid wife.

Zion was proud to have a barbershop again. Not many towns our size did, and our barber was something of a celebrity. Frank, in his fifties, stood about five feet six inches tall, slim of build, but handsome and gregarious to a fault. He loved to entertain, and he wanted people around him all the time.

He knew a thousand jokes (mostly connected with sex), but he also told long stories about an imaginary town—Chicken Switch—peopled by wildly interesting characters such as Grandpappy Banks and Puece Lindar. His characters often reminded us of someone in Zion.

Frank could not read, but he scanned the newspaper each day, and it was uncanny the way he could look at a person's picture and tell you his profession. People said he was a student of human nature. Frank always had the best-weighted and balanced horseshoes around, and we wore calluses on our hands and deep holes in the slack-covered road with our intense play.

Frank also prided himself on making the best slingshots in the county, which we could buy for a dime each. If all this didn't entertain his customers enough, he would send his mixed collie and German shep-herd dog chasing the few airplanes that flew overhead. Frank would yell,

"Whooeee, sic 'em!" and the dog would run at breakneck speed after the planes. We often speculated what the dog would do if he caught one.

Every month or so, Frank's school recessed for a few days. Frank would have drunk himself into a stupor.

Business and Industry

In Zion I studied business and industry a short distance up the road from the barbershop—at Cousin Ed's blacksmith shop. Ed Henderson, a short, broad-shouldered man, was a first cousin to my Granddaddy, Tandy Henderson.

Cousin Ed's dark, sprawling shop reeked of smoke, hot metal, and animal odors. Everything revolved around the huge forge. Metal was everywhere, and the predominant colors were rust and coal gray.

The teachers at the blacksmith shop differed sharply from those at Spud Cinnamon's and Frank Reid's. The blacksmith crowd taught as they worked, and they always seemed to be in a hurry, especially in the spring, summer, and fall.

Cousin Ed's customers usually drove in from the fields, caked with dust and dried sweat, needing a machine fixed so they could get back to work. They often helped repair the broken equipment, or they took part in the shoeing of the horses and mules, for not many farmers had tractors.

Sometimes the farmers came by just to use Cousin Ed's tools, for which he never charged. The talk fit in with the work—mostly about crops, animals, machinery, the latest prices and why they were going up or down. I learned of the men's concern for a living, and from my experience on an uncle's farm I knew how hard they worked—from sun-up to sundown.

Ethics and Religion

I studied ethics and religion at Zion Baptist Church, which had traded the hundred-plus-year-old frame building with its small steeple and bell for a brick building that housed a growing congregation. As in the past, the church was more than a school for faith. It pulled the community together, for only here did town and country families gather at one time.

Community events were planned and sponsored by the church, like the all-day picnic at Adkinson Park in Henderson.

Frank and my Daddy were not the only hard drinkers in Zion. The owner of Crafton's General Store was one, too. I remember women from the church corralling either Frank or Mr. Crafton in plain sight on the side of the road when one or both of them was drunk.

The women would lecture them, pray with them, and usually get them to promise to give up drinking. The problem was when they became sober they didn't seem to remember those promises, and when sober they wouldn't let the women talk or pray with them.

I started attending most of the functions for youth at Zion Baptist Church, and they filled a strong social need as well as attracting me religiously. Our pastor was Clel Rodgers, a man who loved people and communicated it. His theology was mostly conservative, but his expression of God's love was not.

Clel began to pay a lot of attention to me, inviting me to ride with him when he visited members and finding things I could help him with around the church. Although we did not talk about it, he sensed that Daddy's drinking and frequent absences left a void in my life. Clel began to fill that void with his companionship. He became one of the most influential men to touch my life, leading me to what we called "full-time Christian service." Of course, that usually meant being a pastor, for we heard little of any ministry other than preaching or singing, and I couldn't carry a tune.

What was unique about this informal education from its many sources was the fact that generations mixed. I did not realize my generation would possibly be one of the last in America to have this experience. Children were allowed to hear day in and day out the conversations of adults. Not all of my friends found it as fascinating as I did, and maybe it was just as well, for none of these schools was large enough to handle many teenagers.

I had found treasure mines of folklore, and I worked those mines with intensity. It is possible I appreciated these classrooms because we had lived in the city of Henderson where it was absent, and I found it in Zion.

Back out on the highway past Cinnamon's was Newman's Garage, nestled so far back it was easily missed by travelers. Finally, there was the grade school at the intersection of the two highways, sharing its playground with the parking lot of the Baptist church.

However, in 1939 when Mother and Daddy were looking for a place large enough to house the growing family, none was available in Zion. No relative had room for a family of nine, seven of them children, and the family had no funds with which to rent a dwelling. Finally, as a last resort, Daddy rented a three-room shack, usually occupied by farm workers, on the Shelton farm four miles east of Zion, halfway to Hebbardsville.

I thought then this phase of our lives was the low point of our troubled family history. The small house slumped close beside the two-lane highway with just enough room in front to park and turn a car. The paint had long worn off the gray boards, and the back and side yards were marked by a wire fence that held off the cattle grazing in the surrounding fields.

We drew water from an old well and relieved ourselves in a two-hole privy that stood beside the coal shed. No electricity was available, even though the Rural Electric Consumer Cooperative had brought it to the county in 1937.

We had to use kerosene or "coal-oil" lamps. Heat for the thin-walled house came only from a fireplace and cooking stove, but we had plenty of coal. Daddy, now thirty-seven years old, had found a job driving a truck for the Zion Coal Company.

We made the move during the summer while I was again working on the Nichols farm near Geneva. I returned to a family crowded into an inadequate house and very much in distress, but Mother kept our spirits up. "We've got our health," she would say, "and we have each other. Things will get better."

We made the most of our surroundings, exploring the fields and woods of the area. We swam and waded in the small, often muddy pond near the Shelton house. Once Dot had a crawfish get inside her makeshift swimming suit and cried for us older boys to get it out. We stood on the bank and laughed at her discomfort until her dancing and jumping shook it loose.

We scoured the fencerows for blackberry bushes and brought home buckets of the black, juicy fruit for Mother to make into cobblers. When we could get enough, we sold gallons of the berries to others. We located pecan trees and in the fall gathered the nuts by the sack for eating and selling.

When school started, we were excited at getting to ride the yellow school bus that stopped at our front door and took us to Hebbardsville. Dot was in the sixth grade, but had a poison ivy rash so badly she could not start when we did. Bettye was in the seventh grade, Buddy in the ninth, and I in the tenth. We carried our lunches in brown paper sacks, consisting mostly of peanut butter and jelly on biscuits or crackers.

When there was meat, which was rare, we might have sausage or ham or bacon sandwiches, or occasionally even an egg sandwich. We carried silver, collapsing aluminum cups from which to drink at the school pump. We did not feel deprived over our lunches, for most of the other students brought some variation of the same things. However, some did have lunch pails and brought meat more often than we did.

While Hebbardsville was the site for the county's largest school, the village was not much larger than Zion, and the area was not nearly as prosperous looking. Hebbardsville always appeared a little seedy to me. The homes were not as inviting, and the farms and roads seemed overgrown. However, economics had changed the year before: Oil had been found on a farm near the town.

The Green River ran its deep, muddy course less than a mile to the east. On the highway one could continue on to Owensboro by crossing the river on the ferry at Ranger's Landing, but we seldom did. It was simpler from Zion to go by way of the Spotsville bridge, and one didn't have to pay the ferry charge.

The Hebbardsville School included all grades, one through twelve, but not all children in that part of the county came to Hebbardsville. There were other local schools for children through five or six grades at places like Zion. At Hebbardsville all grades met in the rambling white frame building that seemed to go off in all directions, and classes met also in daylight basement rooms. A barn-like gym with three deep bleachers on each side stood to the left and back from the school building, as though the fun that went on there might taint the seriousness of the other building.

On the right side, down a short hill, was the boy's toilet where we gathered to tell jokes and smoke, always with someone on watch for the principal. Nevertheless, he would often outsmart our lookouts by sneaking in from another direction than the school.

The principal was mostly trying to keep us from smoking, but he only slowed us down. We rolled our own cigarettes from sacks of Bull Durham or Golden Grain that cost a nickel each. We were impressed whenever anyone had "tailor-made" cigarettes, usually Lucky Strikes or Camels or the cheaper Twenty Grands.

All of us Knights immediately fit well into the school's routine, and we were accepted by the other students. We knew most of them, including a number of our relatives, especially Aunt Mary's children: Coonk, Mary Jon, and Mot. Russ had already graduated.

Coming from the city schools that were much larger, we enjoyed the smaller classes and student body. My class consisted of only twenty-four students in the entire tenth grade. It allowed me to excel, but it provided no challenge.

I went through the three grades at Hebbardsville without ever taking a book home to study. When assignments were made for the next day, I would either complete them before the class was over or do them in the study period. I soon worked my way through all of the novels in the small library as well.

At math, one of my favorite subjects, I enjoyed the contests the teacher often held. He would place a few of us at the blackboards where we wrote down numbers as he called them out. The contest was to see who could add the fastest. By the time he quit calling out numbers I would usually have the answer on the board. I would then remain at the board and a new group would join me, with the same results. However, I did not do as well at spelling or memorizing dates in history. English literature ranked high on my list of favorite subjects, but the teachers spent most of their time on English grammar.

Daddy's drinking had improved with the heavy work of driving the truck and unloading the coal he carried to homes and businesses. He found us a larger house on a hill southwest of Zion. We were disappointed not to be in Zion proper, but the four-room house, privy, and small barn were not only more spacious than the tenant house but also warmer.

Electricity had not been strung there either. From the hill at night we could see the lights of Zion about a mile away, and it was comforting to know that Granny and Granddad were so near.

On wash days Mother would often take her large bundles to Granny's to use the new electric washing machine with the automatic wringers on top. "Watch your fingers," Granny would warn us when we fed the clothes through the rollers.

Those of us in school had to walk to Zion to catch the bus each morning, a task that had us getting up very early. The seven-mile drive to Hebbardsville took a long time with the bus making all its stops and covering the route. We loved riding the bus. There was little adult supervision, since the driver had his hands full up front.

I wanted to sit beside Jean Bennett, the school's prettiest and most vivacious girl, even though she was a grade ahead of me and a popular cheerleader. The best chance I had was on the ride from Zion to about three miles near Hebbardsville. Then Charlie Tillotson, her boyfriend, got on and I would have to move, but I would try to reclaim the seat beside her on the way home after he got off.

The tangled relations of Zion families in and near the town were illustrated by my connections to Jean Bennett. Her grandfather, John Bennett, was a brother to Cooksey Bennett for whom Daddy was named. One of John's sons, Miles, married Bett Nichols, a sister to Peck, Touie, and Johnny Nick, all of whom were married either to one of Daddy's sisters or Mother's. Uncle Doot and William Evans Bennett, Jean's cousin, were lovers. And there were other Bennetts and Nicholses scattered throughout the county.

If I couldn't sit beside Jean, then I sat with Ben Crafton, who was in my class and the school's wit. Ben also came from a large family, but he wasn't the oldest. He was the third child of twelve. Like me, he was small and thin. We would usually gather with other boys in the back of the bus, playing games, telling jokes, and going over plans for the day, especially deciding what we would do when we got home from school.

Ben lived at the other end of Zion from our house, near Crafton's store, owned by his uncle. I seldom visited that store, preferring to spend my time at Cinnamon's Store nearer our house. However, Daddy had applied for welfare, and we were given "commodities" by the government. Crafton's was one of the distribution points, and it was my responsibility as the oldest child to go pick up the commodities, sometimes with Buddy's help.

I hated the task. I was embarrassed that we were so poor as to require government help, and I would take the back streets and cross the fields to avoid anyone seeing me on my way home.

Because of the size of our family, we qualified for a large amount each Thursday. "Commodities" consisted mostly of staples: navy beans, white flour, oatmeal, peanut butter, sorghum molasses, cheese, and large cans of some vegetables I never much liked. Mother made a lot of biscuits. It was rare for us to have "light" bread or sliced bread bought at the store.

We were forever eating navy beans, which we spiced with mayonnaise or tomato catsup or both. At the time we didn't know how healthy oatmeal was, nor that beans and rice provided the protein our growing bodies needed. We just knew that when we ate them we didn't get hungry as quickly as when we ate less nutritious food.

Being on welfare affected me in other ways than just being embarrassed. I would find it difficult to allow others to give me things or do things for me. I was much more comfortable being the one who did the giving. I came to feel I should earn what I got, and grace from others was difficult for me to accept.

With a barn available and pasture nearby, Daddy bought a rangy, brown cow. Her teats were small and difficult from which to press the milk or to get the cow to stand still and quit swishing me with her tail. I didn't enjoy milking for it was a twice-a-day chore that placed some restrictions on my freedom. We didn't always have corn or feed to supplement her diet, so her milk was not as rich as we would have liked. Mother seldom got enough cream with which to churn butter, but it may have been because the nine of us drank the milk so fast.

I loved fresh butter, and only got it on the Nichols farm where they milked many cows and were always churning for butter after using a separator to take the cream from the milk, instead of skimming it off the top after the milk sat for a while. They gave the skimmed milk, called "blue john," to the hogs, pouring it into a long, V-shaped trough.

We bought oleo margarine as our substitute butter. It came in one-pound loaves looking like lard in its whiteness, but with each package was a small folder of coloring. It was said the dairy industry would not allow the margarine to look like butter. Mother didn't always take the time to add the coloring, and we used it white. When we didn't have cow's milk, we used the condensed canned Pet Milk, which I detested. I would use it on my oatmeal, but nowhere else.

By the middle of the school year, we were rejoicing at home again. Daddy had been given his job back at the *Gleaner & Journal* when they found no one could do as much work or do it as well as he. The hard manual labor on the coal truck and reduced income had slowed his drinking. A back shop man told me one day, "They found it would take three people to replace Ben, drunk or sober."

At Hebbardsville I was too small or too inept at basketball, the major sport of the school—and the entire state, for that matter. Our tallest boys were barely six feet, but that seemed huge at the time as few grew much taller. I thought I was fast, so I tried track. When one of the Peckenpaugh girls beat me twice in the hundred-yard dash, I gave that up.

I was fascinated with cheerleading. Bill Crafton had broken ground as a boy cheerleader, and he would be graduating. Hebbardsville had three cheerleaders: Jean Bennett, Marie Keach, and Bill. All three were from Zion. I determined I would try to take Bill's place.

Tryouts for those who wanted to be cheerleaders were held on the stage of the school auditorium before the entire student body, and the students voted. Those receiving the most votes on the first ballot were selected. This year there were two openings, as Jean was the only one continuing. The competition was not too stiff for me, as only three boys tried out. Most of the boys thought it was a "sissy" thing to do, or they were too shy to do anything so public.

I had no problem with either, and besides I wanted to do anything to be noticed by Jean. For the competition we did solo leading of cheers, making moves we thought were appropriate. In the voting, my classmate Eva Long and I were selected.

Walker, cheerleader for Hebbardsville High School in 1940.

I worked hard at odd jobs to earn the money for my uniform: white flannel pants with big pleats and cuffs, a white wool V-neck sweater on which Mother sewed the blue and white H, white shoes, and white socks and shirt. For pep rallies or if we were traveling to another school on the day of a game, I sometimes wore the uniform to school. The white was difficult to keep clean, but I thought I looked great. I was proud to wear the uniform, and prouder still of my new status at school.

Jean taught Eva and me the cheers during study periods or after school when we were waiting for the bus. We would have practiced at Zion, but Eva lived on a farm. Most of the time I got a ride to the basketball game with some friend, as we played county teams at Spotsville, Roberts, Sebree, Niagra, Cairo, Holy Name in Henderson, and Weaverton—all high schools near our size.

If we got into the county tournament, we might play some of these teams again. But in the district tournament we would usually face the always-tough Corydon, actually the oldest school in the county. The games were always held in tiny gyms like ours, and we cheerleaders had little room on the sidelines from which to lead the yells that we kept going throughout the game.

At quarter and halftime breaks, we had the floor to ourselves. No one team dominated the sport, so we won some and lost some. When Jean graduated, Agnes Mills, another classmate, took her place.

Both Eva and Agnes were attractive and outgoing. I enjoyed being with them, and we had a lot of fun together, both as classmates and as cheerleaders. Our times together were never characterized by pettiness, spite, or arguments. However, we never dated each other; in fact, I did very little dating. This was due in part because I could not afford it, and with Jean committed to Charlie Tillotson, I had little desire to date other girls.

When we boys did date, most of us found girls a year or more younger than we were, probably because the girls matured physically earlier than we and because we boys were not as shy around younger girls.

For a short while I dated Mary Martin Musgrave, a pretty, intelligent girl three years my junior. We sometimes double dated for a movie or to a school function, and we talked a lot on the telephone, but I never had a car available for solo dating. Mary Martin, because she was so young, tended to be reserved and not as outgoing as girls I was used to being around, like Eva and Agnes, so our short period of dating never blossomed into romance.

Although I didn't date much, I learned about proper relationships by observing my pastor and his wife. I was a frequent guest in the Rodgers's home, playing with their young children. I was allowed to drop in any time I wished, and when I was with them I marveled at the relationship Clel and Lucille had with each other.

Clel teased her in subtle, quiet ways, and she responded in kind. They were not bashful about showing their affection for each other, and they wore their faith in such comfortable ways that I was pulled to them like metal to a magnet. Clel had a Will Rogers-like demeanor, almost shy at times and both sharp and gentle with his wit. The community seemed as attracted to him as I was.

One summer Clel planned youth week at the church, a time when all of the offices of the church were to be held by youth. We would be Sunday school superintendent, BYPU director, WMU director, teachers, choir members, song leader, deacons, and, of course, pastor. Not too surprising to anyone because of my association with Clel, I was asked to be the youth pastor.

The other boys were probably relieved. I was honored, fascinated, and frightened. What would I talk about? How was I to prepare a sermon? How long did it have to be? Would Clel help me? Of course, he said he would, and I started weeks before the date of Youth Sunday working on my message.

When the day finally came, and I was dressed in my only suit, Mother and some of my siblings were in the audience. Finally the time came, and I delivered myself of that sermon—all ten minutes of it, but it seemed like two hours. I do not remember my theme or topic. When I gave the invitation, six of the young people made decisions by coming to the front and registering them—so I was considered more than the usual success as a preacher.

My earlier sense that I was to be a minister was thus strongly reinforced, but I did not talk about it, even to Clel. I still was telling everyone I wanted to be a journalist, and my lifelong dream was to work as a reporter on the *Gleaner & Journal.*

Daddy's drinking was consuming him, and he was fired again. He was out of work for a long time, then got a low-paying job at the Audubon State Park selling tickets at the entrance booth. The Audubon Museum had been completed by the CCC, and the park attracted visitors from a large area. Daddy looked good in the uniform he wore during work hours, and he didn't seem to mind the menial job, for he never complained in my presence.

Why did Mother endure the agony of living with Daddy, with the drinking, the abuse she personally suffered at times, with the uncertainty of daily life, and with one pregnancy after another? I can only speculate.

Divorce was not something respectable people did in those days. Also she had almost no alternative to provide for a large family, whose responsibility would fall on her or upon her parents. Possibly she continued to love him through it all, as difficult as that might seem. A psychologist might say that she contributed to his alcoholism by constantly taking him back and standing by him through all of his firings and problems with drinking.

Sunday night, December 7, 1941, my senior year at Hebbardsville, I was in church when I first heard the news that the Japanese had bombed Pearl Harbor in Hawaii. We would spend most of that night and every possible moment the next few days glued to the radios.

Our first thoughts were of Coonk and Russ Nichols, who had joined the Navy. Coonk was somewhere in the Pacific, and it would be weeks before we learned that indeed they had been at Pearl Harbor, but had escaped injury. One of my strongest memories is hearing Aunt Mary sing "His Eye Is on the Sparrow" in church during this time of uncertainty about Russ and Coonk. The war was to change all our lives immediately.

Chapter 6

WAR

With war declared and the nation mobilizing, it seemed half the youth and young men of Henderson County were suddenly gone, including Uncle Doot who became an officer in the Army. All males age eighteen and older had to register with the Selective Service, and I was eighteen that February of 1942.

I was classified 1A, which meant I was subject to immediate draft once out of high school. The county was introduced to rationing, and the war seemed immediately to bring an end to the depression. With men going into the service, there was a new demand for workers and wages slowly began to increase.

Daddy, employed yet again at the *Gleaner & Journal*, lost a reporter, and he asked me if I would consider dropping out of high school to work at the paper. I was thrilled beyond words; at last I would get my chance to work as a reporter on a real newspaper. Daddy talked with the high school principal who arranged for me to get my assignments from the teachers and to turn my papers in each week for grading. The principal thought I would learn as much from the work as from schooling.

I had no problem with the arrangement about homework. I usually could do the work in less than an hour each day, typing out the assignments at the office. I graduated that year, 1942, but I did not attend the graduation exercises; instead, I visited the principal and received my diploma at his office.

For the most part I rode to work at the *Gleaner* with Daddy, if our schedules matched. Otherwise, I caught a ride for the six miles with someone I knew who would be coming into town. At the paper I had my own desk and typewriter in an open area marked off by a fence-like railing. Daddy presided over the space from a corner desk.

Becoming a reporter, however, was not as easy as I had thought it would be, especially since Daddy took little time to give me any instruction. He seemed to think I should pick up the skills on my own, as he possibly had done during a less intense time. I was often embarrassed to have to call back on an interview when I had failed to ask the right questions or I had written my story with an important fact missing.

My beat included city hall and the county courthouse. I would check on the arrests, the filing of deeds, marriages, trials, and other such recorded events. From these I either would write articles, calling and interviewing officials or people involved, or simply type up the lists for publication. Luckily, I had taken typing in high school and did not have to learn that.

I was introduced to a side of life in Henderson I had only vaguely known existed. I also got to meet and to know Francele Armstrong, the youngest Harris daughter, who began writing a column for the paper and did some reporting.

The few months I worked for my father did not prove to be as rewarding and as fulfilling as I had hoped. His expectations of me were so high that I did little to please him. His constant criticism hurt, even though I knew he wanted me to do well. And the agony of being so close to him while he continued to drink throughout each day became more than I could stand.

I received the chance offer of a job at a restaurant paying me $10 a week instead of the $7 the newspaper paid. I took the other job, to my father's disappointment. However, Mother understood this as she seemed to understand most of my other decisions.

Growing up as the child of an alcoholic affected me in many ways. One of these was an emotional numbness. I learned early to protect myself from emotional damage by avoiding strong feelings. I would not allow my hopes to soar too highly for fear they would be dashed on the rocks of another family crisis. On the other hand I did not become too despondent. Encouraged by Mother to see the brighter side of life, I always thought things would become better.

My involvement at church had reached a new level. Mr. and Mrs. Al Burton had moved to Zion into a house down the hill from ours. They became very active in the church, especially Mrs. Burton. She was an attractive, soft-spoken woman who radiated the most intensive spirituality of anyone I had known.

I kept expecting to see some flaw, some Achilles' heel, but she never revealed one to me. She invited a few of the young people to come to her home on Tuesday nights for Bible study and prayer. We started going mostly for social reasons, but then we discovered an entirely new dimension to our faith.

We were surprised that we came to enjoy these sessions when all we would do was read the Bible, with little commentary from Mrs. Burton or anyone else. After the Scripture study each of us would pray, then we might have light refreshments and some time talking and joking with each other. We kept going back. In a way, it was unusual but stimulating.

As we began to tell others about what was going on, they asked if they could come and see for themselves. The Tuesday night crowd grew and grew, until we overflowed the Burton living room. During this period all of us became even more active at church.

Once we young people decided that Pastor Clel Rodger's salary should be raised. We attended the monthly business meeting en mass, a surprise to the adults who usually found the business meetings sparsely attended and almost boycotted by youth. They were in for another surprise when one of us made the motion that the pastor's salary be increased, but cautious adults had it referred to a committee for study.

We felt we had done our duty in making the motion and in expressing our feelings about the matter. It worked, too, for the pastor's salary was later increased.

Although he never said it in so many words, I sensed that Clel was not too comfortable with the Bible study sessions at Mrs. Burton's. By summer that year, the ranks of those attending our prayer meetings had swollen to include youth from all over the county, and one meeting at a lakeside attracted more than fifty. By this time our weekly agenda included a short devotional along with the Bible study and prayer, then refreshments and "fellowship."

I'm sure the uncertainty of the war had us all searching for answers to the meaning of life and the significance of faith. Each month our ranks would be thinned by the drafting or volunteering, as one after another of our friends went to war, but we all discovered a more vigorous commitment to a faith we had more or less taken for granted.

In a way, my work at the restaurant became a repeat of what had happened at the newspaper. After hiring me, the owner gave me the keys and told me to open up the next morning. He didn't even take the time to show me where anything was. Luckily it was one of the small restaurants with eight stools and a few tables, and trade in the mornings was not too heavy.

The first morning I was there bright and early, clad with my clean white apron and cap. The first customer ordered cereal, and before he noticed he had poured the buttermilk I gave him into the bowl. It was downhill from there, as I scrambled eggs, made coffee, and otherwise stumbled through the morning until the owner finally showed up. He got a big laugh out of my troubles. I could have choked him.

All businesses were short-handed at this time, and one day the manager of a ready-mix concrete company was eating in the restaurant where I worked. He had known me for years and was a friend of Daddy's. He asked me how I had done in math in school. I told him it was one of my favorite subjects and I had done extremely well.

"How about coming to work for me as a bookkeeper?" he asked.

"I don't know anything about bookkeeping," I answered.

"Doesn't matter," he said. "I'll teach you all you need to know. And I'll pay you $12 a week to start."

The restaurant work was not all that fulfilling, so I quickly agreed and turned in my notice. The next week I was a fledgling bookkeeper for a ready-mix concrete company whose business was booming as the war had set the construction business on a quickened pace.

Once again I was the victim of little or no instruction. The manager handed me the books, told me where to enter the invoices, and lightly explained debits and credits. Then he turned his hand to other, more pressing matters. His business was exploding on him. The phone never stopped ringing, and the stream of workers and customers flowed constantly in and out of his office.

I was left to myself trying to figure out what went on what page and in which column. As the weeks passed I became more and more confused, often making attempts to slow the manager down to explain to me what I should do, but to no avail.

At church Clel started planning a summer trip to Ridgecrest Baptist Assembly in North Carolina for Training Union Week, and he wanted as many of the young people to go as possible. He had also arranged for scholarships for those of us short of funds. I wanted very much to make the trip. I literally ached to go and could think of nothing else.

Finally, I asked the manager of the ready-mix concrete company if I could be off for the dates, without pay, but he said he could not spare me. I was disappointed and depressed, feelings that were probably intensified by my unhappiness at work because I knew I was not doing it well. Casting all caution aside, I quit.

I knew another job would not be difficult to find with everyone being called into the military. I was going to Ridgecrest. The manager of the concrete company told someone later he was years getting the "Bunk" out of his books. I felt he had only himself to blame.

Ridgecrest Baptist Assembly in the lush Appalachian Mountains near Black Mountain, North Carolina, was another world to me—more beautiful than I had expected and much more exciting. I was nearly overwhelmed by the hundreds of youth from all over the nation. I had made only one other trip out of the Henderson County area in my life. That was our senior class trip to Nashville when all twenty-five of us rode the bus for a day's outing that included the replica of the Parthenon and the Tennessee state capitol. We skipped the Grand Ole Opry.

I determined to make the most of my trip to Ridgecrest, getting acquainted with Baptist young people from Texas, Georgia, the Carolinas, and other states. We laughed at each other's accents. They liked the way I said, "Ah cain't hep hit."

In one Bible study class I met a tall, big-boned blond from Corpus Christi, Texas. Her name was Margaret. We found our interests to be very similar and spent hours together at meals and other free time. She was the first girl since Jean Bennett to whom I was attracted, and we couldn't find enough time to get all of our talking done, telling each other about our lives back home and plans for the future. She returned my interest, but after the week was over we were to correspond only briefly.

Each evening during the week at Ridgecrest the entire assembly of nearly a thousand people would gather in the auditorium, the largest building of its type I had ever seen. Usually, Margaret and I would find each other and sit together for the program of music, testimonies, and preaching. It was all fresh, new, and appealing to a small town boy out of the state for virtually the first time.

The custom was to have a well-known preacher speak each night of the week. That week the preacher was C. Oscar Johnson of St. Louis,

Missouri. Dr. Johnson was world famous among Baptists, not only for his long-time pastorate of the prestigious Third Baptist Church, but he also had been the president of the Baptist World Alliance. He appeared to be in his fifties—a big, heavyset man with a low, booming voice he could manipulate like a musical instrument.

For the week he had chosen to preach on the Beatitudes from Jesus' Sermon on the Mount, picking one for each night. The Beatitudes were the characteristics of the Christian life he told us. After each message an extended invitation was given for persons either to become Christians or to register publicly some decision they were making.

Since the beginning of the week I had been thinking more and more about the feeling I should be a minister. Even Frank Reid had once told me I would become a preacher. I talked about all this with Margaret, and I had started praying about it.

On Thursday night Dr. Johnson preached on the Beatitude, "Blessed are they who hunger and thirst after righteousness, for they shall be filled." He said that we should see the thirst, the desire we had for faith as an indication God was working with us, that even the doubt in our minds was a step leading to faith. The verse could also be translated, "Blessed are those who want to see things set right, for they will help accomplish it." At the time I had no idea this verse would characterize my life from that time on.

Emotionally, I already had been prepared to make a public decision that God wanted me to be a minister. Now Dr. Johnson was answering some of my intellectual questions and speaking to my doubts. I stepped out and joined others that night who were also registering decisions.

Some people in Christian vocations say that God has spoken to them with very specific instructions. If God spoke to me in that fashion, I did not hear. I was deaf. What had happened was that what once had been but a slight impression had gradually become a whisper and finally a strong urge. Had there not been a set pattern to follow I might not have responded as I did, and even then it was still an uncertain path. Life then and afterwards was not all that certain.

However, Baptist circles speak of "surrendering" to God's will, and that night at Ridgecrest I experienced a sense of giving in, an acceptance of and a faith in something greater than myself that I felt would have a strong part in my destiny. It is difficult to find the words for the sensation, but the decision would stay with me for the rest of my life, even though my understanding of the Christian vocation would change.

Was it coincidence that Dr. Johnson preached that night on that particular beatitude? Did I respond in part to what he was saying, or had my mind subconsciously already made the decision? I believe most of our important decisions are not made in one brief moment but over a lengthy period. In fact, I had been acting out this direction or decision even before I registered it.

But if this was all coincidence—his preaching on a verse that would characterize my life's work and my registering an intention to devote my life to a religious vocation—then I stand amazed, but to say God planned it all for my sake would be the height of egotism. I prefer to think that God's Spirit utilizes what is present in any situation and gently nudges us without force or coercion, like the caress of a spring breeze, to align our lives with God's will.

Clel and the others from Zion were excited about my decision, and I sensed that Clel was not too surprised. At the time I thought I would become a pastor, for that was the only model of Christian ministry I had ever seen or heard. However, despite my unhappy experience with the newspaper, I felt some regret I would no longer be planning to be a journalist, even though I had not seen Christianity and journalism mixing very well.

With the decision at Ridgecrest I was turning my back on my earlier desire, so there was sadness as well as elation following that week.

While I did not at the time comprehend the importance of the decision I had made, I did sense it was a life-changing event, that my life would not be the same afterwards. In a way, it was not an unusual pattern for young men to take who had grown up in a Baptist church.

It was a pattern repeated hundreds of times each year among Southern Baptists, and there was within the decision a ritual that one followed: a sense that I was being "called" by God to the ministry, a decision we were encouraged to make by teachers and ministers, and this was followed by a public registration of the decision.

I knew that it was a decision I had considered for a long time and one that had been in my mind for years. There was a sense of abandonment of self to God's direction, which meant that no matter what, I would seek to serve as a minister. That did not mean I knew what I was doing with certainty and without doubts. Doubt always walks as faith's shadow.

Once, Clel and I discussed the doubt that every person has who is honest with himself. Clel said he had decided that even if the Christ story were false, what he was giving his life to was yet worthy of all his energy and time. And that if the Christ story were true, then all that he did was doubly blessed.

I did realize then that my decision eventually would require my having college and seminary training, but all of that was but dreams. When I returned home, the family was pleased but not too excited.

Once when someone asked Mother, "Aren't you excited about your son?" she replied, "Which one?" I had briefly become the talk of Zion. I was not the only one from our church at that time to announce he would become a minister.

Joe Priest Williams, a year older than I, also did, and later his younger brother Robert made the same decision. Their father, Frederick Williams—a tall, slim farmer who spoke softly and deliberately—had long been a deacon and leader at the Baptist church in Zion.

But I would not become a minister immediately; I went to work at another Red Front grocery store in Henderson. In September the bottom dropped out of our family's world.

On Labor Day the phone rang. Someone from the *Gleaner & Journal* asked, "Is Bennett coming to work?"

Mother answered, "I don't know. He did not come home all weekend."

Daddy's not coming home was not unusual, for he often found somewhere to drink and drink and drink. Mother told the person at the paper we would try to find him and let them know.

"Walker Leigh, go by the Checkerboard, the American Legion, the pool halls, and any other place you can think of, and see if you can't find him at any of those," she told me, knowing we couldn't get the truth out of anyone who might answer the phones.

"Meanwhile, I'll call the sheriff's office and the police in case he has had an accident," she added as I left.

We searched throughout the day to no avail. I went to every place he was known to haunt. No one appeared to know where he was, and none had seen him since Friday. The next day we notified the police that he was missing and asked for an investigation. Later that week the police found he had sold the Ford. They suggested he might have left town. The next week Mother reported his absence to the draft board, and they said if he was found he would probably be drafted.

I felt numbed at his desertion of the family. I could not understand it, and I could not really feel a strong emotion at the time. I was not overtly angry. If anything, I was saddened. We had been abandoned by the one who provided for us. Why?

I had seen up close the grip that alcohol had upon him, but nevertheless I was shocked that he had left without a word to us—without telling anyone, for that matter. He was only forty-one years old, but he could not go for a day without drinking. He knew he was failing at work, for he had been fired twice, and he could not control his drinking.

Was this enough to cause a man to leave his wife and seven children at home? Or did he think he could go somewhere else, turn over a new leaf and possibly send for the family or at least send funds back?

Had he felt trapped in Henderson with a family this size, with a job that held no promise of advancement after twenty years? Had he met someone with whom he left? How long had he planned to leave, or did he suffer a blackout that is common to alcoholics and take this action during such a period?

I would never have my questions answered. We were never to hear from him again, and we did not have the funds to employ a private investigator to search for him.

Walker's father, Cooksey Bennett Knight, in the late 1930s.

In fact, I do not remember anyone suggesting it seriously. The assumption was that alcohol had caused Daddy to leave.

During this traumatic period I kept a small diary. Each day I wrote about three sentences, mostly telling one or two highlights of my day. I was working at Red Front Store Number 11 from 7:30 a.m. until 6 p.m. during the week and until 10:30 p.m. on Saturday. I refused to work on Sunday on religious grounds.

At the time I was active at the Wednesday prayer meeting at the Zion church and at the young people's prayer meeting on Thursday nights.

It was no wonder that I frequently admitted to being late to work, especially since I had to "catch a ride" or hitchhike to Henderson going and coming. One night I noted that I had walked three miles, with the comment, "Guess I'm getting in shape for the Army."

I was a very religious young man, recording guilt feelings when I went to a movie, refusing a promotion because I would have to work on Sunday, and closing each diary entry with a prayer for Daddy. The sentiment about Daddy was admirable, but I know now that I was suppressing anger that I thought a "good Christian" would not express.

I actually did not express emotion of any kind toward him, and not until thirty years later would I realize that I never cried for my father. I did express one emotion again and again in that brief recorded period. I was brokenhearted because Jean Bennett had married Charlie Tillotson, and I wrote, "My devotion will never die."

Making things worse, Daddy had left Mother pregnant with their ninth child. There were seven of us children living at home. I was 18, Buddy 17, Bettye 15, Dorothy 13, Bubba 11, Hiram 7 and Jane 4. (Mary Ruth, living with the Nicholses, was 9.)

Daddy had deserted us, but none of us would ever hear Mother complain or degrade Daddy. The closest she ever came was to say, "If Bennett Knight were to walk in that door, he would expect me to take him in as though nothing had happened."

I was the only one with work, as those old enough were still in school. Granny and Granddad, with Doot gone to the Army, were living by themselves. They moved their furniture out of two rooms, and we moved ours in. At the time, although I did not know about it, Granddad already was looking for a larger place for us.

The John Bennetts lived on a high hill overlooking Zion in the old ten-room, two-story Bennett mansion. It was a deteriorating frame structure almost falling in on itself in places. The aging Bennetts could not take care of the place, and their children did not want to spend the money to repair the building. Granddad asked if we could rent one of the upstairs wings while he constructed a house for us in Zion.

We had plenty of room, but wind whipped through the cracks like the walls were not present. Later, Granddad traded his two acres in Zion for the ancient mansion and twenty acres surrounding it. Being a carpenter and a contractor, he planned to restore the structure. Granddad knew we could not stay there long, so he was already sawing the lumber for a house on a lot he owned near Aunt Mary's.

Since I was the oldest and the one working, I began to assume more authority with the younger children. I am sure that I was not too pleasant to be around some of the time. My brothers and sisters had strong minds of their own, and they began to call me "Bossy-boss-ass-Bunk." Buddy, frustrated with it all, decided he would join the Navy, even though he was only seventeen and Mother's permission was required. He was quickly accepted and almost as soon gone, promising to send money home. On November 9 I rode with him to Owensboro where he caught the bus for Louisville.

The next night, November 10, feeling the sting of his absence and my having to stay at home, I wrote in my diary, "If I don't get to go (to the Army), I believe I will miss something that I have been wanting." I also knew that I

In the early 1940s Mariah Griffin (Granny) and William Tandy Henderson (Granddad), parents of Rowena (Anna) Walker's mother, stand beside the old mansion for which Tandy had traded their house in Zion. Walker's family lived in a portion of the mansion until the community built them a house on two acres in Zion.

might be inducted any day, for Congress had passed the "teenage draft bill," lowering the age to eighteen.

But the trauma of war struck our extended family on November 13 with word that the *USS San Francisco*, on which both Russ and Coonkey Nichols served, had been hit by a falling Japanese airplane and thirty were killed. The announcement, of course, did not carry any names.

The word came on Friday and that Sunday, Aunt Mary stood in church and sang "His Eye Is on the Sparrow," not knowing if either of her boys were alive. The next week President Roosevelt, in a radio message, bragged on the *USS San Francisco* for its leadership in the great naval battle for Guadalcanal, but it would not be until December 8 that we learned that Russ was fine but Coonkey had been burned severely over his upper body, including his head.

As if we didn't have troubles enough, one day Mother and Bettye took me aside and told me that Bettye was also pregnant. I had wondered at her size, but when I had questioned Mother she had told me Bettye was just gaining weight. Bettye had been dating Raymond Sigler almost from the time she started at Hebbardsville. He was nineteen and the son of an established farmer.

After Mother and Bettye told me this startling news, I talked with Bettye and Raymond, sitting outside the house one night in his Ford car. I asked Raymond what he was going to do about Bettye's being pregnant, and he said they wanted to get married immediately, before he was called up for service.

I was pleased and relieved. They were married November 21, and Raymond moved in with us because Bettye at fifteen years of age did not want to leave her mother while she was pregnant, knowing Raymond was subject to being called into the military at any time.

On November 24 I was told I would be inducted, despite my appeal— at Mother's request—that I be given a deferment because of our family's need. Getting this news, I enlisted for immediate induction since it gave me the choice of which branch of the Army I would serve, and I chose the Air Corps. Raymond was notified that he would be in the same group to leave on January 21.

Meanwhile, all of us who could use a hammer or carry a board, along with a number of others in the community, including Clel, were helping Granddad with the house in Zion. I also learned that I could actually send home nearly as much money from my pay—I was earning $20 a week—as I was clearing at the grocery store.

I'm not too sure about my motives. It is possible I could have gotten a deferment if we had been more persistent. The Selective Service had not offered Raymond a deferment, so I did not expect one myself. I may have been looking for a way out of all the pain and misery, and Mother was looking more to Granny and Granddad than to me.

January 1943 was a pivotal month in all our lives. First, Raymond and I both quit our jobs to spend full time building the house, which under Granddad's supervision and ingenuity finally neared completion.

Granddad had bought old buildings that we razed, then we cleaned the lumber to be reused. The same process was followed for old brick with which to lay the foundation and construct the chimney. Men and boys from all over the nearby county came to help erect the dwelling, making the event a festive affair.

Granddad, before he died, would give each of his four children a house and lot. Our house had three rooms across the front and a kitchen and porch at the back with nearly two acres for a garden. The worse problem was that Mother and the children would have to go to the well at the blacksmith shop about 300 feet away for water.

James Lynn Knight was born January 11. We called him "Jimmy." By the time Mother was on her feet after the birth, we had finished the house and were moving things into the new, well-constructed home. However, Raymond and I were never to live there.

We were inducted into the Army and the Army Air Corps soon after Jimmy was born. We were both sent to the induction center at Indianapolis. Without Raymond and me, Mother moved into the house with six children, all under fifteen years of age and one of these newly born. Mother was still cheerful and determined.

As I was leaving, Clel told me, "Your mother is the most remarkable woman I have ever known."

Over the years I have pondered those words, along with my own questions. How could she have nurtured us all? How could she see the bright side to any disaster? Where did she find the time to express her love in such ways that we all can never express how much we love her and revere her memory?

I have always felt secure in who I am, have had the strength to take risks, and been willing to care for and share with others. The only answers I could find were in God's Spirit and in my mother's love.

Chapter 7

U.S. Army Air Corps

No one in Henderson County questioned whether or not the United States should be engaged in a world war, not that I ever heard or read about it. After all, had we not been attacked by the Japanese? Was not Hitler a fiend who should be destroyed? Was this not a just war by any definition? It was a struggle between the forces of light and darkness.

I enlisted with no questions as to the rightness of our involvement or that this was a proper way for a nation to settle its differences when threatened by another power. Actually, I gave very little thought to matters of the morality of war. I had a very parochial view of life at eighteen, finding the struggles of family life sufficient unto the day.

There was in my enlistment something of the adventurer, wanting to see more than Henderson County, or Evansville, which I had visited only rarely. My travels had taken me once to Nashville and once to North Carolina. I had enlisted so that I might escape the infantry and serve within the U.S. Army Air Corps.

I was sent by bus to the Army induction center in Indianapolis that cold January of 1943, leaving a family very much in turmoil but now settled in a house they owned, thanks to Granddad. Both Buddy, who was in the Navy, and I were to send home an allotment from our meager pay. I first drew $50 a month, of which I kept less than half, and the Army matched what I allotted for Mother. Knowing this much had been done, I was able to turn my attention to the business of being a soldier.

The induction center swarmed with recruits. The place was over-flowing, with more coming in than they seemed prepared to ship out. Consequently, I was introduced to the time-honored practice of standing in line—for meals, for tests, for clothing, for mail, for shots, for examinations, and sometimes even to use the latrine. I learned early to battle the boredom of waiting in line by taking something to read with me, or I would get acquainted with those nearest in line and learn from them. I was not shy, and I was born curious.

The first gift the U. S. Army gave me was a serial number: 357-225-99. It is a number I will never forget. This was before much emphasis was placed on Social Security numbers. The serial number became more important than my name.

Two or more soldiers might have the same name, but they could not have the same serial number. Every time I went for a test, every time I filled out forms, every time something was issued, I was first asked for my serial number. I soon had my personal serial number memorized.

Along with the number I was issued "dog tags"—metal identification tags to wear on a chain around my neck. The dog tags were stamped with my name, serial number, blood type, and religion. For the Army there were only three religions—Protestant, Catholic, or Jewish—and a dog tag had either a P, C, or J.

Some of us pure Baptists resented these classifications, for we claimed none fit us. We were not Protestants. We claimed Baptists pre-dated the Reformation when former Catholics were protesting the pope. We had never been Catholics. However, I never thought it made all that much difference, for we had protested Catholicism long before the other Protestants. I accepted the "P" classification as readily as I did "AB" for blood type and the serial number that had now taken the place of my name. I wonder to this day how they classified those who were Buddhist, Muslim, or otherwise, even Native American religion.

The first day those in charge started our physicals—including the infamous "short-arm" inspections (milking the penis for venereal disease before a doctor)—when it seemed all they wanted to discover was if we could see, hear, and walk. We didn't learn of many men flunking the exam. Standing around naked for an hour or more did not phase me, one of the benefits of a large family and hanging out with the boys at the mine washhouse or swimming in the Ohio and Green Rivers.

After making sure I would be accepted, the army issued my clothing and gear. Along with a dark green duffle bag that would hold everything when packed correctly, I was issued black shoes and a belt, greenish underwear, a heavy overcoat, a blanket, towels and a washcloth, a hard plastic helmet liner (the helmet would come later, they said), sheets and a pillowcase, socks and a light khaki jacket, then two each of hats and summer khaki and winter wool outfits. The winter outfit included the dress blouse that I proudly wore on leave or on parade. Because I was so small, nothing fit me well, but I considered myself well clothed with all the new apparel.

Other than clothing, I received an aluminum mess kit whose top and bottom were held together by a long handle that swiveled to clamp over the two parts, and inside the mess kit I placed my knife, fork, and spoon. I was issued a canteen with a cloth cover that fastened onto a three-inch wide, heavy fiber belt. The canteen also was designed to fit snugly within an aluminum cup that held a pint of liquid and could be used for drink or stew.

The next day I took the I.Q. tests, which were more pleasant and challenging than the physical tests. I scored well, but they did not bother to tell me what my score was at the time. I learned that men were retained who scored as low as 75, but I felt that the higher the score the greater would be my options in regards to assignments.

I was unceremoniously introduced to close order drill and kitchen police, as well as "policing" the grounds. Policing the grounds was going over every inch of the area for cigarette butts and other trash. Drilling had three purposes: first, to keep us busy; second, to teach us to do things together; and third, to learn to obey orders on command without questioning them. Drilling, nevertheless, was preferred to kitchen police or KP.

For KP, I and the others on duty were awakened at 4 a.m. in order to have breakfast ready before the camp heard reveille. Getting up that early was torture for me. I sometimes had trouble going to sleep on the double bunks, but once asleep it was very difficult to awaken me. I remember feeling almost drugged in the mornings. I came very close to getting in serious trouble because of it. They would call for us, and when we did not respond, they would come shake us. I would answer but never actually wake up. They would find me missing in formation, and come back to the sack to chew me out royally.

KP lasted from 4 a.m. until 7 p.m., and we worked hard all of the time: mopping floors, washing pots and pans and dishes, peeling potatoes, and serving food. The abusive cooks could always find something for us to do during the entire fifteen-hour day. When I reached the barracks at night I could do no more than take off my clothes and drop into bed. Besides having to take a turn at KP, the Army used the duty as punishment for infractions, and punishment it was. The only good feature was that it did not occur very often.

During those first few days I was introduced to another feature of the Army: rumors. Someone always knew the inside "dope" about what was going to happen next or where we would be going or even what might be the next ordeal we would undergo. We knew we would not be at the induction center long. Those in charge had to move us out to make room for the next wave of inductees.

We would be there only long enough for them to make up their minds about our next assignments. What followed this phase, we all knew, would be basic training. Everyone had to have the dreaded basic training, and no matter where we were sent we did not expect it to be pleasant.

Orders affecting those in our barracks were posted daily on bulletin boards near our buildings. We were told to check them each day. In addition, at morning assembly when we answered roll call before being marched to breakfast, the non-commissioned officer would read out the names of those whose orders were being posted for the day.

Roll call those first days was an experience, for corporals and sergeants had been trained in barking drill orders, not necessarily in reading names they had never seen before. Of course, the ethnic names from Chicago or even the Germans from Evansville were the hardest, but often when they came to Knight I would hardly recognize my own name.

Just ahead of me would be someone named "Knipe" and they would call out "Kee-nipe"—correctly pronouncing that name. Then when they came to "Knight," they shouted "Kee-nite" or some other corruption. I quickly learned who was in front of me, so I knew when to expect my last name to be shouted, and I could shout back, "Here!"

Part of the impersonal nature of military service was the loss of our first names. We referred to each other by family names: Jones, Smith, Knipe, Knight. Only with long-time acquaintances or close friends did we become Walker or Bill or John.

Finally, my name was called for orders. I was to be shipped out to Atlantic City, New Jersey, for basic training. Atlantic City? Not even the smartest of the rumormongers had predicted this.

No one knew of an army base at this resort area. They wouldn't ship us overseas without basic training, would they? Could this be some trick or ruse? If so, why? One consolation, if I could call it that, was I would have plenty of company. They were sending a train full of us. We carefully packed our duffle bags and carried them aboard the train. I spent my nineteenth birthday en route.

February snow and ice covered the streets, houses, and sidewalks of Atlantic City. The wind had gathered force racing across the frozen land, and by the time it reached us it had a sharp sting to its breath. At the station we were loaded into trucks and driven to the ocean.

"My God," cried one soldier, "They are shipping us out!" But the trucks rolled to a stop before the huge fifteen-story Ambassador Hotel, sprawling alongside the boardwalk like a worn-out movie set abandoned for more glamorous dreams.

"Are we going to stay here, Sarge?" more than one of our party excitedly asked, with visions of fancy rooms and plush beds dancing in their heads. "Will they have room service?"

"It's your home for the next four weeks. Make the most of it!" the nom-con answered, without any explanation.

Vision met reality once we walked through the wide doors—darkened with blackout curtains against lurking German submarines—and we struggled with duffle bags to our floors. The wide halls, stripped of hotel furniture and carpet, were crammed with bunks. Bunks were everywhere, especially in the once spacious rooms. My bunk was in an alcove along the hall of the fifth floor. The boardwalk's largest hotel was only a fifteen-story barracks. We ate and pulled our KP duty in the mess hall in the large basement.

And the boardwalk was a drill field. When the wind whipped across the churning ocean, we could not find enough clothes to stay warm. We put on layers of pants and underwear. We wore our huge, heavy coats and blouses, but the wind found our most vulnerable spots and bored into them. The wind even came from below, through the cracks in the boardwalk. We welcomed movement, for the worse moments came when we had to stand still.

We spent long, torturous hours drilling on the boards beside the sea, or in open areas near the famous walk, whose shops and restaurants were all closed. One small advantage came my way because of my size. Each platoon was formed by placing the tallest at the front and grading downward to the shortest. I was most often on the back row, so if we were headed into the wind, I had some protection, but otherwise the wind was at my back.

I was issued an M-1 rifle for drilling purposes and some training in taking it apart and cleaning it. We also used it on the rifle range until we were able to earn the Sharpshooters Medal certifying our ability to hit a target some distance away. I had used BB guns, .22 rifles, and shotguns back home, so I had little trouble qualifying. We learned the proper positions for holding the rifle, to keep the left arm underneath for support and to squeeze the trigger when firing to avoid jerking it off target.

I welcomed the days we were marched to the armory, the site of the Miss America Pageant, now stripped bare of seats. The enormous cavern held stacks of military supplies with trucks moving in and out, and platoons moving through, around, or standing in place. The stage area often became the site for lectures or movies about Army life, venereal disease, or the enemy.

At the armory we were also given more tests. But one test sealed my fate. We were asked to write yes or no if two sounds were alike or dissimilar. Always one to compete for a high score, I succeeded, and my file noted that I had a high aptitude for radio operation using the Morse Code.

After three weeks on the boardwalk, I received a day pass to explore Atlantic City away from the army resort camp beside the sea. I jumped at the chance, and I felt I deserved some treat. Along with two other buddies who had also been released from "prison," I went searching for something to do on Saturday afternoon. We had to be back by dark. We window shopped for some time, but soon despaired of finding much that was exciting.

"Let's eat!" someone suggested. "I'm sick of Army chow."

We were close to a small restaurant, with counter and tables, reminding me of the café in which I worked when I left the *Gleaner & Journal*, only this was fancier. I determined I would order something I had never eaten before, feeling both adventurous and risqué.

The menu surprised me by its elaborateness, and even more so by its prices. Finally, I found an item that matched my feelings: Oyster Cocktail—$1.50. It was a lot of money, but "What the heck," I thought, "I've never had a cocktail. I'll try it."

Preparation of my order did not take long, and soon a large platter, big enough to hold a pot roast, was placed before me. Six large oyster shells surrounded a small bowl holding a red sauce. On each shell lay a grey, raw oyster, and on the plate was a tiny fork. The plate was garnished with a slice of lemon.

I looked at that plate for a long time, hoping neither of my buddies was watching too closely. They didn't know that I had not known what an oyster cocktail was, that I thought it was something to drink. Now, what could I do? I had blown $1.50, half a day's wages at the grocery store where I had last worked.

Anyway, how do you eat oysters—raw oysters, that is? Do you swallow them or slowly chew them? I knew the fork was my only utensil, so I speared one of the slimy creatures, drug it through the scarlet sauce and placed it in my mouth. I almost gagged, but it quickly slipped down my throat. I made my way through two more, then gave up. My friends had been watching, and now they started laughing. Embarrassed, I pushed the plate away and said: "Give me a hamburger, please." So much for risqué adventures . . .

I had been in Atlantic City long enough to receive mail. From my first day in service I had written Mother each night. I found it a way to settle down and a way to ward off homesickness, and besides, we could mail all our letters free of postage. Mother's letters were interesting and informative. Through them I began to see another side to her life. We corresponded as adult to adult, not as parent to child, and I looked forward to mail call.

I came to see that Mother had given me more than my physical life. She had freed me to be myself. She had not imposed upon me her expectations. Her love had never demanded, had never smothered, but had set me free. From the distance of a month and hundreds of miles, sitting in a faded resort hotel hallway, I had a clearer view of our relationship.

I now could see that I alone had made the decision to volunteer for the Air Corps, as I had earlier made the decision for a Christian vocation. If she had said anything to me with her silence and the lack of pressure, it was, "Be yourself. Make your own decisions, for you are the one who will have to live with them throughout your life."

She gave me the freedom to fail without rushing to hold me up or to burden me down. As I write this, I realize I might not have been able at nineteen to verbalize it, but I do remember feeling it and being grateful to her. How she could accomplish that in the midst of her great needs, I shall never know.

I learned that Mother had taken a job in Henderson, working at the lunch counter of J. J. Newberry Variety Store. Bettye took care of Jimmy and Jane at home while Dot, Bubba, and Hiram were in school. My allotment checks had not started, but the Zion grocery store, now owned by Johnny Haynes, was extending Mother credit against the time the checks would come. The ones from Buddy in the Navy had started arriving.

My mail, however, faced another delay. Orders came for me to attend a radio school in Texas. Secrecy always surrounded all troop movements, and we were usually the last to know when and where we were going. This time we were on the train before we discovered the destination was somewhere in East Texas, a town I had never heard of—Tyler. I was being assigned to the Army Signal Corps for training purposes and would be there nearly ten weeks.

Those being assigned to Air Corps units were being promoted to private first class, meaning a stripe on the left sleeve, but more important, a small raise in salary. I remained a buck private, since I was not assigned to a unit but was on detached service. For some reason only a military mind knew, advance in rank could come only while a person was assigned to a unit.

We were going west to a warmer climate. Anything that took me away from the frigid boardwalk was good news. A small group shared my travel plans, and I was not alone for the three-day trip. We were required to change trains in St. Louis. I wanted to take a day's delay and go home, just 200 miles away, but it was not allowed.

I did not even telephone. We had a thing about long distance telephoning, preferring to send telegrams so there would be a written record and the knowledge it would eventually reach the party desired. Telephoning long distance was only done in very serious emergencies, like a death. And most of the time, we felt we could wait until a letter could be delivered.

Money was so scarce we would not spend it on something as frivolous as small talk on a telephone. Besides, Mother did not have a phone at home. I would have had to call Cousin Ed's house across the road. Then he would have to try to get Mother to the phone, and by that time it would be fifteen minutes or more. So, in St. Louis I only sat in the station and thought about being that close to home.

On the train we slept sitting upright on the seats or, if lucky enough to have an entire seat to ourselves, stretched out. It was not unusual for soldiers to be sleeping on the aisle floor or in the exit areas. Meager meals were served in the dining car, and we were called in order of our cars.

Even then we stood in line forever, but, of course, there was nowhere else to go. The lines moved so slowly, we would sit on the floor, passing the time reading, playing cards, or talking. We speculated about what the accommodations would be like in Tyler: barracks, tents, etc. The Army had taken away hope. We expected the worst.

Tyler won our hearts at first sight. In March the trees were budding. Flowers seemed to bloom everywhere, and we could wear khaki. The weather was wonderful. Compared to Atlantic City, we were in heaven. Tyler, a business and banking center of some 30,000 people, was near the biggest oil field in the nation, but the wells were in other towns such as Kilgore and Longview.

The wealthy had fled the muddy and crowded boomtowns to build their huge homes in Tyler, whose sandy loam deposited by ancient seas made the soil ideal for—of all things—roses. The chamber of commerce billed it as the Rose Capital of the World. They grew roses like we had grown tobacco back home. Each fall they crowned a rose queen during the rose festival.

The bus took us directly to our quarters: another hotel, the Blackstone, a five-story structure a block east of the county courthouse. The old courthouse, like an English manor house, majestically presided over a two-block grassy area of small trees (by Kentucky standards) and park benches. This was the center of town, and businesses were gauged in importance by how close they were to the square.

We entered the hotel expecting another stripped-down Ambassador, but the Blackstone was still operating as a hotel. The Army simply rented rooms for us. We had regular beds and bathrooms—no bunks in the hallways. There were even pictures on the walls and comfortable chairs.

We were told we would be trained at Tyler Commercial

Walker in the U.S. Army Air Corps in 1943-1945.

College, a block west of the square. The Signal Corps had taken over the entire college for its radio school. We would take our meals from a cafeteria. No KP!

Our evenings and weekends were ours. All we had to do was report for classes from 8 a.m. to 5 p.m. to become radio operators. If we flunked out, we would be reassigned. To stay in Tyler as long as possible was incentive enough to succeed at the school. I don't remember anyone failing, although some struggled to become proficient in gaining the required speeds in Morse Code and in typing.

Tyler in 1943 was a serviceman's oasis. Our student body of less than 100 was the only military stationed in the area, and we were seen as an above-average group because we had been screened by our potential to learn.

Under construction about five miles east was Camp Fannin, scheduled to house thousands of infantry. A small service center, sponsored by churches, was housed off the square on the second floor of a business building. The center was staffed by some of the city's most cultured and wealthy women and young ladies, and we spent as much time there as possible.

I missed out on one week's activity, however, because my tonsils became infected, swelling so much I could swallow only liquids. The Army sent me to Dr. William Bailey, whose office was near the square between the hotel and the courthouse. Dr. Bailey, a friendly man in his fifties and somewhat on the plump side, took one long look at my throat and asked: "How often you had this type of illness, Son?"

"I usually get a sore throat every winter, and my glands swell on each side of my neck," I answered.

"Those tonsils need to come out right away. Come back Friday, and we'll remove them. You can have the weekend to recover. Take these pills on Thursday. They will help your blood to clot."

On Friday I was in his office by 9 a.m. When my turn came, he had me sit in a barber-like chair, draping me with cloths. Using a long needle, he deadened each tonsil. Once they were past feeling anything, he inserted an instrument with a wire loop at the end that he placed over the inflamed tonsil. With that holding the culprit in place, he cut first one then the other out. I coughed and gagged from the blood, at times spewing it out against the wall. I remember being fascinated with the spots that hit the glass on one of his diplomas.

He painted my throat with medicine, then he had me lie down in another room for an hour or so in order to check if the blood was clotting properly—I guess to make sure I would not bleed to death. Then he sent me to my hotel room, telling me to take the prescribed medicine and to stay on a liquid diet until I felt like eating other things. I stayed in bed until Monday, and on another visit to Dr. Bailey's office, he checked his work and declared it was good.

When the officers agreed that I might have a week's leave to go home to Zion, I immediately caught the train, bundling up well against the spring weather, and used two of my seven days getting home. It would take two to return, so I had three wonderful days of seeing Mother, the kids, and everyone I could find in Zion and Henderson.

Mother was enjoying her work at Newberry's, and Bettye was making an exceptional mother. She should; she was getting enough practice. Gene had been born in March. Everyone was healthy, and I was healing fast but still not talking more than I could help. Those days blurred in my mind with the pain of a sore throat and the happiness of being home again.

Later, as I walked the streets of Tyler, I experienced the sensation that I was looking for someone. I had felt the same way in Atlantic City and briefly in St. Louis when we changed trains. I was examining every man I met. Almost subconsciously I was looking for Daddy. Sometimes I would quicken my pace in order to overtake someone who was about his size.

I had now been in four states within a few months— Indiana, New Jersey, Missouri, and Texas—and I knew that somewhere across the vastness of the United States, Daddy would also be walking the streets. I began to visualize what it would be like to meet him. What would I say? What would he say? Would we recognize each other?

I came to realize that Daddy's leaving had left a deep, dark hole in my life, not unlike a death. In some ways it was worse than a death because I did not grieve, because I did not understand, and because there had been no closure.

It was all so uncertain. Daddy was still alive I felt sure, but where was he? And why was he there? If any emotion bubbled near the surface, it was anger. But for some reason, I could not or would not surrender to that.

In Tyler I attended Queen Street Baptist Church on Sunday mornings and Wednesday nights, having been invited by members who volunteered at the service center. But Sunday nights I went to First Baptist Church, which was also only a block off the square's north side.

Big, heavyset Porter Bailes, reminding me a lot of C. Oscar Johnson of St. Louis in his speaking manner, was pastor at First Baptist. I had never been a part of a church this size. It was at least three times as large as Immanuel in Henderson, and Zion Baptist was about the size of one of their adult Sunday school departments.

My favorite activity was BYPU—Baptist Young People's Union—which met each Sunday night before worship services. In Sunday school we studied the Bible, but at BYPU we studied church history, missions, and the work of the Southern Baptist Convention. BYPU in Tyler, Texas was not all that different from BYPU in Zion, Kentucky. Each used the same material prepared in Nashville, Tennessee.

I joined a union of about fifteen young people near my age who gathered in a basement room after a ten-minute opening assembly. We spent the time presenting "parts." Those willing would take a portion of the quarterly material, reciting it from memory or paraphrasing it or simply reading it aloud. A person was considered inept if he simply read it.

I relished the opportunity to try out my speaking skills and usually embellished the material. Unlike the others still in school, I had no homework during the week so there was ample time for preparation. I was one of the few servicemen to attend church regularly, and the only one at Training Union at First Baptist. I was not only welcomed but also felt fussed over, even honored.

In Tyler I discovered a new personal freedom, which came in part because I was now treated as an adult, but also with new friends I stood entirely on my own, as though I had a new slate on which to write. In Tyler I was myself, at least the self I chose to present to others, and the one I presented was the self that had made the decision for the ministry at Ridgecrest Baptist Assembly. In a way, I guess, I was trying on the role outside of Zion and Henderson, and I found myself comfortable with it. Also the reaction I received from new friends reinforced the decision I had made in the Blue Ridge Mountains of North Carolina.

On the other hand, I was Zion and Henderson, from my country accent to the memories of Granny and Granddad and Frank Reid and Cousin Ed and John Wilkerson and Jean Bennett, and Mother and Daddy and the hundreds of others—the people I loved, who had loved me, and who had changed my life for good or bad. Through them—and the memory of them—came the strength and the variety of my life. I could not deny who I was or who I had been, but I was also reaching out for a new life that would be built on what all of them had given me.

I became friends with Kenneth Howard and Charlene Waller. Both were freshmen at Tyler Junior College. Kenneth, a lanky handsome youth a year my junior, was a leader in the union, and had been an above-average student at the large Tyler High School where he was still remembered as an outstanding drum major.

Charlene was Miss Personality, a bundle of boundless energy, whom everyone loved and flocked around. In the high school band she had been notorious. She had played the big bass drum—flinging the mallets up and around with the same abandon that Kenneth threw the baton. Kenneth and Charlene did not date, but they were the closest of friends, and they took me into their circle.

BYPU socials were high on my agenda, and for days we had planned a skating party on May 13. I had not skated in years, but skating was something one never forgot. We planned to meet on the steps in front of the sanctuary of First Baptist at seven o'clock on Thursday night. I was there early, waiting for the crowd to gather, especially looking for Charlene and Kenneth.

Finally, they drove up in Kenneth's car, and three people got out: Kenneth, Charlene, and a small, dark-headed girl with large bright eyes and the biggest, most engaging smile I had ever seen.

"Bunk," Kenneth started in, using the nickname I had shared with them, "we've been trying to get in touch with you. We want you to meet Iva Nell Moseley, one of our closest friends. Iva Nell, this is Bunk Knight from Kentucky. We've told you about him."

I was smitten. She was beautiful and even smaller than I. She had been a cheerleader at Tyler High the same year

Wedding announcement photo for Iva Nell Moseley to Walker Leigh Knight, November 10, 1943, in the *Tyler Morning News Telegraph*.

I was a cheerleader at Hebbardsville High and had also graduated in '42. She had graduated at sixteen, having skipped one grade early in school, and the Texas school system required only eleven grades for a high school diploma. Even our birthdays were close. On February 12 that year she had become seventeen.

When she climbed into the back seat of the car, I climbed in after her, determined not to let her out of my sight for the rest of the night. Only later that evening did I discover Kenneth and Charlene had brought her as my date, but because they could not get in touch with me earlier I was uninformed. They had not mentioned it during introductions for fear I had made other plans.

The only hitch for the night was Iva Nell did not skate. So I showed off, using all the skills I had learned while working at the skating rink in Henderson—skating backwards, skating fast, jumping, squatting, and even halfway dancing. At five-to-ten-minute intervals, I either brought Iva Nell a Coke or came asking if she wanted one. Only half my time was spent in the rink; the rest of the time I was at her side.

We shared all the quick introductory type information. I learned she was a Baptist and was a clerk at the Cotton Belt Railroad Headquarters in Tyler. She had briefly attended Tyler Junior College, but had quit when the general manager of the railroad had come to the college asking for workers to replace the men being drafted. Until then almost all the positions had been filled by men.

Before that she had worked briefly at McClellan's Variety Store immediately after graduation. Then the family had left Tyler for a few months and had lived at Troy, near Temple in Central Texas, while her father, Marion Matthew Moseley, helped construct officers' barracks at Fort Hood. With the barracks completed, they returned to Tyler and she entered Tyler Junior College.

She told me she had a married brother, Kelly Green Moseley, twenty-three, who had a daughter, worked at a filling station in Tyler, and was married to Ava Nell Martin. She also had a younger brother, Jack, fifteen, still at home, but he had quit school and was working at Lasiter's Grocery Store.

They lived on the outskirts of Tyler near the airport and attended a newly formed church, Dixie Baptist. Both parents were raised on farms near Ben Wheeler, about twenty miles west toward Dallas, in Van Zandt

County. She was amazed at the size of my family and laughed when I tried to tell her all their names and ages.

Before the social was over, we agreed to meet the next night after she got off from work. I wrote in my diary of meeting this "swell" (the word of choice then) girl, adding, "I have fallen in love like I never fell before. I only hope she feels the same way."

The four of us double dated on Friday night at a Young Life meeting at the home of Add and Loveta Sewell, and I met her parents for the first time when we drove out to pick her up. Iva Nell had to work Saturday morning, and I had schooling for the morning, but I decided to hang around downtown in the afternoon.

I visited Perry's Variety Store, and Iva Nell walked in looking for her mother. It seemed we were fated to be together. We again met Charlene and Kenneth, spending the day and part of the night studying our BYPU parts. That night I wrote, "Iva Nell seems more and more like the girl I have always wanted."

By this time, I was so in love I could think of nothing else, and, best of all, my love was returned. We kissed for the first time that night. She asked if I would come to their house on Sunday, go to church with them at Dixie Baptist, and eat dinner with the family.

Iva Nell told her mother on Sunday morning that we were planning to be married, "but not any time soon, either after the war or after Bunk has finished college."

Mrs. Moseley said, "I have had a feeling this was going to happen ever since that boy walked in the door." Then she cried.

After church, while we were sitting at the table, I complimented Mr. Moseley on his shirt, a white-on-white design. He looked at me and said, "Thanks, I'll give it to you if you'll leave my girl alone."

"Keep your old shirt," I answered, laughing.

Chapter 8

CALIFORNIA AND MARRIAGE

F ollowing the Sunday dinner at the Moseleys, when I turned down Mr. Moseley's trade of a white shirt for my leaving his daughter alone, Nell and I attended a Young Life chapter meeting at the home of Loveta and Add Sewell.

Almost from our first meeting at the skating party, I had shortened Iva Nell to Nell. Why, I did not know, and Nell made no objections. In a way, it was a special way for me to address her apart from friends and family. The family continued to call her Iva Nell, which had been reinforced after Kelly had married Ava Nell whom everyone called Nell.

The weekly Young Life gathering of about ten youth near our ages was planned for a core leadership who, in Add's words, were "ready to get down to business for the Lord." Nell and I went with Kenneth Howard and Charlene Waller. I immediately found myself a part of the inner circle as the three of them had been charter members of the chapter that Add and Loveta, as newlyweds, had started the year before.

The Sewells were an engaging couple, and Loveta at nineteen was not much older than the youth with whom they worked. Add was twenty-seven and the one who was very much in charge.

In many ways Young Life reminded me of the prayer meetings we had held at Mrs. Al Burton's back in Zion, except here an unusual emphasis was placed on scripture memorization. Young Life had been started as a non-denominational Christian ministry in Dallas two years earlier by Jim

Rayburn, who had borrowed a system of memorizing Bible verses from a
Navy-based group called Navigators.

Members of the Young Life group carried scripture cards on which
Bible verses were printed with the citation of book, chapter, and verse
noted "fore & aft," as they said in the Navy. They carried their cards in a
small leather holder with a slot in the upper left-hand corner revealing the
reference. Thus they could look at the reference, recite the verse as well as
possible, and then look at the card to check the accuracy.

I was amazed at the hundreds of verses Nell, Kenneth, and Charlene
knew, rattling them off with the speed and accuracy of accomplished
actors reciting lines, not that they spent time in the meetings doing that,
but they did have periods of asking about verses that might relate to life
situations. Add would also give a devotional or pep talk and might cite a
reference and ask someone to recite that verse.

Captivated by the process of memorization, I immediately secured
cards and a leather holder and started memorizing, a process continued
during the remaining months I served in the Air Corps. It was another
way to defeat the boredom of standing in line, and many of the verses I
learned then are still seated in my memory, especially those that proved
meaningful in times of concern or crisis.

For example, whenever I was faced with some temptation to go along
with the crowd that deviated from what I then considered model behav-
ior for a Christian, I would think of the words in 1 Corinthians 10:13,
"There has no temptation taken you but such as is common to man, but
God is faithful, who will not suffer you to be tempted above that which
you are able; but will with the temptation also make a way of escape, that
you may be able to bear it."

It was ethics in its most rudimentary form, but for me at this time in
my life it proved very satisfying and a way of growing spiritually. Mother
had given me a fine edition of the Scofield Bible, and I underlined in it
many of the verses I was learning. I had no reference point at the time
to know that the Scofield notes in the Bible were of a very conservative
nature. I took them to be as truthful as the Bible, including a note that
said the world was only some 6,000 years old.

When we began to correspond, Nell and I would regularly add to the
bottom of our letters the reference to a verse we had been studying or had
found significant. Mostly we did not have to look them up in the Bible,
for we would have memorized the verses.

I felt very accepted by Loveta, Add, and the other members of the inner circle of Young Life, most likely because of the sponsorship by Nell, Kenneth, and Charlene. I attended every meeting possible, if for no other reason, as a way to be with Nell.

Meanwhile, my time at Tyler Commercial College was drawing close to the end. The class work there in some ways related to the Bible memorization, for we had to memorize the code and strive to seat it in our mind where the subconscious could take over without a conscious effort at recall. When this happened, our speeds at receiving and sending the code made dramatic jumps.

During our first weeks we found it difficult to "read" at

Walker and Nell in 1943.

the rate of five or ten words a minute. A "word" was five unrelated letters, for all messages were coded and transmitted in five-letter blocks to make it difficult for the enemy to break. This also made it more difficult for us to achieve rapid speeds, for there were no patterns.

I finally got my speed up to nearly thirty words a minute, but my most dramatic jump came in typing. With hours to practice, I could type as many as eighty words a minute on the upright Underwood.

The school published a weekly newspaper, the *SOS, the Signal Corps News*, in tabloid format, and I volunteered for service on the paper. Because I had more experience than any of the others, I was soon named editor and helped improve both the layouts and the news gathering of the publication. The teachers would allow us some class time for working on the paper.

Nell and I had nearly three weeks to be together before I finished my schooling and would be sent to California for assignment to a unit within the Air Corps. During this time we began to discuss our hopes for the future. We would definitely get married, we said, but we felt I first had to complete my Army service, and then it might be best if we waited until the hard times of college, even seminary, were over.

I had no way of knowing how I would finance my education, but I did not doubt that I would secure it. However, even though we talked of waiting until these years had passed, we could not bear the thought of even the coming separation the military would impose.

Quite often chance events determine the direction of a person's life. One may make the wrong turn while driving an automobile and have an accident that disables the person for life. One may have a chance meeting with a stranger who becomes very influential, or on a lark one takes a course in college that establishes vocational direction.

Most often, however, life flows as a stream and it is a series of happenings within our families, within our various communities, and ultimately within our interior lives that gradually form both the questions and the answers of life. A Christian also asks: How does God work within life's stream and within one's life?

I had come to Tyler after having made two life-directing decisions: I had decided on a Christian vocation, and I had enlisted in the U.S. Army Air Corps. Those two decisions established the basis for the decision that occurred at Tyler: to marry Iva Nell Moseley. The rest of my life would flow out of these three converging streams.

At the time I held a rather simplistic view of how God worked in our lives. In many ways I saw God determining what we did, almost that of a puppet master who was imposing a creator's will upon the creation, and my role was to discern God's will and actions and to conform to what God was doing. In this view, God had placed me in the Army, had determined that I would be sent to Tyler, Texas, and had brought Nell and me together. Yet I also would have said at the time that I believed God had given us the freedom to follow or not to follow that will, but I did not see or understand the contradiction or the limiting scope of such a view.

Shortly after I left Tyler, Mr. Moseley was driving Nell to work one day and he started talking about the important events of life. "Iva Nell, two of the most important happenings of your life you have little control over," he said. "Those are your birth and your death. However, a third—your choice of a life partner—you will determine. I hope you will be very careful about the one you marry." That would constitute his one and only word of caution to his daughter.

Leaving Tyler was as hard as it had been to leave Zion when I entered the service, maybe even harder, for I was tied by a new emotion: I was deeply in love. I had not experienced love to this degree before. Nell and I promised to write every day, and we had decided that maybe we might get married as soon as the war was over.

A small group from my class left Tyler by bus, which then carried us to the train for the rest of the trip to California. Our destination was Fresno, in the middle of the San Joaquin Valley, a city of some 80,000 midway between Los Angeles and San Francisco in the middle of a desert reclaimed by irrigation.

Actually, we were not stationed in Fresno but in a tent city called Pinedale (later a suburb of Fresno), and there I experienced a desert life of unrelenting sunshine, swirling dust, and blistering heat. We were assigned four to a tent, sleeping on cots. The nights were not too difficult, for after sunset the temperature dropped. It was the daytime that drained us, as the Army felt we should be kept in shape through calisthenics and close-order drills or long twenty-mile hikes into the foothills of nearby mountains.

On one lengthy hike we took a ten-minute break beside a roadside stand selling apple cider. Thirsty and wanting something other than the canteen water we were carrying, we mobbed the vendor and drank our fill. But we paid for it that night. The cider was contaminated. We had the "G.I. runs." Unfortunately, the latrine was on the other side of the parade grounds, and half of us did not make it all the way. The next day we had extra duty cleaning up the parade area.

During the late summer months this area of California suffered from a lack of rain, and with the dryness came forest fires. When the fires would threaten cities or become unmanageable, the Army would be enlisted. I was called out one night for such duty, transported in Army trucks into the foothills of the Sierra Nevada Mountains. At designated areas we were given shovels, axes, and other equipment to prepare fire lanes or to aid in setting back fires.

My group was stationed near the fire, and we labored in the heat with the smoke billowing around us. I did not know it at the moment, but the smoke penetrated my clothing and affected my sensitive skin. Within two days I was in the hospital with one of the worst cases of poison ivy I had ever experienced.

My face was swollen, and my eyes would barely open. I had the rash everywhere, but nowhere was it as painful and as swollen as around my genitals. For more than a week I walked straddle-legged in a nightgown, carrying lotion to give me some relief from the itching. The episode had one positive side, other than giving me reading and letter-writing time: I developed immunity to poison ivy and poison oak that would last for nearly twenty years.

The Pinedale camp included a number of us who had been trained as radio operators. An officer who was acquainted with Morse Code and the process of learning and retaining what was learned knew we would have a serious deterioration of our sending and receiving abilities if we were not using the code over a long period of time.

Consequently, a refresher school had been established in an old CCC camp at Wawona Point in Yosemite National Park. We were loaded into Army trucks and driven up winding mountain roads, climbing more than 5,000 feet above the hot desert floor of Pinedale to the most beautiful place I had ever seen in my life.

In Yosemite, nature had sculpted everything on a magnificent scale, dwarfing the older Blue Ridge Mountains of my Ridgecrest Baptist Assembly days when I first experienced mountains. Yosemite sent my spirits soaring from that first day.

Our school was housed in four log buildings nestled among tall, stately Sequoia pines beside a clear stream of melted snow on its way down the mountains. At our clearing, the stream deepened and flattened enough that we could swim in it. Often before breakfast I would put on my bathing suit and dive into the chilling waters, scrambling out as fast as I could, but it sent me to the mess hall with a ravenous appetite.

For once the Army had correctly matched skill and aptitude with assignment in our cooks. They were former hotel chefs, and they were cooking for a manageable sized company. We ate royally. At breakfast they often prepared corn fritters, which at more than a mile's altitude puffed out into an airy delicacy. On our way out of the mess hall the chefs stacked baskets of apples and oranges for us to carry with us. With such food and exercise I added fifteen pounds to my thin frame during the weeks I was stationed there.

On weekends we were given passes and transportation to Yosemite Valley, a wonderland of sights and sounds and invigorating pine-laden smells. We marveled at El Capitan's sheer walls, at Bridal Veil Falls' cascading mist, at Half Dome's awesome size, and at just the splendor of such pristine beauty. Along with the few tourists who could find gasoline for the trip, we swam in the Valley's warmer streams and shopped at the old inn. Weekends when we did not go to the valley, we hiked to the higher levels of the Sierra Nevada range, often traveling the road that passed through the base of one huge sequoia tree.

Yosemite was like a cathedral to me, and the great trees pulled my thoughts upward to God. I memorized verses from Psalm 121: "I will lift up mine eyes unto the hills from whence cometh my help. My help cometh from the Lord, which made heaven and earth."

I felt the psalmist must have had some vision in mind such as this magnificent place when he penned those words. I did not know then that the writer was saying he would not look to the hills, where the pagans worshipped. A question mark should have been placed after the first sentence. The King James Version was inadequate. The writer instead would look to the true God for his help, not to Baal.

Nevertheless, the experience seared into my mind the fact that God is Creator and speaks to us in daily ways. I learned that all of life can hold its cathedral moments. Particularly since most of our lives are spent primarily on the plain, I realized I did not have to wait for those rare Yosemite days to sense God's presence. God had also created the Pinedale desert, and it was as important, maybe even more so, to hear God's voice there as in the magnificent mountains.

It was during my days in Pinedale, the desert, that Nell and I made an important decision. We had been writing every day about our activities and our dreams. She continued working at the Cotton Belt Railroad, earning the princely sum of $25 a week, more than I had ever earned. By continuing to live at home, she was able to save a good portion of what she earned. I could not save anything from the little I had left from a buck private's pay after Mother's allotment was drawn. However, I had simple needs and never regretted the allotment. All I needed was money for stationery and cigarettes that were as cheap as ten cents a package.

Nell continued to attend the Young Life meetings, sharing with Kenneth and Charlene the depth of our relationship. We did not know at the time, but they were busy trying to discover some way to cool down our engagement. They felt they were responsible, and they had had no idea we would act so rashly, would so quickly fall deeply in love and talk of marriage.

In our letters Nell and I revealed more and more of ourselves to each other. After all, we had been together for only a little more than a month and we had a lot to discuss. With my assignment overseas possible at any time, we found separation those few months difficult to bear. We decided we would not wait until after seminary for marriage. We would not wait until after college. We would not wait until I was discharged from the Army.

We decided to get married as soon as I could arrange for a furlough to Tyler. We would snatch what happiness we could from the jaws of uncertainty. Always hanging over us was the fact that I might not escape the war unharmed.

Back in Pinedale after Yosemite, I found that the summer heat had passed and the weather was endurable. Those in charge were also open to my having a furlough, and it was arranged that I could have a ten-day pass in November in order to get married. With travel time to and from Tyler, that would mean only four or five days with Nell.

When I got to Tyler and we applied for the marriage license, I discovered I was underage at nineteen. I would have to have parental consent. I had written Mother of our plans to marry, not thinking that I would need her permission. I promptly sent her a telegram, since she still did not have a telephone, and she promptly wired back her consent. Mr. Moseley signed for Nell who was seventeen, and we were issued our marriage license.

Nell asked Charlene and her parents if we could have the wedding at their house on Wednesday evening, November 10, since the Wallers had a piano and Nell did not think we could have a proper ceremony without music. They agreed.

One year previous to this date I had written in my diary, "If I don't get to go (into the military), I believe I will miss something that I have been wanting."

We asked Add Sewell to officiate, and he used the traditional wedding vows. It did not enter our mind that we had any choice in writing our own vows, but at least Add suggested we take the unusual step at the time of omitting "obey" from Nell's vows.

Loveta sang "Beneath the Cross of Jesus," which had also been sung at their wedding. I wore my uniform, and Nell bought a new, medium blue, street-length dress with a V-neck and fabric bows tied in front just below each shoulder. Charlene was the maid of honor, and Marcille Barnette the bridesmaid.

Marcille and Nell were in high school together but did not become friends until they worked together at the Cotton Belt Railroad. Fifteen-year-old Jack was substituted as best man when Kelly was hospitalized on Monday to have his appendix removed. Kenneth Howard had enlisted in the Army.

Charlene's sister, Jean, got permission for us to use her in-laws' cabin on a nearby lake for our honeymoon. We were driven there by Add and Loveta, after someone had bought us some groceries, and we were left there for three nights. We forgot to bring any of the wedding cake, and so never ate more than the traditional bite.

Add and Loveta realized both of us were innocents and had taken us aside separately for some counseling. The advice Add gave me as to foreplay, tenderness, and timing set a tone to our marriage that was invaluable. Loveta told Nell that she was to forget all she had heard about the evils of sex, that on the contrary it was a gift from God and that she should relax and enjoy it. Someone had also given Nell advice on a form of birth control, a small cone-shaped pill she inserted before intercourse, called Boro-phenoform.

The cabin had a large fireplace, and I soon built a roaring fire. We sat before it, with Nell in my lap for a long time. Too long, in fact, for when I finally stood up I fell to my knees, embarrassed before my bride, but we were laughing. My legs had gone to sleep with the blood circulation cut off.

At breakfast the first day we hit two snags. I discovered Nell did not know how to cook, since her Mother had never insisted she do anything in the kitchen except wash dishes and make a green salad. I was going to fix pancakes, but there was no syrup. I eventually made syrup with sugar, water, and flavoring, but with our paying more attention to each other than to the cooking I overcooked the syrup and it turned back to sugar. For the rest of the meals, I cooked and started teaching Nell at least how to boil water.

We began planning the rest of our lives during those few days in Tyler, and the immediate problem was to be together. Parting was painful, but I left Tyler on Monday to return to California with the intention of getting permission to live off base just as soon as I reached Fresno. I also would apply for an allotment to be sent to Nell at her mother's address, knowing we might be moving frequently.

If and when I got permission to live off base, I would receive a cost-of-living supplement, since I would not be eating on base or sleeping there. All of this took weeks, but I finally received the needed permission and went looking for a room in downtown Fresno.

I found a ground floor, furnished room with a Mrs. Fox, who also rented other rooms to military couples in her large white, frame house on a corner lot. A deep porch reached across the two sides that faced the streets, and our room was down a wide, short hallway near the baths. I was most impressed by the lemon tree and its ample fruit in the back, side yard. The rent was $6 a week without kitchen privileges. We could have rented a house for that in Zion or Tyler.

As these arrangements neared completion in mid-December, I wrote Nell to join me. She bought a ticket for the train, leaving from Mineola, about eighteen miles south of Tyler. The trip was four long days to Los Angeles, sitting and sleeping in a crowded coach car, buying her meals either in the diner or from vendors who came through the cars on a regular basis. During the entire trip she was unable to change clothes or take a bath.

Nell made friends with a young soldier, who thought she was fourteen years old and needed looking after. She welcomed his company, especially when she found that he was also going to Fresno. She was especially glad she had his company when they reached L.A. where they were to change trains. They found the train was overbooked, and they would have to wait until the next day. He got the idea that they might complete their trek by Greyhound Bus, and he made the needed arrangements, including getting a taxi to the bus station.

I was unaware of when she would arrive, since all travel was uncertain, but I had sent her a phone number to call to tell me where I could meet her. On arrival at Fresno, she and her soldier friend, who was stationed at another camp near the city, had gone to the USO for the phone call and the wait, since it was a more comfortable place than the bus station. As soon as I received the news, I took off for downtown Fresno and our reunion at the USO. Her friend had stayed until I got there. We met and I added my appreciation for his help.

When Nell told me the story of her trek to Fresno, I got a new insight into this young, small beauty I had married. She had the strength of a mature woman, and her love was as deep and as strong as the Cherokee blood that ran in her veins.

Nell and I gradually settled into joyous married life, even though I had to get up at five each morning to be in camp for roll call. Nell began looking for work, and soon found a job in the office of a fruit and vegetable wholesaler, Levy and Zentner's, making $30 a week—even more than she had earned at the Cotton Belt Railroad. Nevertheless, we had a difficult time stretching this over our needs, for we had to buy Nell's meals out along with my supper since our room rent did not include kitchen privileges. (I ate breakfast and lunch at the base.) The shortage of funds lasted only about a month, until I could draw my supplement and she could receive her allotment check.

I decided that I wanted to be an Air Force pilot and applied for pilot training. After filling out the necessary papers, I was given the mandatory tests and the physical, and I was accepted for Air Cadet Training; but I would have to wait until a school had an opening. Nell and I both were willing to wait in Fresno just as long as they wanted.

We checked out the Baptist church, affiliated with the Northern Baptist churches, but we were not too impressed, being somewhat put off with the lack of friendliness. We tried the Methodist Church and despite the fact the minister wore robes, we liked what he had to say and the friendliness of the congregation.

By the end of the second week, I discovered I had sores on the end of my penis and, fearing the worst I reported on sick call. When my turn finally came, the doctor examined me carefully and shook his head. He did not know what it was. He called in two other young doctors to examine me, and the three of them stood in a semi-circle around me wearing question marks on their faces. Finally the oldest began to ask me some questions about what I had been doing recently.

I told him that I had married a little more than a month ago, and that my wife had recently come to Fresno. We were living off base. He then said, "What type of contraceptive are you using?"

"It's called Boro-phenoform," I replied. "It was recommended to us by older friends of my wife."

At my answer the three doctors began to laugh, and when they had quieted down the oldest said, "That's just like throwing sand in there, son. It might be fine for an older couple, but not for newlyweds. Have your wife fitted with a diaphragm."

When I finally got my supplement and Nell got her first allotment check, relayed by her mother, we decided we had the funds for a trip. I had learned that my first cousin, Coonkey Nichols, was also in California. I wanted Nell to meet one of my very own Kentucky kinfolks, so we planned to visit Coonkey and his wife Mildred in Valejo, California, about forty miles north of San Francisco.

Without calling or writing, we boarded a bus early one Saturday and knocked on their door that night. Were they surprised! Coonkey, a four-year Navy veteran, was undergoing plastic surgery to restore his ears and rebuild his face from the severe burns he had received when the *USS San Francisco* was hit, but he was staying at home during this period.

They had only one bed, so the women slept in the middle and the men on the outside. The first time Coonkey saw Nell in Kentucky after that, he embraced her and said, "Nell, it's so great to see you again. The last time I saw you we were sleeping together."

In March I learned that the Army had a surplus of pilots in training, and they were shutting down the cadet program for the rest of the year. I was to be sent overseas as a replacement radio operator. By the middle of April I had orders to go to Greensboro, North Carolina, with an eight-day delay in route, which meant I could take Nell to Zion.

But getting her there at the same time I would arrive would take all of the ingenuity and contacts I had made in camp. Finally, I talked a sergeant into revealing the train I would be placed on, and we packed Nell's trunk and suitcase and bought her a ticket for the same train and destination. However, we had only the sergeant's word that the train she was boarding was the one on which they had placed me. She scrambled on board by faith, with the understanding that she was to proceed to Zion no matter what.

Once on board and moving, she began to walk through the lengthy train, which had troops in separate cars from the civilians. After stepping over soldiers and pushing through crowded aisles, she arrived at my car. We had boarded the same train!

For three days we traveled east, and we managed by begging and hiding to keep Nell in the military cars so we could be together, sleeping on the floor in the dining car along with all the others who could crowd into the area.

I proudly took Nell back to Zion like a trophy of my fifteen months of travels, and the family fell in love with her, as much for her difference as for her grace and gentleness. As I paraded her before the scores of kith and kin, they commented on her youthfulness, her size, her combination of shyness and strength, and her inherent beauty both physically and spiritually. At first they treated her like visiting royalty, but when they discovered she was easily embarrassed, they teased her—actually a form of testing—finding that while she did not often tease back she could take it, and that communicated to them a strength and self-assuredness they admired.

Against their aggressiveness and competitiveness, she appeared meek and mild, but they soon found that beneath the veneer she was tough and resilient. The teasing could go just so far before she would cut it off.

And on Nell's side, she found few surprises in the family. Johnny Nick and Shack were no more profane than I had told her. Mother was as quick to play as to work, and she was the hub around which the family revolved for its strength and love. Granny and Granddad presided over the extended family from their old mansion on the hill, and Granddad had lost none of his ability to tease and Granny still set the best table in the family.

All my brothers and sisters revealed an energy that amazed Nell. Whereas her family was content to sit and talk, mine wanted to "do" something, to "go" somewhere—anything to burn off energy—and Mother was always in the middle of anything the group wanted to do.

While Nell never grasped the finer points of card games, she was often drawn into the simpler ones such as Hearts and Old Maids or Spit or Canasta. She left Self Pitch, Rook, and Pinochle to the others. When the family played such games as charades, it was like a circus—loud, laughing, and competitive—and she joined in even though she felt they had a genetic headstart on her. If she hadn't been a cheerleader, she would have been overwhelmed; as it was, she just picked her place and let the family flow around her.

Nell and Walker in 1944.

The war had continued to change Zion. Clel Rodgers had left Zion Baptist Church to serve as an Army chaplain. Buddy had been discharged from the Navy for incompatibility, a combination of his age at the time—seventeen—and the years of turmoil in the family. I believe he suffered more from Daddy's drinking than any of us. He had married Ruth Willett and was working at a White Castles restaurant in Henderson.

My friends, John Wilkerson and Walter Farley, were both serving in the Army, but we had not kept up with each other by writing. It seemed everyone who could walk had been drafted, and more and more women were now working outside the home.

One day we drove to the western end of Henderson County toward Geneva and Smith Mills to meet Daddy's sisters, Ninnie and Mary Lou, and their extended families, especially my sister, Mary Ruth, who was now eleven and very much the proper young lady, loved and treasured by them all. The Nicholses were still the hardworking, earnest farmers with whom I had often stayed in my teenage years. Only now, led by Mary Ruth, they were more and more active in the Baptist churches in the area.

There was a difference in tone between Zion and this end of the county, a difference brought about by the physical location as much as anything. In Zion there was closeness and community; here the farms were large and scattered, so families did not get together as often, requiring more planning and effort than the casual dropping in that happened in Zion.

On Sunday at Zion Baptist Church I "showed off" Nell to the congregation, where she met Jean Bennett, whom she had completely replaced in my affections, and the scores of other youth who had been active in the prayer meetings and the BYPU, but now most of the young men were in military service. Nevertheless, the Burtons continued the prayer meetings, which centered their praying on those of us in the Army and Navy.

Nell was thus introduced to a congregation that was more than 100 years old and had never had a serious split, quite a contrast to the newly formed Baptist church of which she was a member in Tyler.

These few days in Zion passed as a quick excited blur, and all too soon I had to continue to Greensboro, North Carolina. We were determined to squeeze in every precious moment together. Nell remained with Mother until I had found a room in one of Greensboro's fading southern mansions downtown. We occupied a long, narrow, second-floor porch enclosed with huge windows and shared the house with other military couples who filled every room of the spacious house.

We lived together in Greensboro for three anxious weeks, very much the victim of rampant rumors, each declaring we would be shipped out the next week. Nell did not seek work, because we knew at best the time would not be long. On Sundays we attended the large First Baptist Church where J. Clyde Turner, a nationally known minister, was pastor.

Finally, we succumbed to one of the more persistent rumors, and bought a train ticket back to Tyler for Nell, fearing I would be shipped out without notice and she would be stranded in Greensboro alone. However, it was several weeks ahead of my departure date, and we felt we had been cheated.

Back in Tyler, Nell almost immediately found a good job at Montgomery Ward, then a strong competitor to Sears Roebuck. Her task was to receive and tag most of the merchandise the store received, working with Mr. Bolucher, a small middle-aged man who became a close friend and instructive workmate.

My orders to ship out finally arrived. We were sent by train to Norfolk, Va., to board ship for some unknown destination. Rumors had it that we were going to Europe, but some even said we would travel to the Pacific.

The huge, gray troop ship held 5,000 of us positioned into four decks and stacked as high as five berths deep. I had never suffered from claustrophobia, and I knew I never would if I survived this. I felt like a bee deep within a honeycomb or a worker ant assigned to the colony's lower section.

It seemed to take forever for us to board, find our berths in the hot stuffy lower decks, and then to wait and wait some more for the ship to move, but it finally did, and my journey to another side of the world had started.

Chapter 9

CHINA

The mammoth, gray troop transport slowly moved away from Norfolk, Virginia, and once in the sea lanes, to our surprise, turned south instead of going east or north toward Europe. Of course, we thought this could be a maneuver to evade the German U-boats, but our speculation soon ended. Now that we were at sea and unable to reveal secrets, we were told the ship was taking us to Bombay, India. Our route would carry us through the Panama Canal, then south below Australia, and finally to our destination.

The voyage, lengthened by zigzag patterns to avoid being an easy target for submarines, took seven long, boring weeks—most of fifty days. Nearly 5,000 of us were crowded into varying levels of the ship and stacked in bunks four or five high, having to climb to the highest level by using the lower bunks as steps. We fought the boredom every way possible, mostly reading from the Armed Services Series of paperback books, said to be the start of the paperback industry—only most of these editions had rather plain covers and were printed on a fairly good grade of paper.

Most were classics of world literature and were distributed free: *War and Peace, Jane Eyre, Vanity Fair, Wuthering Heights, David Copperfield,* and scores of others. One soldier on a nearby berth appeared to be reading the same book for a long time. He was a heavyset, olive-complexioned, balding Jew from New York City, a couple of years older than I. I asked why he was so long reading the novel.

"It's a murder mystery," he answered, "and this is my fourth time to read the book. I plan to be a writer, and I am studying this author's technique because I admire him." I always regretted not remembering that soldier's name as I might have checked on his success as a mystery writer after the war.

When not reading, we often played cards—Hearts, Pinochle, or Bridge. But the universal favorite was Poker, which I did not play but often watched, especially when the stakes were high among the big gamblers.

Standing in line became a ritual that reached new heights in time consumption, even though those in charge staggered our meals throughout the day and called us to eat by areas. We even stood in line to take the cold, saltwater showers that left me feeling afterwards like I had a film over my body, and the soap refused to make suds. We envied the sailors their freshwater showers.

At times we were assigned the task of chipping off the old paint on the ship's deck, using a dull chisel and hammer and a stiff wire brush. It was slow, tedious work, redeemed only by the fact that it was on the open deck. The Navy regularly chipped off the paint to reach the bare metal where rust would begin to form, and once exposed the metal was treated with a rust preventative and then painted with a number of coats of the blue-gray enamel.

I also volunteered to work in the ship's laundry, for which I was paid a meager sum, but it was something to do. My assignment was to operate a large mangle, a machine with heated rollers through which the laundry was passed to remove the wrinkles. The work was hot and repetitive, but one of my rewards was an occasional freshwater shower.

After an overnight stop in Sidney, Australia, for fresh water and supplies and a glimpse of the city from the ship, we proceeded through the Indian Ocean and the Arabian Sea to Bombay, avoiding the more dangerous route to Calcutta by way of the Bay of Bengal.

Once unloaded at the Bombay port, we had only a couple of days to lose our sea legs and swagger on board a train bound for Calcutta. We had reached India at the end of the hot season and the beginning of the rainy season, and I was always willing to trade the heat for rain.

The long train ride of more than a thousand miles across the continent gave me a lengthy look at the Indian countryside and when we stopped, some contact with the people who were eager to sell us something or to beg. The beggars, especially the children, were persistent and clingy.

"Baksheesh, Sahib. Baksheesh, Sahib (gifts, Sir)" they pled repeatedly with hands extended, and to reward one was to invite others to swarm around you. We learned that begging was honorable among certain castes.

We were starved for fruit, but we were told not to buy any that had cracks on the skin. I remember the wonderful taste of the small, tree-ripened bananas we purchased, but only after we had carefully examined every part. We were also warned against drinking untreated water, to drink only from our canteens of our bitter chlorine-dosed liquid. Each of us was issued chlorine pills to treat water ourselves in case we ran short.

At Calcutta we were housed in tents on the outskirts of the city while we awaited our turn to be flown over "The Hump"—the Himalayan Mountains—into China. During the wait we were granted passes to visit the swarming, crowded streets of Calcutta. We were astounded to see hundreds sleeping in the streets and to witness the appalling poverty.

We could not comprehend the gentle treatment of the sacred cows that wandered casually through the streets and market places. Thanks to Great Britain's long rule, everyone spoke English, which made shopping easier, but we still had to grapple with an entirely new monetary system based on the rupee. We walked the bazaars open-mouthed at the wares of the mysterious Far East, occasionally buying cheap knives and jewelry as souvenirs. India, however, was not to be my final destination.

After only a few days of enduring the heat and rains of Calcutta, I was loaded into a C-54, a four-engine cargo airplane. Our duffle bags were tied down at one place, and we were belted to the floor throughout the stripped interior for the bumpy ride over The Hump. The trip required a high altitude flight without oxygen, but luckily it was not lengthy.

After a few hours we were in China, landing at the enormous supply base at Kunming, through which all personnel and materiel for the war effort in China were funneled. Kunming was as American as baseball and apple pie. If one did not leave the base, he would not have known it was China. One of the few major concessions to the influence of England was that traffic moved on the left side of the road.

Once in Kunming, I discovered it was my fate again to be placed on detached service to the Signal Corps and assigned as a replacement to an outpost at Ipin on the Yangtze River about halfway between Kunming and Chungking, the capital of free China.

I was still a buck private, and being on detached service meant I would not be considered for an advanced rank. But the good news was that I would draw per diem pay from the U.S. government, despite the fact the Chinese government was furnishing all our food and lodging.

The flight to Ipin, which meant river town, was made in a C-120, the two-engine workhorse of the Army Air Corps. The pilots chose a low altitude just high enough to miss the tall pagoda temples, probably to avoid Japanese fighter planes. The low altitude and the warm weather thermals made for one bumpy ride to the short grass strip just outside the outpost compound. The plane was also carrying supplies, and I was holding on to whatever I could grab that seemed stationary.

The walled compound at our base housed a company of twenty men, supervised by a young, green second lieutenant and a seasoned staff sergeant. We were billeted in two barracks, two to a room, with separate buildings for the kitchen and mess hall and for the radio station.

Chinese men did all the cooking (using U.S. recipes and supplies), cleaning, and maintenance, even to making our beds and washing our clothes. We had a barber in the compound who would provide a very close shave and a haircut for the equivalent of ten cents. Once again I had stumbled into near ideal accommodations, and this time they were even paying me extra.

We also received weekly rations of beer and cigarettes. I let others have the beer but I took the cigarettes, which I quit smoking when I found they could be sold for $2 a package. I once traded a carton for a large, handmade, man's tea jacket, which at the time was said to be more than fifty years old.

Finally, I had stopped traveling long enough for my mail to catch up with me, and I was the envy of the entire compound. From Nell I received nearly three months of letters, one written each day, and Mother had written once a week. I opened all of the letters and arranged them in the order in which they had been written. It was like getting books of love letters from home. I would go to my room, climb into my bed and read and re-read those wonderful letters, while my heart ached to see those who had written them.

My roommate was George Riley, a wild Irishman from the Bronx who had been taken out of the stockade to be shipped overseas. I soon learned why he had been jailed. When drunk he practically lost control of himself and was known to ram his fists through panel doors and otherwise release a rage that came near to consuming him. A handsome man of bulldog proportions, Riley lived with an abandon I had never before witnessed.

The highlight of his week was to visit the prostitutes in Ipin. Our outpost was five miles from the city, requiring at least an hour's walk alongside flooded rice patties or beside the Yangtze River, often on paths high above the swiftly racing and churning waters. If Riley left our compound drunk, he arrived at Ipin sober from the walk, and the same coming back.

Ipin, a city of more than 100,000 people, was surrounded by a twenty-foot stone wall, with entry only through massive, wooden doors at the gates. Robber bands roamed the countryside, and these doors were shut each night. But the closed doors did not stop Riley.

We were instructed to carry our carbines at all times, and if Riley arrived after the huge doors were locked, he would stand straddle-legged before them banging with the butt of his rifle until someone gave him entrance. Then he proceeded to the whorehouse. He was the talk of Ipin, and recognized by half the town.

One of the prostitutes either fell in love with Riley or thought through him she might escape her fate by marriage and getting to the United States. She frequently followed him to the compound and more than once I entered our room to find the small, beautiful woman in his bed. On occasion when Riley would describe some of his escapades with prostitutes, I was appalled at his beastly treatment of them. I could only imagine how bad their lot was that one would want to follow him to America.

The lieutenant was frightened of Riley, not without cause, and avoided him at all times. But the staff sergeant kept him in line most of the time with threats of shipping him to an area where there was fighting. Riley and I became good friends, and often when drunk he would place his huge arm around my shoulder and say, "Knight, I loves ya."

Our outpost existed to assist planes on their way between Chungking and Kunming to maintain communications, since our transmitter was much larger than what a plane could carry. We worked in shifts—eight hours on and twenty-four hours off, or at times, four hours on and twelve hours off. The duty was not difficult; in fact, we often felt useless. Usually by the time we had made all of the relays, the airplanes would be close enough to their destinations to handle the communication themselves.

Our transmissions were either in Morse Code or by voice. The lieutenant, who was there more as an administrator than as a radioman, did not know Morse Code well but would come by the station to check on what we were doing.

If we were working with code, he hardly noticed. But if we were having difficulty with someone on voice, he invariably would grab the mike, saying, "Here, let me do it," as though his voice could penetrate the airwaves better than ours. We called him "Golden Voice Tommy" behind his back.

I was very curious to know more about the Chinese, quite in contrast to most of the other soldiers who seemed content to spend their time within the compound. I made friends with a young Chinese civilian who worked at the Chinese side of the tiny airport as a radio operator. His name was Wang Sey Gin, about my age, and he was married with a two-year-old son. His mother also lived with them.

Wang was intelligent and eager to learn English, and quickly asked if I would be his teacher. I agreed and we began one-hour classes in my room at least twice a week and sometimes more often. I had no textbooks. We began by simply pointing to objects, naming them, and then having him learn the spelling for the word.

At the same time it was agreed he would teach me Chinese, but I never proved to be the quick student he was, possibly because I was not as motivated and because Chinese, with its tonal variations, is much harder to learn. Nevertheless, I once knew about 750 words in Mandarin Chinese.

Soon all of my fellow soldiers were speaking to me as I spoke to Wang, slowly, clearly, and loudly, for they heard our conversations through the open doors. When they would first see me in the morning they would say, "HOW ... ARE ... YOU ... TODAY, ... KNIGHT?"

Before many months, however, Wang had passed this awkward stage and we were conversing with some normalcy, if haltingly. When some of Wang's friends heard of the classes, they came to ask if they might study English. At one time I was teaching as many as twenty of them, meeting in the dining area.

I had found a mixed-breed Chow puppy that I raised as a pet and called Tabby, feeding him mostly from the scraps left from our meals. He became a mascot for the outpost, but I feared losing him to one of the Chinese. They would come sit in my room and pat Tabby, who was not only friendly but chubby. They would say, as they patted his broad back, "He would be good eating."

Wang searched for ways to thank me for my instruction, often bringing me a gallon jar of shelled, oiled peanuts, and more than once inviting me to his home to eat with his family. They lived in a three-room stucco house with dirt floors and chickens strolling in and out of the open doors. On occasion he served me rare Chinese delicacies, many of which I did not know the contents and I was embarrassed that he was spending his limited resources on me. Consequently, I would not accept his invitation often and would try to find a way to supplement their menu with something from our kitchen.

Clarence, one of the few college graduates in our group and one of three translators of our secret code, wanted the experience of eating in a Chinese home. He encouraged me to ask Wang if he could accompany me the next time I went. I finally agreed, provided we take something ourselves.

Wang went the extra mile and served us Thousand Year Eggs, a rare treat for someone of Wang's status. The eggs had been buried in lime for years and when prepared for the table were multicolored from being cooked in the lime. Their flavor was so delicate that we could not appreciate them fully, and the thought of their age did nothing to enhance the taste, but politeness demanded that we eat one. However, I told Wang that Clarence just loved those eggs, and no amount of refusal on Clarence's part would allow him to get by with just one. Clarence could have killed me.

I became close friends with Marlin, another radio operator who lived with flair and passion, and whose healthy good looks and high intelligence made him a favorite with most people. Marlin discovered that if he could secure a transfer back into the Air Corps as a radio operator on one of the bombers, he could get home to Illinois after so many missions— twenty-five, I think.

He was very persistent in his appeals for the transfer, and finally left us to fly the not-so-friendly skies of China. It was a very sad day when our supply plane brought the news his plane had gone down and the entire crew was killed.

Two families of missionaries of the then Northern Baptist Convention—the Doors and Masons, I think—lived in Ipin, and I took every opportunity to visit with them and to attend their church services, making the long walk each way.

The most difficult part of the journey was through the rice patties, for without fail we would meet a Honey Dipper, and the narrow path with flooded fields on each side provided no escape. Honey Dipper was the term we gave to coolies who carried large buckets on the opposite ends of a long, stout pole. This was a common sight throughout China, but the Honey Dipper had a special cargo for the fields—human fertilizer.

We would start holding our breath when we first saw them, until finally, having to have more oxygen, we would gasp air as quickly as possible and try to keep from fainting as we passed.

The missionaries introduced me more completely to Chinese life, on occasion taking me to visit one of the wealthy families in the city who lived, as did the missionaries, in large stone houses within a walled compound that included a servant's house and manicured lawn.

Once I was asked to speak to the young people of the church about the activity of Christian youth in the United States. It was my first attempt to speak through an interpreter, whom I completely stumped when I told of a "wiener roast" that was part of our weekly prayer meetings.

I wanted Wang to understand my faith, and because of the barrier of language, I introduced him to the missionaries, asking that they answer some of his questions more fully than I had been able to answer. Whether it was out of politeness or commitment, Wang did become a Christian.

The missionaries also introduced me to the Chinese pastor of the Baptist church in Ipin, and he gave me a Chinese name—Lie Dgu Lee—which means "Trust in the Lord's Strength." The pastor wrote the Chinese characters for me, and I had them made into an ivory chop, actually a signature stamp.

I attempted to hold religious services in the dining area at the compound for those of our group who wanted to attend, and a few did. I fear that my competitive nature appeared in conflict with some of their views of Christianity.

We all played Pinochle and Hearts, and I won my share of the games—maybe more than my share, according to some. Once the staff sergeant, who also loved to win, threw down his cards with the comment, "Hell, you are no more a minister than I am," as he stormed off, implying I had been cheating. He did have one effect upon me; I played cards less often.

But it was this same sergeant who led us all in crying when word came that Franklin Delano Roosevelt, the only President most of us had ever known, had died in Warm Springs, Georgia. The voice that had told us that the only thing we had to fear was fear itself was now quiet, and his passing left a hole in my life not unlike the far deeper hole left by Daddy's disappearance.

Like all of the world, we worried about Harry Truman, the little man from Missouri, himself a Baptist. But we sensed that the tide of tyranny had been turned back and sometime soon we would stop its flow altogether, and Roosevelt deserved much of the credit for his leadership.

Those of us at Ipin were slow to hear of the dropping of the atomic bomb on the two cities of Japan. We were never fully informed about what had happened, but we were thrilled with the results: Our war was over! We found it hard to believe.

Some of us went around saying, "Is it really over? Then why can't we go home?" We wanted to know why we couldn't return to our Zions and our Tylers and once again, embrace our Nells and our Mothers. Now that this war business was over, we wanted to get on with our lives. We wanted to make the decisions, right or wrong, about what was to happen in our lives instead of being directed by some unknown, distant powers.

I have always found it difficult to comprehend fully something so long hoped for and passionately desired when it was finally mine. It might suddenly happen, but my mind would not completely grasp the event or its significance. It seemed to require a series of realizations for a present reality to replace a past reality.

The ending of the war was just such a process for all of us at Ipin, and, no doubt, our isolation from other Americans delayed our full comprehension that the war was, in fact, over.

When Wang and my other students learned that the war was over and that most likely we would soon be leaving, they gave a banquet or dinner party in my honor. I did not dare ask for too detailed an explanation of what I was eating. I only prayed it was not Tabby whom I had given to one of the students.

In deference to my tee-totaling habits, no wine was served—unlike the Chinese dinners some of our personnel attended where the hot orange wine would suddenly strike with enough force that men would fall out of their chairs.

I had also learned during my first months at Ipin to use chopsticks, for we were given no options when dining with the Chinese: It was chopsticks or the china spoon for soup, and we would have lost face eating with the spoon. I had even purchased a personal pair of ivory chopsticks, and when I used them I ate the way the Chinese in this area ate.

I held a small deep bowl in my left hand, filled near the top with the brown, unpolished rice. From common dishes we used our chopsticks to add vegetables and meats to the rice. I then held the bowl to my mouth and proceeded to eat, both raking the food in as I gently sucked it from the bowl or picking up the food with the chopsticks. It was a noisy way to eat and would not have been polite back home, but here the noise indicated how much we appreciated the food.

We found that even with the war at an end we could not immediately, suddenly leave China or even Ipin. Transportation was at a premium. There were no planes to fly us back to the large supply base at Kunming. The powers-that-be eventually told our lieutenant that our small contingent was to use the Yangtze River as our highway for the first leg home. Hire a sampan (a flat-bottomed, skiff-like boat), the orders suggested, and float the crew the 300-plus miles to Kunming.

The lieutenant and the sergeant, as eager to leave Ipin as the rest of us, proceeded to do just that. The sergeant found a motorized sampan large enough to sleep us all under its bamboo-covered forward deck. We crammed all our personal belongings into our duffle bags, and taking only our rifles, papers, and secret-coding equipment, left all the other materiel to the local Chinese officials.

We left early one morning before the mist had cleared from the river, and, despite having to move against the current, made good headway up the muddy stream that nature had compressed within many deep gorges in the Szechwan and Yunnan provinces.

We spent the day observing life along the river, occasionally seeing evidence of a coal mine slanted into the banks. More than once in my walks into Ipin I had passed a similar coal mine—having to step around one or two naked corpses sprawled at the entrance. The bodies probably had been left following an accident deep within the mine. The callousness with which life was viewed in China often shocked me.

On the sampan, as it churned its way against the current of the Yangtze River, we speculated on how the war had ended, on the process of changing to a world at peace and, above all, how long it would take for us to reach the United States.

Some of us joined the Chinese in drinking the hot green tea prepared on a small, low charcoal grill. No matter the size of the boat, each was equipped with the charcoal grill, for the Chinese loved their tea above everything else. The Chinese also prepared their rice and vegetables on the grills, tempting us with the pungent aroma while we mostly ate from our stock of C-rations,

Robber bands were a threat in this area, and we feared stopping anywhere except at one of the walled cities. Even though it was early, we knew we couldn't reach the next city before dark, so our sampan pulled to shore before the open gate of a river city. We immediately disembarked to stretch our legs. Gawking residents outside the massive wooden gate became very excited and ran into the city, evidently to tell of our arrival.

Eventually we decided to visit the downtown business area as something to do before turning in for the night. It was a typical river town with all businesses and residences located inside the towering walls. By the time we reached the center of town, which was built around a small open park, hundreds of people were gathering.

We could hardly make our way through the crowd, and none of us spoke enough Chinese to learn what was going on. The people were pressing around us, struggling to get as close to us as possible. We were becoming more than a little apprehensive.

To our great relief, a well-dressed man in his late thirties approached, and speaking in easily understood, if somewhat broken English, welcomed us to their city. He informed us that we were the first Caucasians to visit the city, and it seemed everyone wanted a look at the "Foreign Devils," as most outsiders were called. The spokesman told us they were honored to have representatives of their ally, the United States, to visit them.

Some of our men, always looking for an occasion to drink, told him we wanted to celebrate with them the end of the war and the defeat of Japan. He steered us to a small, open-front restaurant to one side of the square and proceeded to order Wan Jo, the hot orange wine.

Our young lieutenant was somewhat shy, but the older sergeant took over. With glass in his raised hand, he announced, "I raise a toast to China and to all the brave men and women who have fought to defeat the enemy."

The Chinese spokesman translated the words to the crowd who smiled and clapped. He then took a glass of orange wine, and in turn raised it to speak words in Chinese to the crowd, which he translated, "I raise a toast to the United States and to all the brave men and women who have fought to defeat our common enemy, and have freed us from the Japanese."

These were but the first of a series of toasts. The next was to the glorious end of the war and the great role each nation had had in defeating Japan. As the hot wine warmed our men to their task, some stood on a table, making short speeches as though their hearers understood English, but they paused occasionally and the translator shouted the message to the crowd.

Roosevelt was toasted. Then Chiang Kai-shek. Then Truman. Then other Chinese officials. Then this city. Then each of us and all of them. A wonderful and glorious time was had by all.

Actually, for the first time we had celebrated the end of the war in a significant way and with someone other than Chinese servants—with a whole city. Even for those few of us who did not get drunk, it was a night to remember. These friendly Chinese, curious about the visit of strange foreigners, had given us a gift. More than anything that had happened recently, they helped us to comprehend emotionally that indeed the war was over.

The rest of the journey to Kunming was uneventful, with the last leg from river to base traversed in Army trucks. Our hopes of immediate shipment home soon became the victim of reality. Each of us had to wait his turn, and there were hundreds of thousands of us in the China-Burma-India Theatre.

We had to fly over "The Hump," and there was a limited number of airplanes. Once in India, I supposed there were a limited number of airplanes and ships. This time the line extended from Kunming to the United States, and we would stand there for a long time waiting our turn—or so it seemed to us.

In Kunming I was given the task of operating one of the base telephone switchboards, rugged equipment designed for field operation but now overloaded as it served a huge air base. When a party wished to speak to someone, he cranked a small lever beside the receiver. This dropped a tiny, flat, metal piece on my board and I inserted a line into the hole beside it, asking, "Number, please?"

My problem was that when several persons rang at the same time, I could not get to them quickly enough and each would continue cranking the lever. If I inserted the metal end into the hole at the time they were ringing, it shocked me. And I was constantly getting shocked. I wanted to crank one in their ear with my more powerful battery. It was by far the most frustrating job I was given in China.

Meanwhile, I had become friends with the base chaplain, a Southern Baptist named Sidney Burnette. He had in John Dunn one of the most incompetent assistants of anyone who ever tried to type a bulletin, place an order for supplies, or do any of the hundreds of tasks an assistant was required to do.

His problem was that he was unskilled. It was as though some classification officer could find no spot for him and had said, "Give him to the chaplain." He had just barely scored high enough on the I. Q. test to be drafted, and he had no feelings for religion whatsoever. He was a pleasant person but slow, and he could barely type, whereas I could type as much as 100 words a minute with very few errors.

Chaplain Burnette wanted me to become his assistant, but the problem of getting John transferred somewhere had us baffled until I took him to work with me one day. John was fascinated with the switchboard. I let him put on the headphones and try it out.

He eventually grasped the concept of what was going on, and I started telling him how exciting he might find this work. He agreed it was fascinating. I hope God forgave me my lying, but I eventually talked John into trading jobs. And I was forever grateful that we remained friends. I realized that the chaplain's assistant position had been as frustrating to John as operating that jangling switchboard had been for me. It was a swap made in heaven, as far as I was concerned.

Working with Chaplain Burnette was as fulfilling for me as operating a switchboard had been emptying, and the chaplain knew the military ropes well enough that he immediately put through a request that I be given the rank of corporal. I had gone thirty-three months as a buck private, nearly three years. I think I set some kind of an Army record. It was approved, and I would leave the service with a rank higher than buck private.

Burnette was an energetic and creative chaplain, and ministered to the military personnel effectively. He decided one week that we would organize a small party to visit missionaries of the China Inland Mission who served the Hau Miao tribes high in the Himalayan Mountains. Despite the fact that only four of us wanted to make the trip, it was scheduled anyway.

Chaplain Burnette secured a Land Rover for the journey over the narrow dirt roads back into the interior. We drove most of the day, taking a beating from the heavy transport and the rough roads, but finally reached the base of the mountains where one of the missionaries met us.

The rest of the journey, some fifteen miles, had to be made on foot up the twisting mountain trails, and we were carrying bedrolls and clothing. Each mile of the climb opened larger and larger vistas, and when we stopped at the top at last, we gasped at the sweep of the mountains with seven ranges unfolding below us, fading away in mist and clouds. While our bodies rested, our spirits feasted.

The Miao tribes were thought to be the aborigines of China, said to have once occupied the islands of Japan. But when the Mongols swept into China, the Miao were driven back and back. Fiercely independent, they refused to compromise or submit and eventually fled to the Himalayan Mountains, gradually moving higher and higher with their goats.

The Chinese occupiers in time found that salt—almost nonexistent in the mountains—was the key to their control of the Miao. Without salt in their diet and salt to preserve their meat, they could not survive. They submitted but continued to live, virtually independent, on the mountaintops.

The most striking features about the Hau Miao women were their hair and their blouses. Before marriage a maiden wore her long, jet black hair wound around two large cones at the back of her head with the points of the cones directed downward past her back shoulders. The core of the cones consisted of old hair. Once a woman married, she removed these two cones from the back of her head and wound her hair around a single cone at the front just above her forehead. It was a unique marriage symbol of two becoming one, and none was never in doubt as to whether a woman was married.

The colorful blouses were the source of the Hau Miao tribal name, for it meant "flowery," and they distinguished this tribe from other Miao groups. We were astounded at the process by which the cloth was made and dyed.

The thread was created by taking the white, fuzzy underside from the eucalyptus tree leaf and spinning the substance into thread, which was woven into cloth. By some long process of discovery, it was found the cloth could be dyed into designs by using beeswax to seal off that portion one did not wish to be colored. The wax was removed after each dying and repositioned for the next color. The result was a primitive print cloth with reds and blues dominating the designs. Each extended family identified with a particular pattern.

China Inland Mission (CIM) missionaries, sent to the area from Great Britain, had worked among the Miao for more than twenty-five years. While the tribal families had devised a complex society, they did not have a written language. Once the missionaries learned to speak the Miao tongue, they had created a written language, using mathematical marks, asterisks, and other symbols for unique sounds. By the time of our visit, the missionaries had opened a school, teaching the children to read, write, and do basic math.

The missionaries had also translated all of the New Testament and much of the Old Testament into the Miao tongue, along with many of the traditional Christian hymns. We recognized the tunes during worship services, and we sang along in English when we could remember the words. The accompaniment was on Miao instruments, a variation of the lute or guitar.

The worship service was informal, following closely to a traditional Protestant service of hymns, testimonies, sermon, and prayers. Chaplain Burnette was invited to preach with one of the missionary men translating. I always found it both inspiring and a little clinical to be a part of such worship services, clinical in the sense that I found myself more observer than participant, a sensation heightened by the language barrier.

We did not visit any other village, but the CIM missionaries told us they had a circuit around the mountain tops that they made regularly, spreading not only the Word of God but also the word of the Miao in its written form. Villages could now communicate better with other villages, families with their scattered members, and friends with friends in ways other than orally. The missionaries had drastically changed the Miao society, and I prayed that it was for the best.

Once back in Kunming I was finally told that it was my turn to leave China. My plane crossed The Hump in a violent thunderstorm, with the airplane at times dropping and rising as much as 500 to 1,000 feet, tossing those of us sitting on the floor in the cargo area about like chopsticks in weightless space. I decided there was nothing I could do about the storm or the flying, and when the weather settled down somewhat, I went to sleep for the rest of the flight to Calcutta.

In the hot, steaming caldron of Calcutta we were once again billeted in a tent city similar to the one in which we had stayed on the journey into China, only this time everything was more relaxed. One day as a group of us discussed our varied experiences in China—especially the food we had eaten—we learned that John Dunn, the same person I had talked into trading jobs, had spent nearly two years in China but had never eaten a Chinese meal.

I had come to love the Chinese and their food, and I felt not only some surprise but also was indignant that someone would leave the United States for two years but would never escape its culture. "You are not going back to the States without having eaten one Chinese meal," I declared, "even if it has to be in India."

The thought inspired the entire group, and we decided we would make an excursion into Calcutta in honor of John Dunn, who of course was cautious about it all but agreed to go. I found a Chinese friend who would act as both interpreter and guide. Our instructions to him were to take us to a fine Chinese restaurant and to order us the best meal he could have prepared for that night. Some feasts require two days' notice.

Our party of six arrived at the restaurant about 6 p.m., finding it an imposing display of traditional Chinese dining with each party assigned its separate small room, where we sat on mats around a low round table, similar to the Japanese. The interpreter started our meal with the customary colorful rice cake, a delicate dessert to soften the appetite and thus avoid eating too much. He also ordered Wan Jo, the orange wine, and for once I had a glass.

For the next four hours we were treated to one elaborate dish after another—a whole fish, a Peking duck, varied vegetables, and a series of traditional Chinese delicacies. We continued the discussion of our experiences in China, and I found that very few of the others had had much contact with the Chinese and neither had they sought to learn anything about the language.

Before 11 p.m. we left the restaurant, having spent the princely sum of $6 each on the meal, but it was worth every rupee. John not only had eaten a Chinese meal to remember, but we all had.

For our voyage back to the States, we were able—with the war over—to board ship at Calcutta and not have to repeat the long train ride all across India. We took the shortest, most direct route home: the Indian Ocean, the Red Sea and Suez Canal, the Mediterranean, and finally the Atlantic Ocean. From the deck I saw the dry Egyptian desert and small dusty settlements as we waited our turn through the Suez, and leaving the Mediterranean I glimpsed the Rock of Gibraltar.

Once in the Atlantic, however, there was nothing to see but waves and occasional porpoises as we weathered severe storms. At times the seas were so rough, waves washed over our ship when we dropped into the troughs between them. At the height of the storm only those sailors with duty on deck were allowed topside. The storm lasted for days, and two-thirds of the soldiers were seasick. The lines to chow shortened drastically, and while I never became sick, I did skip a meal or two.

From Calcutta we were twenty days making the trip home, giving me a total of seventy days onboard ship—more than a lot of sailors. I had completely circumnavigated the earth—the long, hard way.

I would soon be twenty-one, and the U.S. Army Air Corps had given me a crash course in world affairs, a strong experience of crossing cultures, a camaraderie with others from throughout the U. S. and the world, and a testing of myself in new roles and against other persons.

I had lost much of my provincialism, and in its place I had gained an invaluable global perspective—or at least the foundation for a worldview of life.

When our ship docked at New York City, our elation knew no bounds at seeing the United States and the Statue of Liberty's welcoming torch. There had been many times when we thought the war would never end and we would never see our native country again.

I was given a half day's leave before being placed on a train to Indianapolis, I headed for a small restaurant where I ordered a quart of milk and a half head of lettuce—both foods denied us in India and China because of sanitation problems, among them the Honey Dippers. Never had these simple foods tasted so sweet, and I savored every sip and bite. Then I topped the strange meal off with a pint of ice cream.

I spent Christmas Day in Indianapolis, finally getting a phone call through to Mother and Nell, who was in Zion waiting for me. Nell had quit her job at Tyler's Montgomery Ward in November, since we thought I might return at any moment.

She had been in Zion for a month, working at the candy counter at Kresse's, the store where Mother worked. I told Nell I didn't know how long deactivation would take, but I would be home as soon as possible. As usual the Army took its own sweet time with the process of giving me my discharge.

One whole day was spent hearing lectures about the Army of the future and being asked to stay in the reserves. There was no way I would continue with an organization that took thirty months to promote me to private first class, not to mention a few other things I held against the military mindset. I gave them a quick and loud, "No."

I left Indianapolis on New Year's Eve by bus and arrived in Henderson that night, having to take a taxi to Mother's. I did not dare to call

Cousin Ed that late. Everyone was asleep when I beat upon the door, and Nell was embarrassed that my first sight of her was in a nightgown with her hair disheveled, but I did not care.

She looked wonderful to me, and so did all of the others.

Baby Jimmy was 3 that month. Jane was 8, Hiram 11, Bubba 14, and Dorothy 16. It was almost incomprehensible that I was out of the Army and home, but seeing and hugging all of them made it believable at last. I didn't even mind—well, not much—that Nell and I had to share the bed that night with Dot.

Raymond, who had gotten out of the Army earlier, had moved Bettye and their son Gene (to be three in April) to the house behind Cousin Ed's blacksmith shop, a house once owned by Mama and Papa Knight. Also Dorothy was talking marriage to her long-time boyfriend Jimmy Cunningham, who had just returned from the war. Buddy and Ruth (nee Willett) were living in Henderson where he was working.

Daddy still had not been heard from, and no one knew anything about him. Mother's only knowledge that he was even alive came in an Internal Revenue Service document indicating he had worked in San Francisco.

Mother was being "called on" by a coal miner named Roy Crenshaw who lived in a house trailer on the lot next to Frank Reid's Barber Shop. Roy Crenshaw, ten years Mother's senior (she was only forty-two), was an uneducated, taciturn man whose short, heavy-set features and strong upper body made him an ideal miner.

His specialty was setting the charges of dynamite that blasted the seam of coal out of the rock. Some of us older children thought Mr. Roy "beneath Mother's station in life," but Mother kept her peace and did not respond to our comments.

The families of Zion and Zion Baptist Church had not lost a son in the war. Only Coonkey, of all those for whom the Thursday night prayer group had prayed, had been seriously injured. But not so for my two dear friends from Henderson: John Wilkerson and Walter Farley had both been killed.

As the war came to a close, Congress had passed the G. I. Bill, providing tuition and a monthly living expense allotment for all servicemen who wanted college or advanced degrees. The bill was thrilling news for me, assuring me of a college education.

Before I met Nell I had planned to attend Georgetown Baptist College in Kentucky, but the Moseleys had told me about Baylor University in Waco, Texas, the largest Baptist college in the world and, by Texas standards at least, the best. I wanted to check it out.

Baylor's spring quarter would start in March, so Nell and I remained at Zion for only two weeks. I promised to help Mother as much as I could from our limited resources, and we caught the train for Tyler. Mother, characteristically, supported us in the decision even though it meant her life would be more difficult now that there would no longer be the small allotment checks through the Army.

Nell and I had been married for nearly twenty-seven months, but we had been together only a little more than six months total. The times of separation, however, had given us the gift of revealing ourselves through writing—a process that may have allowed us to express the inner life more profoundly than we might have revealed had we been together.

In a way, those months of separation had substituted for the courtship we never had, allowing us an important time to become acquainted, to express values, to make plans, and to share expectations. Now we were launching our life together with the assurance of some stability, when we, not the Army, would be deciding our fate.

Chapter 10

BAYLOR

Returning to Tyler and to the Moseleys was like a second home-coming that January of 1946. I was treated as one of the family, but a family that was still separated by the military. Kelly had joined the Navy when it appeared he would be drafted by the Army, and had not yet returned to Tyler.

Jack was still at home and working at a grocery store. The Moseleys lived in a duplex on the Dallas Highway about five miles west of Tyler. The house was owned by the Hortons who occupied the other side, and for the time being I moved with Nell into her room.

Mr. Moseley worked for his friend, Buck Thompson, as a cabinet-maker and framing supervisor in the construction of homes. With the war's end, building materials were again available and the demand for housing had increased.

The primary item on my agenda was arrangements for college. So we planned a visit to Baylor University in Waco, one of the largest private schools in the state as well as one of the oldest, having been chartered by Texas Baptists in 1845. Pat M. Neff, a former governor of Texas, was president.

The Moseleys offered the use of their car for a one-day visit to the campus for us to check things out, and if we were pleased with what we found, to start the process of enrolling.

Mrs. Moseley and Jack decided to make the trip with us, Jack to help with the driving and Mrs. Moseley just to keep us company. Jack and I nearly drove the two women crazy by singing "Life's setting sun is sinking low, a few more days and I must go, to meet the deeds that I have done, and there will be no setting sun."

Then we said, "Second verse, just like the first . . ." We sang a hundred verses. Nell said she would never forget it. Jack had an excuse. He was just seventeen, and maybe I was just excited about going to college.

Baylor, located in the center of the state, proved to be all that I had hoped it would be with its spacious campus and varied studies, including a large religion department and even a good-sized journalism department. Other veterans, taking advantage of the G. I. Bill, were enrolling every quarter, and many were married—a new phenomenon for the university.

The school was in the process of building the first units of housing for married students, and we were told one of the new units would be available to us before the spring quarter ended. We would need temporary housing until then, but we were assured rooms were for rent throughout the city. We made the commitment to return in March to start my college education as a ministerial student, a category that included more than 150 other men (no women then).

Nell and Walker on the streets of Waco, Texas in 1946, his first year at Baylor University.

During the wait of more than a month before spring quarter began, I worked as a carpenter's helper with Mr. Moseley, earning a little money and getting myself into better physical shape after the idleness of the last few months. During this time both Nell and I celebrated birthdays, her twentieth and my twenty-second. The time finally came when Mr. and Mrs. Moseley drove us to Waco. There we moved into a furnished room with kitchen privileges on the west side of town, a bus ride of but a few miles to the university.

We decided to attend the large, college-oriented Seventh & James Baptist Church, located one block off the campus and near the site of the married student housing under construction. The church, because of its location and ministry, attracted hundreds of students.

During the bus ride to church one Sunday morning we met another couple also on their way to Seventh & James, "Stormy" and Jerry Ratliff. We were immediately and profoundly attracted to each other. Stormy was a vivacious person who radiated charm, and redheaded Jerry was a laid-back drama major who specialized in comedy.

Both had attended Baylor before the war, and Stormy (her maiden name was Clarice Storms) had gone on to graduate after Jerry was drafted. Now she was three months pregnant, and they also were expecting to occupy one of the units for married students. We decided to request adjoining accommodations.

At Seventh & James, Jerry and I were members of the same Sunday school class, and Stormy and Nell attended a women's class for wives of veterans.

I declared a major in religion at Baylor and that spring immediately took a survey course in Old Testament, to be followed the next quarter by a survey course in the New Testament. In fact, these two courses were required of all Baylor students, along with compulsory chapel.

However, the student body had grown so large following the war that the auditorium would not hold all the students. Veterans, who were seen as more mature and less in need of whatever they did at chapel, were exempted. The only chapel service I was to attend at Baylor was when President Harry S Truman was awarded an honorary degree.

Also enrolled in the Old Testament course was another veteran, a Seventh Day Baptist—they stress Saturday as the Sabbath—named Bill Lathrop, a tall, gangly Scandinavian from North Dakota whose hands were twice the size of mine. If the adage, "still water runs deep" could be applied to anyone, it fit Bill Lathrop.

He seemed to speak only when he absolutely had to, but once he warmed to his subject, he waved those big hands in your face like punctuation marks. Bill was a person who cared very deeply about people and issues.

Maybe it was a case of opposites attracting, but we found common ground from the first day we met, and we looked like Mutt and Jeff walking around campus together. He was the best student I knew.

For example, in history when he received his textbook, he immediately read the entire volume. Each day as assignments were made, he re-read the pages, underlining the important facts, then he memorized what he had underlined. But in class Bill never volunteered to answer a question, responding only when called on. If I had studied that hard, I would have had to let someone in authority know it.

In the Old Testament survey class each student was expected to complete a notebook consisting of class notes, summaries of outside reading, class assignments, and other material related to the Old Testament. Bill and I worked together on the notebooks, with my typing all the material and both of us researching magazines and reviewing books.

Near the end of the quarter we turned in our notebooks consisting of more than 100 pages each. The teacher was overwhelmed and returned them to us with the comment, "Your notebooks have exceeded anything I have ever had before, and I gave others A-plus. I have given both of you A-double plus."

I felt fortunate when I signed up for English grammar and discovered the textbook was the same as one I had used in a correspondence course I had completed during my stay in Ipin, China. Needless to say, it made that class easier, but I had to watch my punctuation very carefully.

If I used a comma—when it should have been a semicolon—to separate two independent clauses in which one clause had some internal punctuation, I automatically received an F for that paper. It was called a "comma blunder" and made for some very stilted punctuation, but I never forgot the rule. (Every chapter of this autobiography would have received an F.)

We had been in Waco for only a short while when Nell missed her menstrual period, and by the time she missed the second one we knew she was pregnant. Conception had occurred in Tyler the last of January. The baby was due in November. We had been careful, but not careful enough.

So once again we would be doing things the hard way, but we had plenty of company. Seventh & James had a post-war baby boom. The church proved to be the focus of our community life, and it was within walking distance of our housing after we moved.

Woodson Armes, whose dry sermons droned on for about thirty minutes, was the pastor. However, his violin-playing and poetry-writing wife, Sybil, spread some water on Woodson's arid dessert.

Sunday school added the excitement and interest lacking in the worship services. My large class, composed mostly of students, was taught by P. D. Browne, a droll professor who taught the interesting combination of math and Bible at Baylor. Nell and Stormy's teacher was the young, attractive Lillian (Lil) Brown, whose husband was still overseas as a chaplain with the occupying forces.

Lil, the mother of two young sons, was studying for her master's degree. Her class became a close-knit community, sponsoring showers and parties, and the experienced Lil provided a strong source of advice and comfort for new mothers.

Many of Nell's class members moved with their husbands into the veterans' housing area at Eighth and Speight Streets. The university had secured used mobile apartments from the government, the type of temporary housing that eventually becomes permanent. Each of the furnished units was constructed around a narrow kitchen, with the two side rooms folding in on hinges for moving purposes.

Each side room was eight by fourteen feet. Our bed occupied one side, a couch that converted into a bed was on the other, and the dining table graced part of the front area. There were no partitions. In the hot Texas summers the low ceilings and small windows made the units almost unbearable.

Since we couldn't afford expensive air conditioning, which was rare then, I finally rigged a water-cooled window fan for some relief. This project consisted of building a window box about three feet square, lining the outsides with wood shavings between chicken wire, and letting water drip down over the shavings. As the water evaporated, it produced cool air that the fan blew into the unit—a little damp at times but worth the trouble.

Because they had been movable at one time, we called the units trailers, and there were twenty-eight in the five rows. A laundry room, complete with coin-operated washing machines and large tubs, took the space of two units at the south end of the middle row. We dried clothes on lines between the unit rows.

I was always amazed at how quickly clothes dried in the Texas heat and wind. Later when we were hanging out diapers there would be times when once we were through pinning the wet clothes to the line, we could go to the other end and take down the dry ones.

Six of the units were strung together in a row, and there were five rows. We shared our bathroom with Stormy and Jerry (being sure to lock the door when using it and for sure unlocking it when through), and we shared the small front porch with Don and Carlene McGregor.

It was not long before someone observed, "You either become close friends or quit speaking to the other families." Luckily, we became friends with the Ratliffs and the McGregors.

I saw no reason to take a summer break, having just enrolled, so I continued my classes. As a freshman I was taking basic courses anyway, and enough of these were offered during the summer to give me a full load. I usually carried more than the average number of subjects in my eagerness to get the college education behind me so I might move on to seminary back in Kentucky.

I was not attracted to the clubs and organizations of campus life for some reason, probably because of my age or demanding time I did not have. I did take part in the mission programs of the Baptist Student Union, which meant going to the jails and to some of the poorer areas of Waco to hold Bible study classes and worship services among the blacks and Spanish-speaking population. Along with Bill Lathrop and Lloyd Gibson, I attended a few meetings of the ministerial association to hear speakers and to meet other students.

Mother came to visit us that summer, riding the train to see Texas for the first time in her life. We were thrilled to introduce her to all our friends and to take her on a tour of the university. She was impressed.

She also told us that she and Mr. Roy Crenshaw were "seeing each other." So it was not that great a surprise early in the fall that they were married, almost four years to the month after Daddy had left. Actually, she had waited this long, most likely, because a missing person in Kentucky can be declared legally dead after five years and no contact.

Although we older children, if not the younger, thought Mother was marrying "beneath" herself, we were pleased that she would have a companion in raising the four children at home. After all, she was only forty-three years old.

Quiet almost to the extreme, Mr. Roy appeared to be well adjusted to the solitude of being a bachelor, but he did hang out listening to the men who gathered at the nearby country store or sit with another group at Frank Reid's barber shop. It was evidently the only community he knew, other than those with whom he worked.

Two or three years after Daddy's disappearance, Mr. Roy (as the family would always refer to him at Mother's request) began to take an interest in Mother, attention that she tolerated but did not encourage to any great extent. However, Mr. Roy was persistent, if nothing else, and Mother eventually began to see that he was not only quiet but also steady, hardworking, and even-tempered, if not affectionate and generous. She was able to consider his proposals of marriage when they came.

Mr. Roy sold his mobile home and moved into Mother's house. It was the small one the community had helped granddad Henderson build with lumber from houses he had razed and on land he had given Mother. The house and land were but a half of a city block from where Mr. Roy had been living.

Mr. Roy brought with him a steady income, a car, and a man's influence into the house of three boys (Jim, 4; Hiram, 11; Bubba, 15) and Jane, who was 9 years old. Actually Bubba would spend little time at the house as he moved in with Dorothy and her new husband, Jimmy Cunningham, on the Cunningham farm.

Mr. Roy's car became an important addition to the household, and he immediately gave serious attention to the large garden covering most of the two acres of land.

"He had his potatoes in the ground by Good Friday every year, no matter what the weather," the boys remembered. While he showed little affection toward the children, he did not abuse them in any way but left all of the disciplining to Mother.

He faithfully brought to Mother his check of the week, and she managed the affairs of the household. She also was working as a clerk/cook at a Henderson drug store. For the first time in years there was some financial stability for the family.

Mr. Roy imposed few rules upon the children, but one important stipulation was they were not to "mess with my tools." He kept his car in good working condition, adjusting the valves once a week and doing all the other mechanical tasks as needed.

Other than being a miner, a mechanic, and a gardener, Mr. Roy had the ability to "witch" for water, a skill often used for others in the county. His method was much like that of Pa Sexton in Texas. "Witching" was done by the cutting of a forked stick with branches of nearly three feet. Mr. Roy would hold the ends of the branches, bent somewhat in his hands in a way that forced the third end to extend forward.

As he walked around in search of the water, the forward end would suddenly and mysteriously bend rapidly toward the ground. "Here's the water," he would say, and when a well was dug, the water was there.

While he would only speak when spoken to, Mr. Roy could be enticed to tell briefly of his experiences in France during World War I when he drove a motorcycle as a messenger for general headquarters. He escaped any serious harm and had only good words for the officers and generals whose messages he carried.

While Mr. Roy seldom drank to excess, he did enjoy beer and whiskey at times. One Christmas when Jim came home from Coast Guard duty that had taken him to Newfoundland, he brought as gifts for many of the older men fifths of duty-free whiskey. Mr. Roy came upon the liquor, and he proceeded to drink it bottle after bottle until he was unable to stand.

Drunk and limber, the others found him very difficult to move but managed to get him into a bed until he sobered up. Everyone was thankful it was a rare occasion for him to become so intoxicated.

Mr. Roy was older than Mother, had lived a very difficult life as a miner, and suffered from the black lung disease of most miners who had little protection once inside the mine. He died in 1971 from the effects of that disease. I think one of the last pictures of all of us nine children with mother was taken on the occasion of his funeral.

Back in Waco, Stormy gave birth to Rosalyn, a 9½ pound girl, in August. Going through the birth process with them helped to prepare us for our child's delivery. Nell learned from the doctor that her blood pressure was high and was told to drop all salt intake while staying off her feet to keep them from swelling.

Because Nell's blood pressure was so high, the doctor put her in the hospital ten days before her due date and induced labor. After more than sixteen hours of labor, she delivered on October 24 a 6 pound-10½ ounce boy, whom we named Walker Leigh Jr.

But after seeing the size of Rosalyn I remarked, "He's so stubby." We all began to call him by that nickname, and with my background I thought everyone should have a nickname.

Mrs. Moseley agreed that she would come to Waco and stay with us the first week that Nell and the baby were home from the hospital. I'm sure her time there was marred by my preconceptions on how one should raise a child. I had always heard that a child could be spoiled, and the doctors at that time were into strict feeding regiments.

I foolishly insisted, over Nell and Mrs. Moseley's objections, that we stick to such periods and let Stubby cry. I'm not very proud of my know-it-all-attitude of those days, and Mrs. Moseley went home earlier than she had planned.

In December we all visited Tyler for the wedding of Jack, who had enlisted in the Army Air Corps, to Allene Piggott. They asked me to officiate, and I was pleased to do so. It was not my first wedding, for when we were stationed at Fresno in 1944 an Army buddy from New Orleans had asked me to perform the ceremony for him and his bride.

Since we were staying in Tyler that December for the Christmas holidays, we gave Jack and Allene the keys to our trailer that they used for their honeymoon since they lacked the funds for anything else.

In Waco I had been working at a grocery store and delicatessen, but I did not like the owner who berated his workers and cursed at them in front of others. Once when he verbally attacked me, I told him no one could talk to me that way and the next time he did it I was quitting.

Consequently, I looked for some other way to generate additional income. When the opportunity came, Lloyd Gibson and I bought the stock of a feed store on the same block as the housing units and took over the operation from an older man who wanted to quit working.

Lloyd and I arranged our classes so that one of us would be there most of the time, and we began the process of learning about feed for horses, cattle, and pets and about the use of the few other items the store sold. We also jointly purchased an old black 1934 Chevrolet sedan to use in the business and personally.

The business did generate some income, and we had a lot of slack time in which to study. When we tired of our books, we started playing chess, and learned more about that game than the game of business. When Stubby began to crawl about, I would keep him sometimes at the store, but the building was in such bad shape that I could have him in the store only when the weather was fair.

We were the proudest of parents of our baby and showered him with attention. He was small, wiry, and strong and took his first steps at seven months, well ahead of the older but heavier Rosalyn. He was the talk of the housing units. And he talked early as well. As competitive parents, we had won round one.

One week Lloyd drove the Chevrolet to Austin to visit his and Helen's parents. He failed to check the oil, which the old car used a lot of, and he drove it back dry. The car had to have rings and inserts if it was to be used any longer.

Not having the money to pay a garage to rebuild the engine, we enlisted Bill Lathrop, who seemed to know how to do just about anything, to supervise our overhauling the motor. He agreed, and to our surprise, we completed the work ourselves and everything worked.

I could not get away from my love of newspaper work, so I volunteered to help staff the *Baylor Lariat*, then published twice a week. It awakened within me the old longing for a career in journalism, and I began to review my calling to a ministerial vocation.

As I studied the Bible for some direction, I decided that God gave me my talents to be used; that God had given me the experience and the inclination I had for journalism. Could there not be a way to use my gifts in God's service? I decided to shift to a double major in religion and journalism, taking as many courses in both fields as I could.

I was soon named an issue or "night" editor on the *Lariat* when we changed frequency to five days a week. The publication received All-American honors among major college newspapers. We were organized like a big city daily, had our own Associated Press wire by teletype, and the students were assigned beats for coverage of the university. And, of course, we rode the edge of tension often in editorials and coverage that did not always please the administration.

By the summer of 1947, I was through with my sophomore work and ready to launch into my junior year, but Nell and I decided that a summer break would be appropriate. Since I expected to be a pastor, I decided some experience as an associate pastor would be worthwhile.

Clel Rodgers had returned to Zion after his Army service as a chaplain, and he and the Zion Baptist Church extended an invitation for me to work there during the summer as an intern.

It was also an opportunity to stay with Mother and Mr. Roy, even though it meant crowding them a bit, for Hiram, Jane, and Jimmy were still at home. (Bubba was working at the Cunninghams' farm. Bettye and Raymond, with their son Gene, had moved to his parents' farm.) My Mother's house had been enlarged since its original construction, so with some of the family members sleeping in the living room, we managed.

Jane was quite the tomboy. At the last Christmas Hiram was given an air rifle, or BB gun, and Jane was given dolls. She was heartbroken, threw the doll down, and cried for a BB gun. "What am I going to do when he shoots me?" she demanded of the adults, "Throw my dolls at him?" Uncle Johnny then gave her an air rifle.

Mother did not work that summer, so Nell and Stubby spent the day with the family while I worked at the church with Clel. He introduced me to all phases of church life and to his rather casual and comfortable style of ministering. We took surveys of the larger community served by the church, conducted a two-week Vacation Bible School, and ended the summer with a revival conducted by a visiting minister.

Walker Leigh had an eight-month growth of blond hair, and one day I took him with me to Frank Reid's Barber Shop. He was the star attraction of the men hanging out there, showing them he could walk and talk.

On impulse, I had Frank cut his hair. I wanted the barber who had been an important part of my life when I was growing up to be the one who gave my son his first haircut. It was not a wise action on my part, for Nell was crushed when I brought Stubby home. I learned a valuable lesson. Decisions were to be shared.

Back at Baylor we launched my junior year, but we found that our feed store had suffered because of the illness of a partner who had bought out Lloyd Gibson. He had to close it down for nearly a month during the summer, and most of our business went elsewhere. Our business days were over, as we closed the feed store for good.

Our finances were tight, so Nell went to work at the credit office of Montgomery Ward, leaving Walker Leigh with our neighbor Carlene McGregor. However, Nell did not work more than six months because she was again pregnant, and at that time it was not considered proper for a woman with child to continue working.

Despite my indecision about being a pastor or a journalist, I was eager to secure the pastorate of a Baptist church. My wish came true when a friend recommended me to the Dale Baptist Church, some thirty miles south of Austin off the main highway to San Antonio.

Dale, Texas—not as large as Zion—served a farming and ranching community. It was my first introduction to south central Texas, and houses seemed to stand bare and isolated because there were few trees, and those that grew in Dale were very small. I had not realized the role the huge, spreading trees in Zion had played in tying the community together and giving me the feeling of closeness and protection. In Dale I had the feeling of being exposed.

The church's pulpit committee invited me to preach a trial sermon, which I did with enthusiasm, using a number of illustrations from my experiences in China. Contrary to a style I developed later of using manuscripts, at this time I preached entirely from outline notes. The church members voted to ask me to be their pastor, and I readily accepted.

I was to come on weekends and preach morning and night on Sunday, using Saturday to visit among the saints and sinners of the area. For these services and a round trip of 280 miles, I would be paid $25 a week. In my eagerness to test my skills and to serve God in this way, I accepted.

The church, in cooperation with the associational missionary, arranged for a special ordination service one Sunday afternoon, and Nell—pregnant and expecting in August—and Walker Leigh made the trip with me that weekend. An ordination council questioned me as to my beliefs, which at that time did not threaten anyone, and I was duly recommended to the church.

All ordained ministers present proceeded to lay hands on me, and the pastor of First Baptist Church in nearby Lockhart preached. For some reason I did not keep a record of the service.

By this time I had bought a black, two-door 1940 Ford sedan, somewhat the worse for wear but all I could afford, and the trip back and forth between Dale and Waco usually went without incident. The most difficulty I had was with the generator, which evidently did not like going to church even when rebuilt. As with any eight-year-old car, it had its problems with overheating and flat tires.

The drive to Dale was usually pleasant on Friday afternoon or Saturday morning, but the drive back to Waco was painful, for it had to be made after the Sunday evening service. I would leave the church after nine p.m. and get home after midnight—if there were no car problems.

My biggest problem was getting up on Monday for classes, and that summer I had to take a compressed (half the usual quarter) Greek class that started at 7 a.m. and lasted until 9 a.m. Even if I made it to class on time on Monday, I could not keep my eyes open and invariably went to sleep with my head on the desk.

However, the church responded well to my preaching, except for one veteran deacon who always sat near the front and appeared to sleep through every sermon—as I did in my Greek classes. At least he sat there with his eyes closed. When I gently mentioned the fact that he seemed to be catching up on his sleep, he told me the light hurt his eyes. Now, why hadn't I thought of that?

Dale Baptist Church met in a white, frame building with the small sanctuary in front of a smaller education unit across the back. Ceiling fans and open windows were the only defense against the Texas heat, but everyone was grateful for the wind, which never stopped its sweep across the open countryside.

Once, as I was deep within the delivery of an evening message, a stronger than usual gust of wind picked up my notes and deposited them in front of the pulpit. I was forced to stop, descend from the pulpit, and pick them up. I had learned to speak from notes, and found it difficult to preach without them.

An elderly couple, the Jay Dannellys, were my favorites for a place to stay on Saturday night and to rest on Sunday after-noon. I always needed a nap if I was to stay awake on the drive back to Waco.

Dale Baptist Church in Texas, where Walker served as pastor in 1948.

At other homes I was expected to spend the afternoon making small talk, something I have always had trouble sustaining for any length of time. The Dannellys had a son who was a minister, and they seemed to under-stand.

The Greek class difficulty was exacerbated when the church sched-uled its summer revival for one of the weeks when the class was being held. I enlisted Bob Polk, then a pastor at New York in East Texas, to preach and Ford Johnson, a graduate student, to lead the singing. Bob also was an excellent pianist and would accompany Ford when he sang.

We held Vacation Bible School in the morning, visited in the after-noon, and conducted the main services each night. The community rewarded our efforts with one of the highest attendances in recent years, and a number of conversions and other decisions were made. All of the offerings were divided between the three of us, with Bob getting the lion's share.

I was somewhat embarrassed at the small amount, but it was some-thing over which I had no control. My inexperience at stressing offerings may have contributed to the weak response, but I have always had difficulty asking anyone for money—probably a throwback to the times I had to pick up the government-issued food.

By the time I got back to Greek, I was so far behind that I dropped the course and took an "F," the only failing grade I ever had. After nine months with the church I decided I had just about worn out the Ford and myself, realizing I could not afford to continue subsidizing the church. I resigned. Dale was my one and only pastorate.

On August 22 that year—1948—our second son was delivered at Hillcrest Hospital after another long period of labor for Nell. In honor of Kenneth Howard, who had introduced us, we named him Kenneth Wayne. Wayne was also the name of Orene's youngest brother.

By this time I had greatly modified—with more than a little help from Nell—my views on raising children, and we also had decided the doctors were wrong in their rigid patterns of feeding. We fed and held Kenny whenever he was hungry and whenever we felt like cuddling him.

Unfortunately, we had exhausted all savings from the nest egg Nell had put aside during the war. There were times when we did not have food in the house. Once friends, who also lived in one of the trailer units, received a case of ravioli from relatives. They shared their food with us, and it kept us eating until the government check arrived at the first of that month.

While I was enjoying being a night editor on the *Lariat* and being closely involved in university life, I knew I had to find additional work. A senior journalism student told me of a job editing a weekly newspaper in Marlin, about thirty miles south of Waco. I contacted the owner, Sam Pyland, and arranged for an interview. Marlin, the county seat of Falls County, had a population of nearly 5,000 in a farming and light industrial area.

I was surprised to find that Sam Pyland was a young man in his thirties who had started an office supply and printing business some ten years earlier. Sam began publishing *The Falls County Record* as a means of advertising his office and printing business. His heart was not into journalism, and he had discovered he could hire his editors from among the senior Baylor journalism students.

He and I were immediately attracted to each other, and he offered me the position. I arranged most of my classes for the mornings and drove to Marlin almost every day.

Sam gave me a free hand with the paper, and I attacked the work with vigor, more excited than I had been with the pastorate. At least, I knew more about what I was doing than I had with the church. I increased the news coverage of the county, stressing features, because we were also competing with the city's daily, the *Marlin Democrat*. I launched editorial campaigns against sewage pollution and other civic disorders.

Sam had always given the paper away, needing distribution for advertising more than he needed the income from subscriptions. However, I used the telephone as a means of solicitation and finally had most of the people subscribing. Sam commented, "I never thought people would pay good money for my paper."

One day in Marlin I received an urgent call from Bill Lathrop that they had taken Kenny to Hillcrest Hospital when he suddenly turned very pale and was listless. I dropped everything and drove frantically back to Waco and the hospital. The pediatrician—Dr. Charles Shellenburg—had diagnosed the illness as locked bowels, or a kink in the intestines.

The usual procedure was an operation, but he wanted to try a new technique: They would give Kenny a barium enema under gentle pressure in hopes that the barium would straighten out the kink. To our great relief and gratefulness it worked. No operation was needed. In fact, Dr. Shellenburg documented his use of the procedure for a medical journal.

Sam Pyland loved to sell advertising, and he had devised a method where local merchants could get their advertising virtually free of any cost to them. Sam established two rates, one called a national rate and the other, which was 50 percent less, was the local rate. National advertisers, such as Firestone, would cooperate with local advertisers on a fifty-fifty split paying the local rate, which was all Sam required. The local businessmen took out all the advertising the national companies would budget.

The print shop was so disorderly, only those who worked there daily knew where anything was. During all the years of publication, leftover papers had been piled alongside one wall, and the pile had reached significant proportions. The back shop included one linotype machine for basic text matter, but any larger headlines or unusual type was handset from type kept in large drawers. In their hurry to produce new jobs, workers left the old ones tied together with string sitting on top of the huge stone tables on which they worked.

It was inevitable that the workers would soon run out of some letters in each type, and they would go to these old jobs to rob them of the needed letters. The place was covered with these once-used jobs, now falling apart because type had been taken from their insides. Workers spent an incredible amount of time looking for one or two letters of type, sometimes enlisting everyone in the shop to look.

I finally received Sam's permission to let me clean up the back shop myself, for I knew it would save us all time in the long run. One of my aims was to learn to be a printer, which had to start with memorization of the California job case in which the type was placed. As I took each job apart and tossed the letters into the job case, I not only memorized where the letters went, but I could move with some speed in both setting and in replacing the type.

From the mountain of old newspapers I gathered two copies of each past issue, and we bound these by years. The remaining papers we threw away. Sam was amazed at the amount of room he had once the place was cleaned up, and to his credit, he made sure it stayed that way afterwards. When we moved into new quarters on a busy main street, we followed better procedures in the shop.

I had completed my course requirements for graduation after three and a half years, so I participated in the August graduation of 1949. The services, attended by the Moseleys, were held outside. I now had my degree with a major in Bible and another in journalism.

The director of public relations for the university at the time was C. E. Bryant, once an editor of the *Arkansas Baptist* and well known among Southern Baptists. During my last months at Baylor I talked to him concerning a position in religious journalism, and he encouraged me to pursue it, for there were few trained journalists among all those working for the denomination. As I neared graduation, he told me that he often received job offers and the next one coming his way he would refer them to me.

Meanwhile, Sam Pyland offered me a full-time job as editor of the *Falls County Record*, and I accepted it for the time being, since we did not have the funds necessary to move to Louisville to attend Southern Baptist Theological Seminary and had heard nothing from C. E.'s contacts.

We moved to Marlin in the summer of 1949, joined the First Baptist Church, and became very active in its life and that of the community. I became scoutmaster of the Boy Scout troop at the church and worked with youth in Sunday school. Nell taught in the primary department.

Life in the small town was pleasant for us, although we were under some pressure financially, and as usual I was trying to do too much at the paper and the church.

One night Nell woke me up complaining of extreme pain in her left side. We called the doctor, who met us at the hospital. He diagnosed her ailment as tumors on an ovary and a tube and immediately prepared for an operation. Once into the procedure he suggested her appendix also be removed as a preventive measure. After consulting with me and advising that the ovary be removed as well, I consented.

He also had to tie off the tube on the other side. He said getting pregnant again would be very unlikely because the egg would have to travel from one side to the other. No other complications developed, but we were years paying off the hospital and doctor bills a little bit at a time.

Walker was now three, and Kenny was one and walking. We had rented one of our bedrooms to the newspaper's linotype operator, Gaylon Martin. At work Gaylon, an attractive man in his early thirties, was one of the most negative persons I had ever met. He spent the entire day cussing his assignments with an inventive stream of profanity, searching with unusual creativeness for negatives about everything.

He did not require an audience, but vented his spleen toward the clanking linotype if no one was in the room. We all avoided reacting to his tirades; however, he could not be ignored completely and served as a dark cloud over every bright day. If one remained cheerful in Gaylon's presence, he was deaf.

One day at home I was working on the car while Gaylon watched me. Nell and the boys were playing outside also when Walker Leigh needed to go inside. Nell asked Gaylon to watch Kenny until she returned, and he consented.

When she returned she asked where Kenny was, and neither of us knew. I had had my head under the car, and Gaylon had his in daydreams, I guess. We started a frantic search of the area, soon discovering Kenny had walked across the busy street, but he was safe. Gaylon probably hasn't forgotten Nell's lecture to this day.

The last of November, after I had been full time in Marlin only a few months, I received a call from Dr. David M. Gardner of the *Baptist Standard*, the state Baptist paper with offices in Dallas. He said C. E. Bryant had recommended me highly for the position of associate editor, since Horace Burns was leaving to become pastor of a church in California.

Dr. Gardner said he and Horace would like to visit me in Marlin the next Saturday morning. Dr. Gardner, a man in his sixties, had been editor of the paper for nearly a decade, following rather successful pastorates in Texas and Florida, the last at First Baptist Church of St. Petersburg.

Burns had been a pastor but had also worked extensively as a lino-type operator. He continued to have an active union card. Whenever he needed extra money he would substitute at one of the newspapers in whatever town he lived. Burns, however, was one of those persons who could not stay long in one place, and averaged moving every two or three years. He once told me, "I've got more miles on my piano than most people have on their cars."

The three of us met for most of the morning that Saturday, and they visited the newspaper, saw examples of my work, and explained to me the position that was open. The role was actually the number three spot, as R. E. Dudley was titled the executive editor under Gardner and over Burns. The pay would be $4,200 a year—a princely sum in our eyes, for it was almost double what I was making. They would want me to move in January.

After they left, saying they would get in touch within a few days, the time dragged by with painful slowness. Nell and the children were in Tyler while she recuperated from the recent operation, and I immediately called her. I also told Sam of the offer, and he said that if I would stay in Marlin, he would give me the newspaper, with our working out some arrangement on paying for office space and printing.

I was very moved by the offer and the affirmation, but I told him that I felt very strongly that God had called me into a full-time Christian voca-tion, and I would be following that either at the *Standard* or some other place as I was able. When Gardner called to offer me the position, I was beside myself and accepted on the spot, for Nell and I saw this as clearly the leading of the Spirit of God in our lives.

I would turn twenty-six in February of 1950, a veteran, a college graduate, and the father of two sons, but it was as though this was the step into adulthood and a mature future. Suddenly, dreams had become reality.

Looking back I could trace those moments and decisions, at times seemingly not too significant, that determined the direction of my life. First came my conversion and later decision for a full-time Christian vocation. These acts were determining factors in all that would follow.

Next came the close relationship with Daddy and his introducing me to the work of journalism, which I loved and found fulfilling from the beginning.

With Daddy's disappearance and the needs of the family, my life appeared to be bound to Henderson County and possibly a lifetime of work in one of the trades there, such as managing a grocery store. However, the onset of World War II changed that.

As I faced induction into the service, I determined I wanted the opportunities that would be available through the Air Corps, and enlisted. That decision proved to be extremely important, for it led to my being classified as a radio operator and being sent to Tyler, Texas.

In Tyler I met Nell and through her I first learned of Baylor University. While I was stationed in California, I had asked for and was accepted for training as a pilot. The pilot training did not materialize, however, but being placed on the waiting list did cause me to be dropped from the outfit to which I would have been assigned. I was shifted as a replacement on detached service to the Signal Corps to be assigned to China. I consequently avoided engagement in battles in the European Theatre of Operations.

Being in the Army changed my life in significant ways. I was quickly introduced to a larger world, along with thousands of others, shedding my parochialism like a snake sheds its outer skin. I soon learned I could compete successfully on an intellectual level with most of those with whom I came in contact.

I found the friendships, the travel, and the changes extremely stimulating. I found a new context into which to place my life, a context that included a global perspective. Wherever I went I made friends across racial and cultural lines, finding a basic humanity common to all of us.

I reached Baylor University with a more mature attitude than most entering freshmen after high school. I saw the university as a necessary step on the way to fulfill my calling, but I was anxious to put the education behind me, feeling in some ways that the Army had delayed my development. However, in actuality the time in the military had prepared me for pursuing my education, by the experiences and by the G.I. Bill that financed my education.

Going to Baylor was important, because it provided me with a quality education and important contacts within the Southern Baptist Convention, as many of my colleagues would become nationally known leaders through the years. At Baylor I made the important decision to shift from the pastorate to that of full-time journalism, and that decision changed my life's direction.

At Baylor I was able to secure a major in both Bible and journalism, and not many other Baptist schools had a department of journalism, certainly not Georgetown College in Kentucky where I had aspired to go. It was also at Baylor where I asked for C. E. Bryant's help in entering religious journalism, and he had recommended me to the *Baptist Standard*— which set the direction for the rest of my career.

I was well on the way to becoming the person my father had envisioned, maybe short of the religious aspect.

Chapter 11

THE BAPTIST STANDARD

I n Dallas I began work as a religious journalist, a term I never appreciated, for I felt the profession of journalism needed no qualifying adjective. For many, the term "religious journalist" meant a quality lower than the secular journalist, implying that one became a religious journalist when he or she could not make the grade elsewhere.

Such opinions had been reinforced by the widespread practice of employing ministers with no training in the profession of journalism as editors of religious publications. Most of the religious journals were staffed by an editor and one or two office secretaries. Like most sermons, these publications were heavy on opinion and light on information.

The Baptist Standard in 1950 was one of the largest circulated publications in Texas with a weekly mailing to more than 250,000 homes. As one wit remarked, "Baptists and Johnson grass have taken over Texas."

The paper owned a large two-story building on San Jacinto Street near the downtown area, just far enough away from the Baptist Building to keep it at arm's length and yet close enough to stay informed on the latest rumor or promotional project. *The Standard's* building housed not only the publication's staff of some twenty people but also the equipment and offices of Storm Printing Company, a commercial printer that typeset and printed our weekly on a new offset, web press.

The Standard was owned by the Baptist General Convention of Texas (BGCT) and operated under a board of directors appointed by the convention. The editor was elected by and responsible to this board, and only to this board. The directors were not involved at all in the day-to-day operation, only in the financial soundness of the operation, in the setting of policy, and, when needed, in the election of the editor.

Serving on the *Standard* staff were Editor David M. Gardner, Executive Editor R. E. Dudley, and Associate Editor Horace Burns. Dudley, a tall, slightly stooped man in his late fifties had been the editor of a small town, West Texas weekly and self trained as a newspaperman. Burns, trained as a pastor, came to the profession of journalism from the back shop, holding his union card as a Linotype operator. Burns was leaving his position with the *Standard* for a pastorate in the developing Northwest.

Dr. Gardner also had been a pastor for more than thirty years before taking over as editor and publisher of the *Standard*. He spent his time writing editorials and managing the business, leaving the work of news and the publication's production to the other editors.

None of these three had been trained as a journalist, either in schooling or under a professional editor. I soon learned that I was one of the first associates or editors throughout the vast Southern Baptist Convention to have a university degree and practical training in journalism.

The division of labor at the paper was that Gardner wrote the editorials, Dudley handled most of the news and editing of the weekly Sunday school lesson commentary, and my first priority in replacing Burns would be to work with the production of the more than forty church editions, printed on the back page of the magazine-sized regular edition. These church editions had to be produced on Monday and Tuesday, and the rest of the week we worked with the other news.

Dr. Gardner, a small man about my size (5½ feet, 140 pounds) was in his early sixties. He always wore a business suit, white shirt, and subdued ties and drove a large Buick. He loved to smoke big, black cigars, but in deference to the feelings of some Baptists who opposed smoking, he never smoked in his office or in any of the other *Standard* offices.

At least twice a day, usually mid-morning and mid-afternoon, he took a leisurely stroll through the printing plant or visited the office of the owner of the printing company, all the while gently puffing on his big stogie, like a ward boss walking the streets of his borough or a plantation owner checking on his workers. At the time, I was still occasionally smoking cigarettes or a pipe, more at home than at work and never in the office, but I was not invited to take the daily strolls with Dr. Gardner.

I enjoyed my association with Dudley, whose droll wit and easy manner made him a delightful companion, but he was not one given to fast or efficient production. One of his favorite jokes, revealing his irritation with anyone in a hurry, was the definition of a split second: "It's the time," he would say, "between the change of the traffic light and when the driver behind you blows his horn."

I often chaffed at the slow pace and the lack of actual news writing or coverage of what Baptists were doing. Later I would find allies in the public relations office of the BGCT, located at the Baptist Building a few blocks toward the center of town and across from the First Baptist Church.

Alton Reed directed the convention's public relations office. His background was also the pastorate, but he was eager for the news of Texas Baptists to be written and reported. Eventually, the PR office would employ some fine journalists: Leonard Holloway, Lloyd Wright, and Phil Hardberger.

I had recently discovered the writings of Thomas Wolfe, and starting with *Look Homeward Angel* I read almost everything he had written. In Phil Hardberger I found another lover of Wolfe, and we had many luncheons together discussing Wolfe's work. I believe many people are introduced to Wolfe too early. One should read Thomas Wolfe at least when in the middle twenties, at a time when a strong plot is not necessary to stay engrossed in an excellent book.

I also sought ways to improve the production process at the *Standard*, working closely with the printer, at one point helping him to scale his huge offset camera used to photograph the halftones and the line work for the offset plates. As usual, I was trying to organize everything for efficiency.

One project fascinated me more than others. Dr. Gardner, in an attempt to improve the mailing process, had purchased an automatic labeling machine made by the Cheshire Mailing Company of Chicago. For years *The Standard* mailers had used small, arm-held devices that required each man to operate it by perfecting a three-part motion.

Pushing down with the left arm to cut the label, rolling the tape of labels over the glue in the machine with the fingers, and pulling the addressed paper out with the right hand, they proceeded with remarkable skill and speed. It was like patting your head with one hand and rubbing your stomach with the other, only harder. Despite their considerable skill, the five mailers found it difficult to address the 250,000 papers within the four days allotted.

The new Cheshire mailing machine, designed to do the labeling in less than twenty hours, had cost the *Standard* $12,000 two years earlier (a princely sum in that day), but no one had perfected its operation for our paper. After I had been there for some months, I told Dr. Gardner that if he would give me the authority to do what was necessary, I brazenly guaranteed him the machine would work. He agreed to give me the authority.

First, I contacted the Cheshire Company in Chicago, finding its employees were embarrassed the machine was not being used. They agreed to fly a representative to Dallas at no cost to us. The representative checked the machine, found it in good working order, and showed me how it was to be operated.

Meanwhile, I had talked at length with the mailers. The foreman told me, "That mailing machine won't work on our operation. If you get that thing to work, I'll buy you a new Stetson hat!"

I sensed that the mailers were dragging their feet because they thought two of them would lose their jobs if the machine worked as planned. They were protecting each other. However, their major, voiced objection was that if the machine ran at its top speed, they would be unable to read the labels as they came down the conveyor belt requiring them to sort the papers into the bundles required by the post office.

I studied this problem for some time and came up with the solution of placing a large dot on the mailing label carrying the name of the area to which it was directed. All the mailer had to do was to look for the dots; his bundle would lie between them.

Finally I asked Dr. Gardner to assure the men that no one would be fired and when they finished placing the papers in the post office, they were through for the week. This not only allayed the mailers' fears, but it also galvanized them into searching for shortcuts. It was not long before they were running the machine at its top speed, and they were working less than twenty hours a week. The *Standard* was the one to benefit, however, for the circulation grew rapidly, and in a few years we were mailing more than 350,000 papers weekly with the same crew.

To the foreman's credit, he did offer to buy me the new Stetson, but I refused it. My reward was the successful project and not getting embarrassed over my rash promise. Besides, I seldom wore a hat.

In coming to Dallas, we had moved to the east side of the city into a duplex on Military Parkway near the subdivision known as Urbandale. We had little furniture, so we employed a local Marlin trucker to move us for $35. We did not have a television set, and three-year-old Walker Leigh would often watch shows with neighbors, who would ask our permission before inviting him inside.

He was fascinated by the tube, and each day he would come running to announce, "Hop-along Cassidy On," a title he gave to all shows. A black-and-white, fourteen-inch television was one of our first purchases that year. At first we all watched anything shown, including wrestling, Dinah Shore, Sid Caesar, Omnibus Theater, and sports. Many of the shows were only fifteen minutes long, and programming filled little more than half the day. Most of the shows were live and often filled with mistakes, usually good for an extra laugh.

Nell had a scare one afternoon. Walker was running toward the back door when he tripped and fell against the steps, striking his chin. Unfortunately, his tongue was between his teeth and he bit into his tongue rather severely. Nell did not have transportation, and neither did our nearest neighbors, but one resourceful friend ran out on Military Parkway and flagged down the first motorist who would stop.

By coincidence it was the *Baptist Standard* lawyer, Pope Binns, and he rushed them to the emergency room where Walker received stitches in his tongue.

The Urban Park Baptist Church occupied property only two blocks from our duplex, so we attended and soon joined there, at the time feeling we should go to the nearest Southern Baptist church. Besides, it was a new, growing congregation eager to have new members and hungry for leadership and workers.

The core of the church had split two years before from the First Baptist Church of Urbandale, purchased nearly five acres of property less than a mile from the other church, and called a middle-aged pastor, George Steiglitz. The ill feelings of the split continued to dominate the emotions of the older members, but the community was growing and the church grew with it.

The newer members had no part of the bitter history. The congregation's first building was soon overflowing, and plans were on the board for a new auditorium.

The church became the center of our social life, as we found many other couples near our age within the congregation. Two brothers, Doug and Mozell Bailey, had married sisters, Wanda and Margrette Ogletree, when they lived on neighboring farms near Canton, about thirty miles east of Dallas. Both couples had children near the ages of our boys, and both men had served in the Army.

In fact, Doug was working in the offices of the Army Reserves as a staff sergeant. Mozell worked for a wholesale grocer. We became close friends, and Nell bonded with Wanda to a remarkable degree. At the time, none of the women worked outside the home.

Within the first year we were looking for a house to escape the duplex living. Congress had made provisions for GIs to buy housing without down payments and at an interest rate lower than the prevailing prime, all guaranteed by the government. We used this type of loan to purchase our first home: a new four-room white frame on a cul-de-sac less than two miles from the duplex.

It was a pillbox of a house, but a first home is always a pride and joy. The total cost was $6,500, and our payments—including mortgage, interest, and taxes—were almost the same as we were paying for the duplex. A church member, Lester Cunningham, who managed a Babcock store, gave us enough credit to buy living room furniture and a new television. We felt rich indeed. We were true Americans, living on credit.

I was embarrassed over my inability to spell, so for weeks I had Nell, who is an excellent speller, drill me each night. At least I came to recognize a misspelled word, even when I could not spell it correctly.

Meanwhile, at the *Standard* tragedy struck during our first December in Dallas. The city had been hit by one of the frequent "Blue Northers," when temperatures dropped by as much as seventy degrees in a twenty-four-hour period. Ahead of the front had come rain, which eventually turned to black ice and in turn was covered by snow.

Mr. Dudley was descending the steps at the Gaston Avenue Baptist Church sanctuary when he slipped on the ice and fell backwards with his head striking the steps. He died in the hospital without regaining consciousness.

Sometime after the funeral Dr. Gardner called me into his office. He wanted to know if I thought I could carry on without Dudley for maybe a year.

"I have just made a financial commitment to buy all our paper in carload lots," he explained, "and it is placing an unusual burden on us for this first year. After that we will see a significant saving."

I assured him I could do the work, as long as he provided me with some help with the church editions. He agreed, and promised me a raise to $4,800 a year. By the end of the next year, when he was to review the situation, nothing was ever said about the empty position of executive editor. I knew Dr. Gardner did not like the title, since it confused many of the readers about who was in charge.

I would remain the associate editor throughout my tenure on the paper, but I had assumed the role of the executive editor. I hired Don McGregor, a friend from Baylor days, as an assistant editor. He and Carlene moved to the same general area of Dallas where we lived, but they did not stay but a couple of years, for he went to work as a reporter in Midland. Other staff would be added later as assistant editors or as artists. These included Kathryn Allen, Marcia Burton, Mr. Bergman, Orbie Clem, and others for short periods.

The Cheshire mailing machine, the two-story building, the renting of space to Storm Printing Company, and the move to buy our paper in carload lots were all excellent examples of the financial genius of David M. Gardner. Like his wealthy West Texas brother, he had an instinct for good business practices. Not only had he established the independence of the publication by moving it out of the Baptist Building, but he had also placed it upon a sound financial basis, even raising an endowment, with the first major gift coming from his brother.

In 1951 I attended my first Southern Baptist Convention, meeting in San Francisco. Dr. Gardner and Mr. Dudley had previously represented the *Standard*, but with Dudley's death I was given the assignment of photographing and reporting on the events of the week, including the many auxiliary meetings along with the SBC itself.

I had already started changing the format of the publication to more of a magazine look, since it was printed as an 8½ x11-inch periodical and was not at all conducive to newspaper makeup, even though the paper was newsprint. I also had introduced a new look with photography, most often using a full-page picture on the cover and many photographs inside.

We first took pictures using the old Speed Graphic cameras, with 4x5-inch negatives. I would soon shift to the smaller Rollex and a 2½ x 2½ negative. Then finally we became skilled enough in the darkroom—which I was allowed to install—to handle the 35mm single lens reflex and take pictures without a flash, depending upon the available light.

Covering the SBC in 1951, I felt for the first time that I had come into my own as a journalist at twenty-seven years of age. For the assignment

I had traveled halfway across the U.S. I was on an expense account, staying in one of the better hotels of the city, and I was reporting a significant event. I also immediately became friends with reporters from daily newspapers sent to cover the meetings.

An older reporter from the *Fort Worth Star-Telegram* and I teamed up for other activities than work. Together we saw the movie operas, *Tales of Hoffman* and *Red Shoes*. It was my introduction to Offenbach's *Can-Can* in its original setting.

San Francisco fascinated me, not only because of its uniqueness but also because it was the one place we knew that Daddy had gone when he left Henderson. Mother received a report from Social Security showing Daddy had worked in San Francisco, and when the report had been returned from that city they forwarded it to his previous address. As I walked the hills of the city, I could not help but scan the faces of all the men I met, wondering if by chance I might meet my father again.

I reasoned that his experience with a small town daily plus an eighth-grade education would not appeal to publishers in San Francisco, and that he would have moved to another city. I was also curious when seeing homeless men, guessing that his drinking and his skills would make life difficult. I was fascinated by San Francisco on this first visit to the city other than riding the bus through when Nell and I had gone to Velajo to see my cousin, Coonkey.

My first SBC meeting set the pattern for all of the conventions to follow while I was at the *Standard*. I would do the reporting and the photography, and the editor would write his commentary for the editorial page. Previously, many of the state Baptist papers reported the meetings like they were writing session-by-session minutes, without much attention to the importance of the events or breaking the news into separate stories. The trained journalists who were to follow me, as well as myself, forged new patterns.

The strict separation of church and state was a Baptist principle dear to Dr. Gardner's heart: His goal was a free church within a free state. Fully 75 percent of his editorials seemed to touch on the subject, and he was consumed with countering every move he saw Roman Catholics taking to break down the wall between church and state.

It did not surprise me much when I learned that during Dr. Gardner's pastorate of the First Baptist Church of St. Petersburg, he was a chaplain to the Ku Klux Klan in Florida, more because the Klan was anti-Catholic than racist, although a majority of Southern Baptists at the time seemed to fall into both categories.

Dr. Gardner was very parochial, even defensive of Baptists' independence from other denominations, and his fear of entanglement with other Christian groups appeared to be shared by most Southern Baptists.

He was not pleased when Billy Graham splashed across the news media following his large crusade in Los Angeles, coverage fanned by William Randolph Hearst's famous memo to his editors: "Puff Graham." Billy joined First Baptist Church of Dallas and was scheduled to hold a crusade in Fort Worth. I covered our front page with his picture for one issue, and immediately got a call to Dr. Gardner's office.

"Walker, this is unacceptable. I don't like giving Graham that much publicity, when he might lead Baptists into ecumenism, and C. E. Mathews agrees with me," he lectured me. (Graham was open not only to including all Christians in his crusades but also seemed to insist upon it. Mathews was the Southern Baptist director of evangelism, at that time stationed in Dallas.) "Besides, what will I tell those pastors who have written all these articles in my files that I haven't published and they see a whole page given to one picture?"

Walker at the *Baptist Standard* in 1956.

Months later, after Dr. Gardner had grown accustomed to seeing the large pictures and had received favorable comments from readers, we were discussing the paper in his office and he flipped through an issue, stopping at one or two pages without a photograph. "Why didn't you put pictures here?" he asked, "You know how much I appreciate photographs." At least it told me that I had converted him to my new format.

Dr. Gardner also ferociously defended the independence of the *Baptist Standard* from control by the executive committee of the BGCT and its executive secretary. Periodically, someone on the executive committee would move to make the paper a department under the executive secretary, as were the Sunday School, Training Union, church starting, budget promotion, etc.

Most who wanted such a change saw it as a more efficient way to operate, but others wanted to control the positions taken by the editor, especially when they were in opposition to positions held by members of the state convention's executive committee or when not enough space was given to the promotion of some pet project.

In 1953 the executive committee appointed yet another study committee to include a look at the *Baptist Standard's* relationship to the executive committee. The chairman of the committee was E. S. James, pastor of First Baptist Church in Vernon. James was an influential leader among Texas Baptists, and had served as chairman of the executive committee in recent years. In fact, he had nearly been elected as executive secretary the previous year when Forest Feezor had been named to the powerful post.

Feezor's election was sealed when a whispering campaign (no one would say it in public) spread the word that James was not acceptable to many because he smoked cigarettes. James approached most subjects with an open mind, and he came directly to Dr. Gardner to discuss whether or not to make a department out of the *Standard*.

James left Gardner's office convinced that Texas Baptists needed a publication with an unfettered voice. Consequently, when Gardner announced his retirement the next year, he recommended E. S. James to the search committee. The committee unanimously chose James, and he was accepted by the board as editor.

During his last year as editor, Dr. Gardner began to coast, so to speak, not an unusual occurrence when one has announced his retirement and becomes a lame duck. His engagements to speak fell off, leaders ceased to come to him for advice or support of pet projects, and he stopped planning for the future, seeing that as the role of the next editor. Much of the day-to-day operation of the *Standard* fell on my shoulders.

The word got out at the Baptist Building that "Walker Knight's running the paper." I suspect the charge came from some department directors who did not like the decisions I made to limit the space given to the promotion of their work, preferring instead to publish news of interest to a larger audience.

The first week E. S. James came to the *Standard* as editor he called me into his office and asked, "Walker, what's this talk about your running the *Standard*?"

"Dr. James," I replied, "Dr. Gardner has been more or less coasting this past year, ever since he announced his retirement. If the paper was to continue, someone had to make the decisions. I know it's your responsibility to be the leader, but if you don't make the decisions, I will. We can't operate in a vacuum."

That was the end of the discussion. We both knew where we stood. James was not a man to avoid a decision or fail to meet a problem head on. He and I became very close, and we often played golf on Thursday afternoons after I had put the paper to bed for the week—holding out only one page for breaking news on Friday.

In a way Dr. James became the father figure I had always wanted in my life, and I was a person in whom he could confide. His heart was still broken because of the death of a ten-year-old daughter in a car accident some five years previously. He could not talk about her without crying, and he often had the need to talk about her.

Dr. James always attacked any problem head on, never letting it fester in his mind. Once he called me into his office to discuss a conversation he had had with Albert McClellan, promotion director for the SBC Executive Committee and supervisor of Baptist Press.

"Albert told me that you had applied for the position of director of Baptist Press, but he had turned you down. I didn't know you wanted to leave the *Standard*. Do you?" he asked.

I was astonished by the information, for I had admired Albert McClellan from the first day I met him and could not believe how twisted the facts had become.

"Dr. James," I finally answered, "Wait just a minute while I go get a letter from my files."

When I returned I let him read a letter from Albert in which he had offered me the position of director of Baptist Press, and I also let Dr. James read my answer in which I had declined, feeling that I should stay where I was. We both just shook our heads over the way Albert had come to see the situation, for evidently he found it difficult to handle what he must have taken as a personal rejection.

One of Dr. James' first decisions as editor and publisher was to convert part of his large office into a private toilet and study area, more to have a place to smoke than anything else. It was in this study area that he wrote his editorials, did a lot of reading and thinking. He smoked a lot more than Dr. Gardner had or than I did, and he was not about to go walking through the printing plant every time he wanted a cigarette.

When Dr. James had asked me what changes I would like to see in the paper after he became editor, my first suggestions were that we redesign the paper to reflect a new editorship and that we begin publishing letters to the editor. We soon implemented both ideas. He devoted a full page in each issue to the mail, and with a circulation the size of the *Standard*'s we did get a lot of mail. Dr. James proved to be extremely adept at condensing the letters and even better at penning terse and often sharp answers, so sharp at times that I thought he took advantage of the letter writer.

My other suggestion to him was that we start reporting on and commenting on controversial subjects. Most items were those everyone talked about in the corridors of the state and national conventions but that never showed up in any of our publications. In retrospect, I don't think he needed much encouragement here.

As was his nature, Dr. James held to firm and forthright positions, and his editorials brought a virtual flood of letters. By today's standards, those subjects were mild, for example: premillennialism, the Scofield Bible's dating of the world, the Trail of Blood theory of history (that Baptists could be traced in an unbroken line all the way back to Jesus), the separation of church and state, and positions on divorce or gambling.

We did not challenge the racism of the day, but he did endorse Billy Graham. Dr. James thrived on controversy. He was a person with strong convictions, but he was secure enough to allow others their say. Readership reached new heights.

However, personally I was not always pleased with his decisions. He joined First Baptist Church of Dallas and soon was publishing a series of articles by Pastor W. A. Criswell seeking to prove evolution was a false theory. Dr. James also sided with those who forced Ralph Elliott from his teaching position at Midwestern Baptist Theological Seminary, seeing his book, *The Message of Genesis*, as liberal.

He once published an article by an Oklahoma pastor that sought to prove the Trail of Blood theory, causing professors at Southwestern Baptist Theological Seminary to invite him to Fort Worth for an evening meal where they explained the facts of history. Dr. James was convinced enough to publish an apology.

Dr. James, like myself, did not have a seminary degree, and while most of his positions tended to be conservative, mine seemed to be more liberal. I had found nothing in the Elliott book about which to be concerned. I found Elliott to be both honest and intelligent in his approach.

I once asked Dr. James what did he think was the origin of evil, and his reply was, "Walker, you don't ask questions like that?" For my part, I did not think any question was out of bounds or off limits.

Dr. James also followed Dr. Gardner's passion for the strict separation of church and state, but he did not write as high a percentage of his editorials on the subject. However, his stand precipitated a fierce fight among Texas Baptists over the acceptance of a hospital in Texarkana. The hospital had been built with government funds, and when the owners wanted to give it to Texas Baptists to operate, Forest Feezor, the executive secretary, advocated its acceptance, but Dr. James opposed it as an entanglement of church and state. The argument raged for nearly a year, with both sides battling through the pages of the *Standard*. The letters to the editor page almost caught fire.

The hospital issue came to a vote at the annual meeting of the Baptist General Convention of Texas, with Feezor and the executive committee presenting the motion to accept the hospital. Dr. James and others spoke against the motion. It was defeated rather soundly. The result of that division was a shift in power among the leadership of Texas Baptists, with Dr. James accumulating the most power.

After that vote, anyone wanting to change anything within the convention first came to Dr. James to get his support, and especially to find out what his position was. They did not want his opposition. He was not comfortable with this role, often saying to me, "Walker, why don't they just go ahead? They don't need to come see me."

My answer was, "They don't want to be shot down in public by one of your editorials." To his credit, he never abused the power.

The most famous exercise of that power came during the presidential election of 1960 (the year after I had left) when Democrat John F. Kennedy faced Republican Richard M. Nixon. The issue of church-state separation became important, primarily because Kennedy was a Roman Catholic and his opponents were saying he would be under the control of the pope and that he would favor the establishment of an ambassador at the Vatican.

Kennedy, however, publicly took the position of separation of church and state, and said he would not appoint an ambassador to the Vatican. Nixon, wanting to counter the Roman Catholic vote for Kennedy, said he would appoint an ambassador.

During the campaign Kennedy flew to Houston to meet with ministers of all denominations, and Dr. James was among them. It was there that Kennedy promised not to appoint an ambassador to the Vatican and that he would hold to the separation of church and state. Dr. James asked each candidate to write a letter for publication. Only Kennedy replied, and his letter was published in the *Standard* with the explanation that both had been asked for such a letter.

With a circulation of nearly 400,000, the most widely distributed publication in the state, Dr. James's action influenced a lot of votes. Texas became a swing state in the election, and later President Kennedy invited Dr. James to the White House to thank him personally for his part in his election.

Dr. James did not endorse Kennedy through the *Standard*, for such an endorsement would be seen as a violation of the publication's tax-exempt status, which, under today's laws, strictly forbids the endorsement of candidates for public office by non-profits.

(Don McGregor succeeded me at the *Standard*, and I asked him one day who Dr. James actually voted for. He answered: "Nixon.")

Dr. James was to influence more than just national elections. He made a significant contribution to the Southern Baptist Convention, at first, upon other state papers. These papers, many of them functioning as departments under executive committees and thus under the supervision of the executive secretary, seldom took strong positions and few published letters to the editor with controversial positions. When the editors began to see the results of Dr. James's bold stands—the increase in readership and especially the dramatic increases in circulation—they started their own versions of letters to the editor and took bolder stands on issues.

I remember John Hurt, then editor of the Georgia *Christian Index* asking, "Dr. James, how do you get all those letters?"

To which Dr. James replied, "Write editorials on pre-millennialism, on the Scofield Bible, on divorce, and a few other controversial subjects in your state, and the letters will come"

"Yeah," Hurt quickly responded, "if I did, I wouldn't be around to receive them."

However, Hurt, a former Associated Press reporter and editor, did open his pages to more controversy, and he did get the letters. Other editors were also quick to follow, and the entire SBC became a more open society because of it.

Hurt also once observed my doing the hard work of reporting and photographing a Southern Baptist Convention during the time when Dr. Gardner was editor, and Hurt commented, "I'm going to get me one of those."

He meant someone like me, and soon he hired Jack Harwell, a trained journalist, as his associate editor. Jack succeeded Hurt as editor in Georgia when Hurt succeeded James in Texas.

Meanwhile at home, Nell and I were very active at Urban Park Baptist Church where I became the director of the Sunday school and a deacon. One year we taught young people; at other times she taught eight-year-olds and was very active in WMU.

Our old 1940 Ford was about to die on us, and we started looking for another car. Dr. Gardner decided to replace his large blue Buick, so we purchased it from him. The car was loaded, with power steering and brakes, electric windows, and especially air conditioning. I had found that air conditioning in Texas was not a luxury; it was a necessity. The car served us for more than five years, and except for some balky electric windows, gave us no trouble.

We soon found our small, new house inadequate for two growing boys and an expected girl—we hoped. The real estate agent, also a member at Urban Park, who had sold us the first house, found a larger one on Gaylord Street a couple of miles south. The company took our house as a trade-in for the down payment, so we enlarged our debt and monthly payment for the larger house. But I had continued to get a raise each year, and it placed little strain on our lives.

One weekend, when Mr. and Mrs. Moseley were visiting us, the children were playing outside. The boys were across the street while we adults were in the front yard. Walker dashed out into the street from between parked cars and was hit by a glancing blow from a moving automobile. We rushed him to the emergency room, but he was not seriously hurt this time, only badly frightened, as we all were.

Wanda Bailey and Nell had come up with "Nelda Denise" as a name for a girl, and to our wonder and surprise we got to use the name on October 11, 1954, with Nell once again having a long and painful labor. When the doctor told me that we had a girl, I said, "A girl? Are you sure?"

The doctor replied, "If it's not a girl, he's very deformed."

Walker and Kenny welcomed their new sister with joy, as we all did. Having a quiet, tender girl in the family proved to be a surprise for both Nell and me after the experience of two lively, aggressive boys. Nelda quickly became the center of attention not only in our house but also at church.

At two years of age she was especially fond of the church janitor, Mr. Ashmore, a tobacco-chewing man in his fifties, who paid close attention to her every time we visited. He would see us coming and squat to her level for the hug she always gave him, ignoring the tobacco juice dripping from the side of his mouth.

While the young Urban Park Baptist Church was continuing to grow, not all was well between the church and the pastor, George Steiglitz. Word reached the congregation that he had also had trouble at his previous pastorate in Concord, Texas, and I was named to a committee to go investigate. When we returned and confronted him with our findings, he resigned.

Within a year the church called C. H. "Creedy" Jones, a handsome man in his late thirties with an attractive wife, daughter, and son. Under Brother Jones the church flourished, and we were soon able to construct the 400-seat sanctuary as our third building. With the growth the church needed additional staff, and Anita Ashley, a recent religious education graduate of Southwestern Baptist Theological Seminary in Fort Worth, was employed.

I began to have nagging pain in the upper part of my stomach, and my doctor had me undergo an upper G. I. series that revealed I had an ulcerated stomach. I was put on Maalox, an antacid, and told not to eat highly seasoned food and to drink milk often. This was standard treatment at the time for stomach ulcers.

But all the treatment did was to cause me to gain weight, with some easing of the pain. Ulcers came up often in the Knight family, and I think the onset of mine could have been traced back to Baylor days when I was trying to do too much in work and study and starting a family. However, today the medical society traces ulcers to bacteria that are treated with antibiotics.

In 1952 we had gone to Kentucky for me to officiate at Mary Ruth's marriage to Ralph Posey, a high school sweetheart and one of the prize catches of the county. They were married after Ruth had finished one year of college and Ralph three years. After their marriage he completed his and broke her collarbone, but it required only a soft cast or brace and hardly slowed her playing at all.

At church Walker Leigh could never pass a piano without stopping to play on it, trying to pick out hymns or other tunes. We asked if he wanted to take piano lessons, and he did. We bought an upright, mirror piano, and we established a rule that if we paid for lessons, the student's responsibility was to practice without our having to make him. Walker was always faithful to practice.

When Kenny was old enough to take lessons, he stayed with it for a while, but then dropped out, not wanting to do the required practicing. One thing both boys loved was swimming at the pool near their grade school. They received free lessons from lifeguards hired by the city's recreation department.

Kenny remembers the boys and girls had separate times in the water, and they would have to wait until the girls had finished—no "mixed bathing." Also the swimming lessons were so boring, he started going to the deep end with those who knew how to swim. Both boys became much better swimmers than Nell, who would never learn to swim for fear of the water, or I.

Three years later we moved yet again to Riverway Drive into a new brick house with two baths (a great help for a family of five), a two-car garage, three bedrooms, a living room, den, and kitchen—a house that pleased us all. The move was reflective of our improved financial condition, and we bought another Buick, a 1957 red, four-door sedan, to replace Old Blue. However, we were not to enjoy this house long.

One day early in 1959 I received a call at the office from an official of the Southern Baptist Home Mission Board, L. O. Griffith, who was in Dallas on business. Griff, as most people called him, was a pleasant, charming minister who was also from Kentucky. At lunch that day we discovered we had a lot in common.

The Home Mission Board, located in Atlanta, Georgia, had recently reorganized and Griff had been moved up from the promotion department to head a new division that also included the editorial department, the promotion department, and the department of missionary education. He finally revealed to me that John Caylor, department secretary for the editorial department and editor of *Home Missions Magazine*, was retiring.

Griff wanted to know if I would be interested in replacing Dr. Caylor. Indeed I was interested, so he invited me to visit the offices then located at 161 Spring Street in Atlanta. The invitation did not include airfare or degree work and enlisted in the Army Air Corps where he was trained as a pilot.

They were then stationed at Corpus Christi, with their two children, Debbie, who was Nelda's age, and Alan, two years younger. One day in 1956 I received a shattering call from Ruth that Ralph's jet had flamed out over the bay during a firing practice run, and he was killed. I immediately went to her to offer what comfort I could.

In the summer of 1956 we visited Mother and the family at Zion, and everyone saw Nelda for the first time. On this visit we did not have to draw our water from the well at Cousin Ed Henderson's shop. A few years earlier I had borrowed the money to pay for indoor plumbing and a water heater at Mother's house.

Jane Harris had just graduated from high school, and we invited her to come to Texas and stay with us. I secured employment for her in the business office at the *Standard*, for it took a good-sized crew to keep up with the growing circulation, even though most of the names and addresses came from churches, not from individuals.

Jane stayed until December when Mother insisted that she come home to help her with twelve-year-old Jimmy. At this time I had also talked Wanda Bailey into coming to work in our business office. She was reluctant at first because her typing skills were slow, but I insisted and assured her she could do the work. Some years later she was managing the entire business side.

One day after work I took Kenny with me to a park where I wanted to practice hitting golf balls with a short iron. As I was thus occupied, he found a tree to climb nearby. I saw him in the tree and yelled for him to be careful, but he did not know much about the perils of climbing at nine years of age. He tried to crawl out on the end of a branch but fell, hitting the ground with such force that he was knocked unconscious.

We rushed him to the emergency room of the hospital, where he regained consciousness but x-rays revealed he had broken his pelvis. This required a three-fourths body cast from his chest to below his pelvis and down one leg. During his week in the hospital Nell visited each day after leaving Nelda with some friend, most of the time with Margrette Bailey.

Kenny was immobile for months, suffering more from the summer heat than from his injury, but he was a stoic patient and endured his fate with good humor. His best friend, Mike Biko, came over to play with him quite often. About the same time Nelda at two fell off the bed in her sleep expenses for Nell, and since we were always living on the edge financially and Nell was pregnant again, she did not make the trip.

When I visited Atlanta I was impressed with the city, its trees, its beauty, and its climate. I had never adapted to the Texas weather, and in the summer I often played golf at six a.m. to beat the heat. I was struck that the six-story office building in downtown Atlanta owned by the Home Mission Board, a national agency of the SBC, was only slightly larger than the Baptist Building in Dallas.

The lack of expenses for Nell also gave me a clue as to the financial situation at the Home Mission Board, and I learned they would provide only the one trip for me, plus paying for moving expenses. And the salary they were offering, $9,000, was the same I was receiving at the *Standard*, with fewer fringe benefits.

At the agency that day I met John Caylor, who would not officially retire until January 1960. He was a "southern gentleman" of the old school—quiet, polite, witty, and well informed. I met other department secretaries (an archaic term that was later dropped in favor of director) including Jay Durham in audiovisuals (a new name for promotion) who had recently come to the board from one of Atlanta's television stations.

Jay was near my age, tall and extremely good-looking, with one of the finest speaking voices I had heard. He told me that the Home Mission Board was on the verge of a new day in communications, and the reorganization was important not only for that but also for more effective work in missions.

I met Lewis Martin, also a native of Kentucky, cohort of Griff's, and secretary of missionary education, which was primarily schools of missions, a system Martin had developed and promoted throughout the SBC. Then I was taken to the office of Courts Redford, the executive secretary, a long-time missions leader who had been a part of the HMB since depression days when national leaders traveled mostly by rail using free passes. Those sparse times had left a mark both on Redford and the agency.

Finally I was introduced to Arthur B. Rutledge, who had recently come to the agency as the director for the vast missions division. I knew Dr. Rutledge from his work as the state stewardship director for Texas Baptists, and even before that, when he was pastor of First Baptist Church of Marshall.

During his last year in Marshall, at the SBC annual meeting in Kansas City, he had asked Dr. James and me to eat dinner with him. He told Dr. James that he felt his effectiveness at First, Marshall was over and he would appreciate a recommendation to any church or other position that might come open and would appear to be appropriate.

Dr. James received such requests all of the time, and he asked Dr. Rutledge a number of questions, especially as to whether he might be interested in working for Texas Baptists. Not too long after that, Dr. Rutledge moved to the Baptist Building in Dallas, and from there went to head the newly formed missions division at the HMB.

Dr. Rutledge seemed very eager for me to take the position as secretary of the editorial department, and he assured me that the near future would be important times for Southern Baptist missions, and especially home missions.

I came back to Dallas excited and challenged, and when I shared all of what I had seen and heard with Nell, she was as excited as I. Next I told Dr. James that I would be taking the position with the Home Mission Board. He was very disappointed and offered me more salary if I would stay, but I was determined to take the national position, to be an editor on my own. Nearly ten years as an associate editor had only whetted my appetite for a chance to express myself more fully.

My departure time was some weeks away, and Dr. James enlisted my help in finding a successor. I gave him four names: Bill Moyers, a student at Southwestern Seminary; Robert Lynn, an editor with All-Church Press in Fort Worth and a recent graduate of the seminary; Leonard Hill, newly moved to Nashville to work with the SBC executive committee; and Don McGregor, then working as a reporter with the *Dallas Times Herald*. Dr. James began contacting them in that order.

However, Moyers said he wanted to finish his work at the seminary. Lynn said All-Church Press had just financed his master's degree in journalism at Columbia University in New York and he felt it inappropriate to leave. Hill said he had secured permission from the Sunday School Board to use its large computers in his work on his doctorate.

Only later would I know what an impressive list of candidates I had given Dr. James. Bill Moyers would soon move to Washington, D. C., to begin his national career. Bob Lynn completed a doctorate in education and became president of Louisiana College. Leonard Hill finished his doctorate and eventually became an editor of *Baptist Program* and director of convention arrangements and the Baptist Bulletin Service.

Don McGregor later would become editor of the *California Baptist* and then the Mississippi *Baptist Record* and be instrumental in starting the Associated Baptist Press news service. Meanwhile, Don, who earlier had worked a couple of years at the *Standard*, was knocking on Dr. James's door.

"Walker, I want someone who wants the job," Dr. James told me, discouraged that everyone seemed to be turning him down, "and Don seems eager and experienced. I also want someone who will do the work I want done."

I didn't know if the last comment was a reflection on my failure to cooperate or not, but I didn't pursue it. I answered, "Don will do what you want done, and he will do it well."

The Urban Park Baptist Church had become the center of our social life while living in Dallas, and the members honored us with a reception and the gift of an elaborate silver coffee and tea service. The service would grace our dining room for more than two score and ten years—until tired of polishing the silver whenever we were having company, we retired it to the attic—and every time we used it or viewed it or polished it, we thought of the dear friends at Urban Park.

Leaving Dallas had its real estate problems, also. The market was depressed for housing in 1959, and despite the months we had to place our house on Riverway up for sale, we found few interested buyers. Finally, Ed and Geneva Layne, recent members at Urban Park, indicated they would like to buy the house, but they did not have any funds.

Desperate to have something settled before we left, we worked out a second lien on our equity and they assumed the loan with the mortgage company. We would go house hunting in Atlanta with almost nothing down, and only slightly fortified with the $25 a month payment the Laynes would be making to us for the next seven years.

Meanwhile, our thoughts turned to the task of moving, complicated by the fact that Nell was more than five months pregnant and God had blessed us with lively children. Nelda was but four, Kenny was ten, and Walker was twelve.

Like Buddy and myself when we were growing up, the boys would become bored and start picking on each other. They enjoyed each other's company, maybe a little too much. More than once on other trips we would have to stop to separate them, threaten a whipping if they did not behave, or place one in the front seat and the other in the back.

Reinforcement for the trip to Atlanta came from Kentucky. Mary Ruth, living in Henderson with Aunt Ninnie who was also widowed, volunteered to come make the trip with us, leaving her two children with Ninnie.

We were soon Atlanta bound, the six of us riding three abreast in the big Buick. Interstate 20 was under construction in many areas, and for the most part we had to travel Highway 80. The trip required an overnight stay in Alabama. Besides, we did not want our first sight of a strange Atlanta to come at night.

Only two pictures exist of the nine Knight children with their mother. The picture above was taken in 1962 and the one below in 1971. From left to right kneeling are Jane Harris, Mary Ruth, Mother (Anna), Dorothy Rose, and Bettye Jean. Standing from left to right are James Lynn (Jim), William Griffin (Bubba), Robert Hiram, Cooksey Bennett (Buddy), and Walker Leigh (Bunk). The children are shown graded by age. Nine-year-old Jimmy, above, was born after their father disappeared.

Chapter 12

GEORGIA

tlanta, with its amazing canopy of trees hiding narrow, interlaced streets, welcomed us that July of 1959 in the stillness of its summer heat. For weeks we would wonder at the strangeness, the almost eerie quietness, until we realized the wind wasn't blowing, and when it did the covering of trees broke the strength of anything but the heaviest gales.

While the mercury in the thermometer did not climb as high as it had in dry, windy Texas, the higher humidity made us feel almost as hot. However, if we stirred the air it was cool, unlike the oven blasts of Dallas.

L. O. "Griff" Griffith, my supervisor at the Baptist Home Mission Board, had taken a year's lease for us on a three-bedroom house with a carport on Bobolink Drive in the Belvedere section of Dekalb County, some six miles east of downtown. Griff had offered to locate the house for us when I explained I could not afford an extra trip to Atlanta to house hunt, and he had explained that the Home Mission Board did not provide for such an expense.

Griff was wise in picking the location of our first house, even though it was across town from where he lived. At the time Dekalb County was on the growing edge of Atlanta's expanding population, and its schools were rated among the best in the state.

Despite promises to the contrary, our moving company, in transporting our furniture to Atlanta, took a week longer than we took to reach Atlanta. Not having the funds to stay in a motel, we eventually—after hot telephone conversations with the moving company—rented cots, chairs, and a table to camp out in our house.

Mary Ruth soon departed for home, and we promised to follow her to Kentucky as soon as the furniture arrived and was unloaded. That week was misery compounded upon a nomadic family eager to complete our vacation time between the closing of one phase of our life and the entry into another.

One of our first assignments in Atlanta was the location of a church home, knowing that it would become the center of our social life and the context in which we would make new friends. We discovered that Baptist churches were as plentiful in Atlanta as they had been in Dallas—not quite as plentiful as filling stations or grocery stores but almost.

This time we did not feel obligated or desire to affiliate with the nearest church to our house. Instead we sought the one in which the entire family would feel most at home. We rather quickly visited a number of different congregations within a five-mile radius, attending the Sunday morning services at one and the evening services at another. We more or less had our thermometers of friendship out by which to measure the warmth of the churches, and there was a wide discrepancy between them.

A pastor friend in Dallas had told me of a congregation in Decatur—Oakhurst Baptist Church—whose pastor, Ted Dougherty, was a close friend of his. "Don't make a decision without visiting Oakhurst," he had advised.

Visit it we did, and the warmth of the fellowship was far above anything we had experienced at the other churches.

The membership was almost double that of Urban Park, but we did not feel it was that large because of the friendliness of the members. The three children were also pleased and, before August had passed, we had embraced our new church home. Wherever we moved, Nell would work with three-year-olds, and at Oakhurst she taught this age for twenty-one years.

Oakhurst Baptist Church in 1959, located in the southern part of the city of Decatur, was growing and building. The congregation had just completed the construction of two three-story educational units, more than ample space for the 750-plus Sunday school attendance, on a six-acre tract one block north of the sanctuary. Long-range plans included a 1,600-seat auditorium to be erected beside these buildings, and then the congregation would move entirely from the older buildings.

An artist's rendition of the promised new sanctuary, resplendent in full color, graced the back of the old auditorium as well as the fellowship hall of the new educational space. That fall we experienced the excitement of a vibrant congregation at the dedication of the new buildings. I did not have any clue at the time that this congregation would be one of the most significant aspects of the person I would become.

The city of Atlanta and the Home Mission Board at this time in both their histories seemed to mirror the other as each was strongly touched by the past but now held the promise of an exciting future. I had traveled through Atlanta once before when Dr. E. S. James and I drove from Dallas to Athens, Georgia, to attend the annual meeting of Southern Baptist state newspaper editors. When we had left Texas and Louisiana, the highways raced through dense forests, often with the top branches of trees almost touching across the highways.

Dr. James started talking about the open spaces of West Texas where he had spent most of his life. Clearly he was not enjoying driving among the huge, spreading trees and finally said: "I just feel like it's all closing in on me, Walker. I don't think I could live in this part of the country." But for me it brought back memories of my childhood in Kentucky.

Many changes were taking place within the Southern Baptist Convention. Strengthened state conventions had assumed leadership of many of the programs previously held nationally by the Home Mission Board. In an attempt to rescue the HMB from failures of the recent past, the SBC called for and provided new funding for its reorganization. My work with the editorial department of the HMB reflected these organizational changes.

My department published the monthly *Home Missions Magazine* and five annual, age-graded mission study books. For some reason the library existed on the shelves of my office, probably because many of the books had been received for reviewing in the magazine. With my arrival the department would also handle all news releases for the agency.

Because of my strong news background, the department became the first regional office of Baptist Press, a national news service headed by W. C. Fields of the Southern Baptist Executive Committee in Nashville. To publish the monthly magazine, edit and promote the mission study books, and operate a news service, I had a staff of two others—an editorial assistant and an office secretary. Both of these workers resigned soon after I took over the work from Dr. Caylor.

Jackie Durham, a brilliant writer who had recently married Jay, became the editorial assistant, and Anita King, the efficient former Anita Ashley, the education director at Urban Park Baptist Church in Dallas, agreed to work as my secretary. She had just moved to the city, after marrying Atlanta resident John King. I was promised a book editor within a year.

At the *Baptist Standard* I had sensed my role to be the best journalist I could be, leaving the writing of editorials and denominational politics to the editor. At the Home Mission Board, however, I was the editor who would determine what was and was not published.

At first I felt my assignment was to report with accuracy and excitement the work of the agency and its missionaries, but I quickly sensed that I had within my province the tools to influence the pastoral and lay leadership of Southern Baptist churches on both mission and ethical issues.

The major event of our first year in Georgia was the birth of our second daughter and fourth child, Emily Jill, on November 10, our sixteenth wedding anniversary. We did not have relatives who could stay with Nell during the first week, but friends at Oakhurst recommended an African-American woman in her sixties, Olla May Johnson. She actually spent the first two nights with us when Nell came home from Georgia Baptist Hospital, then she came by bus the rest of the week.

As much as we asked and encouraged Olla May, she would not eat her meals with the family. In a way it was our first introduction to the severe division of the races in the Deep South, for Olla May was a well-educated person and had children in college or who had graduated from college. She was an excellent choice as a semi-nurse, and we were proud to have her as a friend. She did eat her final meal at our house with all of us.

Walker, Nell, and their children in 1961: (left) Ken and Nelda, (right) Walker and Jill

Nell deeply loved children, especially her own, a love that was communicated by her tenderness, warmth, and patience. However, Nell revealed the fury of a mother tiger when her children were in danger. Once when Jill was in the second grade, her sister Nelda was asked to deliver notices to each teacher. When she came to the first grade, Jill jumped up and ran to greet her older sister.

The teacher was upset and punished Jill. She came home crying, and when asked told Nell what had happened. Nell took her by the hand and walked her to the nearby school to confront the teacher, who probably remembered for years facing an irate mother.

Within a year we were looking for our own house, but we were severely handicapped by our failure to sell our house in Dallas and then receiving only a small payment each month from the couple who assumed our loan. Our only choices were houses requiring no down payment and no large loan payment.

We did want to settle in the area of DeKalb County where we were. We located a house that fit our finances and our family needs on a spacious lot near the city of Avondale. Although the post-war 1950s house had stood idle for some time, it was well constructed and held the promise of being repaired and enlarged as needed.

In cleaning the leaf-covered backyard, we discovered a large granite patio hidden beneath years of leaves from the many oak trees and pine needles. The trees ranged from seventy-five-foot giants to smaller ones, all denying the yard sunshine. I knew many needed cutting down, but it was painful after living in Texas with its stunted and sparse trees.

Nell, never one to express deep emotion openly, stood in the living room and wept silently. I like to think it was a release from the tension of the move, a fourth child, the move from a new house to this, and our unknown future. As fate would have it, we lived in the house, remodeled many times, for fifty years.

Once a close relative interviewed Nell and me as part of an oral history experience. At one point he asked, "What do you see as your purpose in life?" There was a pause, so I spoke up and expounded on my career, etc.

When I had shut up, Nell quietly said, "I see my purpose in life is to be Walker's wife." I was taken back, in fact, humbled and embarrassed, that she was placing me ahead of anything she might want to do personally. I knew she had left junior college to work during the war, and I had often urged her to take courses at one of the nearby colleges, but she always refused.

I never lacked for her full support in any direction our lives took, and I always sought her advice and support in every important decision.

The house and Home Mission Board mirrored each other: Both were challenges of hard work and creativity. But at age thirty-six I looked forward to every bit of it.

As editor I added full color to the covers of my first issue, in part to signal a new beginning, and I started that first year devoting each issue to a thorough coverage of a major subject. One state paper editor noticed my approach and questioned my reasoning by saying, "You will soon run out of issues." I replied, "If that's so, I'll just start from the beginning again."

The department of work with National (black) Baptists had recently completed a thorough study of attitudes and support with black Baptist churches. I wrote a six-story series from the study for release through Baptist Press and published them in *Home Missions*. The religion editor of *The Atlanta Constitution* reprinted most articles with some modifications.

I didn't know it at the time, but it revealed a theme I would come back to again and again.

I quickly faced the hold that racism held on Southern Baptists, and at one point I was taken to a top supervisor

Walker at the Home Mission Board in the late 1970s.

because (it was claimed) I was threatening the income of the agency with my editorials and coverage of issues related to black Americans. In my ignorance I had not realized that the magazine seldom even ran a picture of a black person.

My approach was explained to the supervisor who reprimanded me with these words, "We have all of the integration in this agency that we can afford. If you want that kind of freedom, you need to go somewhere else."

By that he meant that one black secretary was the limit. I did not answer him other than to say, "Thank you"—and left his office.

I determined that I would proceed as I was doing, and they could fire me if they wished, but I would not change. Actually I was counting on it being too embarrassing for the agency to fire me on racial grounds, and I was careful not to give them any other reasons.

Writing this I recall a time in Albuquerque when four of us were eating an evening meal when we had completed a significant coverage for the magazine. I said to the group, "I do not want us just to be the best writers or photographers we can be. I want us to influence the pastors and lay leaders of the Southern Baptist Convention in significant ways."

Looking back, I believe with that statement I had revealed the one characteristic of a child of an alcoholic that I had neglected to accept: a tendency toward grandiosity.

In 2004, Oakhurst Pastor Lanny Peters recognized me on Reformation Sunday as Oakhurst's "Reformation Man." I was too overcome by Lanny's detailed recognition to respond adequately. But, to tell the truth, it was I who should be presenting Oakhurst with recognition for its influence on my life and ministry.

Not only had the church embraced my family and me, giving my children the insight and experience of a loving, faithful community, but they had given all of us the freedom to be ourselves, and by that I mean to be our striving, seeking selves as faithfully as we could be in a changing, challenging, needy world.

For me personally, Oakhurst had acted faithfully to the ethical teachings of Christ. When I asked the readers of *Home Missions* to accept all races, my requests were reinforced by the costly actions of the church members to do it. The same was true of women in ministry, of missions to the homeless, of the acceptance of gays, of action on world hunger, of lay leadership, and it all was undergirded with deep spirituality.

I was not a voice crying in the wilderness, but one whose home church led the way, even at the expense of being "dis-fellowshipped" from all Southern Baptist organizations: the association, the state convention, and the SBC.

If the church would take such stands with the threat of bombings and even of disappearing through loss of members and the heavy debts of new buildings, could I not do the same?

But the church survived after losing more than half its membership and in the process attracted some of the most gifted of Christians, providing leadership for countless other churches.

Since the pastorate of John Nichol, the church has ordained more than fifty ministers—men and women, gay and straight—and these now form a diaspora throughout the nation. These ministers not only felt the blessing of the congregation but also have carried to other places the truths and courage they found at Oakhurst.

Oakhurst taught me even more: to trust the process of handling diverse opinions in a loving way, taking the time to hear one another and not say it's "my way or the highway." The church found unique ways of giving voice to dissent.

I'm not saying that it was easy or cheap, but it was loving. As a church there was the realization that there were more than two sides to most issues and each of us was likely to be on different sides of different issues at different times. Oh, we had arguments around these changes, but the one most typical was that we were spending too much of our income on ourselves and not enough on missions.

In the early 1970s I wrote a poem, "It Was Here We Cried," that captures some of this:

It was here we cried —
right here in this old room
that the tears came.
They came flowing free
for some and salty hot;
for others there was only a trickle.
It wasn't they didn't feel;
they just weren't used to crying.

We cried those tears
for friends who couldn't understand,
for loved ones who had to leave,
for some whose span had ended.
Those tears,
they hallowed this old room.

We cried those tears
for the joy of new discovery,
for a thought so clearly said
that it took no time to think it.

We cried those tears
for the love we felt for each other,
for the warming touch of friendship,
for a hug so strong
it took the place of a thousand words.

We cried those tears
for the frustration of dreams we didn't have,
for painful vacant nights,
for the strain of visions
so bleak that time stood still.

We cried those tears
for the joy of full surrender,
for the thrill of giving ourselves
to a call so loud and clear
that all others seemed but whispers

Yes, we cried those tears
for love, for death, for challenge,
for friends, for hurts, for celebration.
Those tears,
they hallowed this old room,
and we aren't through crying yet.

I appreciate a quote from *Sojourner* Editor Jim Wallis about the community of faith: "Whenever Jesus says come and follow him, he is saying: I'd like to invite you to join my community. I'd like you to pick up your life, to pack up your bags and come share your life with us. Come join us, come experience the new kind of security that we have found by trusting God together. You'll find people very much like yourselves, people with the same fears, problems, and history, but people who want to learn a new way of living together, friends who will take you by the hand, and together, will be led with you to a new place. Come and live among us and learn what the new order is all about."

Once a church member called me "the gentle rebel." Stubborn might have been a more accurate adjective, but I accepted the remark as a compliment, as I knew it was intended. I want to enlarge the thought here by putting it this way: I am forever grateful for the opportunity to serve among all the stubborn, gentle rebels of Oakhurst Baptist Church.

Chapter 13

BAPTISTS TODAY

In the twenty-third year of my being director of editorial services at the Home Mission Board I had to deal with an unease that was an unfamiliar emotion for me. I shared with Nell on occasion after occasion how a growing unhappiness was filling my heart, and she understood my grief.

The joy I had always found in my work no longer existed. I saw that I would soon have to leave my position at the agency. No longer would I be toiling with the incredibly talented associates with whom I had worked over the nearly two and a half decades, associates whose creativity had placed our work in the magazine, in books, in photography, in news, and in other areas among the best being produced anywhere within the vast Southern Baptist Convention in my opinion.

Quite often I received the credit, but my associates deserved the credit for they were the driving force behind it all. I never had to "push" them. They pushed me.

One associate, who had left for a top position elsewhere, told me, "As I look back over my long career, the three years in the department were the best of all the years. Why? I did my best work because the standards all were setting demanded it."

Creativity seemed always at its peak. I guess one proof of this was that when someone left it was for an outstanding position elsewhere or to seek an advanced degree, and all I could do was to offer my blessing and thanks.

My unhappiness led Nell and me to explore other options, such as selling our debt-free house and using the money for a down payment on a weekly newspaper. We even spent weekends checking out small towns, often wondering how our open views would be tolerated and if we could tolerate their views.

I would be fifty-nine in February 1982 and Nell fifty-seven—too young for retirement. Our four children were now established in their professions.

The problem? Fundamentalists or conservatives had elected their candidates for SBC president the last three years, and the leadership at the agency was identifying with them. More than once I was asked by a top executive, as he pointed at a magazine article, "What's that got to do with missions?"

I often tried to explain that it was part of the context in which mission work was done and we needed to be informed, or it was what our missionaries and church leaders faced every day.

Like the dropping of a heavy chain came the news that we were to draft a written editorial policy. I knew in my heart I would no longer have the freedom to be the editor I had been since 1960.

In October that year the phone in my office rang. The caller was Larry McSwain, a friend from Southern Baptist Theological Seminary. After a time of greeting, he told me that a group of moderate Southern Baptist leaders who had supported candidates in opposition to the fundamentalists had met the night before in Louisville, Kentucky.

Many moderates throughout the nation had expressed the need for a national newspaper to counterbalance the propaganda and bogus charges leveled against denominational employees, seminary faculty, and long-time SBC leaders. The moderate group unanimously agreed that it was time to start the publication to rally those who supported a moderate candidate for president of the SBC.

Led by pastors Kenneth Chaffin and Cecil Sherman, who had gained a national reputation for their leadership of moderates, the group discussed the when, where, and how of the start of such a publication. Proving it is difficult to keeps secrets within a denomination, someone mentioned that I was dissatisfied with the direction in which the HMB was moving under its present leadership and suggested I be contacted.

McSwain went into detail over their discussions, and finally asked if I would be interested. I think Larry was surprised when with a short pause

I said, "Yes, I'm interested." I told him I would need some time to process the information, especially with Nell and close friends.

Along with other journalists, we had seen the need for and had nurtured a dream to create a national newspaper. The news vacuum was usually a topic of conversation at most national gatherings. During the years the void had been partially filled by the influx of trained journalists and the growing leadership of Baptist Press at the SBC executive committee in Nashville that had established bureaus in significant places all connected by a teletype wire service.

In fact, my office had been one of the first bureaus created. The Washington Bureau had gained credentials to the White House news conferences. Baptist Press, however, was not in the position to be the advocate for moderates and always to answer bogus charges.

The election of the SBC president was crucial because he was given the power to appoint the members of the Committee on Committees, which appointed members of the board of directors for all institutions. Committee members served limited terms, but in time with repeated elections of fundamentalists, conservatives would control all SBC institutions. We were already seeing the moderate vote declining each year.

Nell and our friends were excited, concerned, and understanding of my decision. Nell especially knew we were stepping into deep waters with the risks involved, and none of our family members raised objections after we answered their questions.

Later I called Larry back with a tentative yes, and he said the group also wanted me to write out a proposal for the publication, including when we might start and how much money would be needed initially. We met at the Atlanta airport the day after Thanksgiving, and I presented my proposal of an autonomous national newspaper with a vision of establishing a publication with a future.

They asked many questions, especially concerned about political issues, but I was firm in asking for editorial freedom, proposing the paper would be a non-profit organization owned by a board of directors who would have the power of hiring and firing the editor. The editor would employ other staff as needed. We reached an agreement and set a date for the announcement.

The group would raise the $45,000 I asked for by January, and I would announce my early retirement in February. However, a pastor who was raising some of the money but had not attended the airport meeting made an early public announcement of our intentions. Fearful that a distorted version would spread, I announced in December that I would start a national publication with the first issue dated April 1983.

As when Mother and Daddy had faced his firing at the newspaper by moving to Zion, Nell and I turned to Oakhurst Baptist Church. The difference was that theirs was a time of despair, while ours was a dream-filled hope.

Independent Baptist paper planned

By Jim Galloway
Staff Writer

One of the most prominent journalists within the Southern Baptist Convention is resigning to start the first independent, issues-oriented publication aimed at Southern Baptist leaders across the nation.

After 23 years as editor of Missions/USA, the national publication of the Southern Baptist Home Mission Board in Atlanta, Walker Knight said in an interview this week that currently he is looking for financial support to start the monthly publication.

The non-profit newspaper, which Knight hopes to start on a shoestring and $100,000 a year, would operate at first out of the basement of the Oakhurst Baptist Church in Decatur.

In the 1960s, Knight attracted attention from Southern Baptists as a strong advocate of desegregation, an issue that threatened to rip the denomination apart.

Ironically, his hoped-for national Baptist newspaper will be largely devoted to covering the biggest split among Baptists since then — the five-year battle for control of the denomination between moderates and fundamentalists.

See KNIGHT, Page 6-B

DWIGHT ROSS JR./Staff

Knight plans to start an independent monthly publication.

The Atlanta Journal Weekend, December 11, 1982

Missions had become central to how Oakhurst understood its purpose and identity, seeking to use fully the actual and potential gifts of members for ministry in the church, the community, and the world. They sought the leadership of the Holy Spirit in usual and unusual ways, primarily using mission groups formed through a unique process borrowed from the Church of the Savior in Washington, D. C., known as "sounding the call."

Pastors did not need to lead so much as equip the laity. If a member sensed a call from God to be on mission in a particular area and found that no existing mission group or regular church committee existed through which this call could be explored, that person could sound a call at a worship period for the formation of a new mission group.

Before the person was given time at a worship service, he or she was asked to meet with the missions committee, the pastor, and the church council, not for them to say yes or no to the idea but to help clarify the vision. The congregation took the position that only God's Spirit held the veto power. The church describes the process in the following way to its members:

A person sounding a call must answer three questions affirmatively:

1. Is the call incredibly good news to you? God does not call us to do things out of a sense of guilt or dread. No major undertaking should be started without a sense that it is good news.
2. Is the call almost impossible to accomplish? God does not call us to small or simple tasks and does not leave us to our own strengths. The vision of what God is calling us to must be worthy of the Kingdom.
3. Is there a good chance that you will fail? We remember God's love and grace are constant, regardless of the outcome or success. Our responsibility is to be faithful to our perception of God's call.

The church made no promise of financial aid or to rescue the mission if it were failing. It was understood that the Spirit's leading may be saying now is not the time for your vision to take shape. Consequently, many calls have been made and failed to continue. Groups have failed for lack of a "stack pole" leader, and others for the need of members to hear the call as good news.

In this climate and with this understanding, my wife and I sounded the call near the close of a worship service in early 1983 for the starting of a national, autonomous publication, one that would serve as a voice for moderates in the SBC but also one that would hold the promise of life beyond the current struggle within the denomination.

We answered, "Yes" to the three questions. I told the church of my dream of a national publication—and that others saw the need for such a publication that would counter the misinformation being spread by fundamentalists. We explained the backing of outstanding persons among moderate Baptists and their promise to help raise start-up funds, but we expected the publication eventually to be able to stand on its own feet.

Our call was for a mission group dedicated to this end. I quoted the passage from Joel 2:28 on young men seeing visions and old men dreaming dreams. More than forty members responded, including journalists and others skilled in publication work. I was overwhelmed by both the number and the quality of the members who responded, so many that

I would find it difficult to find significant things for all to do. They would serve as writers and proofreaders and help with subscriptions and promotional mailings and other tasks.

However, in the group was Susan Taylor, a fairly new member at Oakhurst. While studying for her degree at Southern Seminary she had worked at the *Western Recorder*. She had come to Atlanta hoping to find employment with *SEEDS*, an award-winning magazine devoted to world hunger that had been started at Oakhurst. *SEEDS* occupied offices on the fourth floor of the old education building no longer needed by the church.

SEEDS was fully staffed, so Susan had become the public relations director at a local hospital. I found she was open to filling the position of associate editor of the proposed magazine, but all we could offer at the time was a half-time position. After pondering the offer for a few days and convincing her parents why she was leaving a full-time position for a publication that had not published its first issue, she accepted.

I knew I would need an experienced assistant on whom I could depend, and Susan was paid half time but worked almost full time. I also knew we would sink or swim on finances. I had taken a salary at this new publication without any fringe benefits at half what was paid to me by the Home Mission Board.

Nell had agreed to keep her secretarial position, and we accepted the fact that we would have to stay in the house with its low maintenance. I realized that the $45,000 start-up funds promised by the moderate group was shaky, but whatever they raised might give us the months we needed before we could gain subscribers. The moderates did secure for us a mailing list of 30,000 persons, mostly pastors and lay leaders.

The Oakhurst volunteers were not the only ones to offer their services. In a brainstorming session, Jim Newton had proposed the name everyone liked: *SBC Today*. Karen Mitchel, an artist, offered to do our monthly paste-ups (used in pre-computer days). Lynn Donham, an accomplished designer, created our format. Hettie Johnson, a retired HMB accountant, offered to keep our books. Other professionals throughout the nation let us know that they would write, draw, take photos, and perform other tasks.

Oakhurst, having lost hundreds of members, had leased its new buildings to Southern Bell and had dedicated the income primarily for missions. The church members said they would keep one third of the lease money for upkeep of the older buildings and distribute the rest for missions. The church gave us an initial $5,000 with which we bought a typesetter, and the church provided office space with utilities on the second floor. Oakhurst also later granted us $3,600 more.

Within two months we were prepared for the first issue, and it was mailed in April 1983. Susan and I told each other, "Well, we have produced one issue, even if we never produce another."

We knew it was a high mountain we were climbing, but we were determined to climb it or exhaust ourselves in trying. It's hard to describe the achievement of putting a proper newspaper together with all the various elements in place without messing up in too many places. The big challenge was moving from a Home Mission Board staff of sixteen to only

Gentle But Courageous 'Crusader' Starts National Paper For Baptists

By Rachel Gill, Southern Baptist Home Mission Board

"I never thought of myself as crusading. I thought of myself as deciding what was the right thing to do."

With this simple, forthright statement, Walker Knight described his past 25 years as director of the Home Mission Board's Editorial Department and editor of *Missions USA*, formerly known as *Home Missions Magazine*.

He recalled: "It was at Training Union Week at Ridgecrest in 1942 that I made the decision for full-time Christian vocation, thinking that it would be the pastorate because I had never seen religion and journalism mixed very well.

"OSCAR JOHNSON was the preacher. I remember he preached on the beatitude, 'Blessed are those who hunger and thirst after righteousness for they shall be filled.' Modern translations say something like, 'Blessed are those that desire for right to prevail.'

"I hadn't thought about it much until recently, but that has been characteristic of my ministry -- wanting that kind of thing -- the right to prevail."

THOUSANDS of people all over the Southern Baptist Convention are grateful.

The firm, loving voice of this keen-eyed Kentuckian challenged the convention's laissez-faire attitude about race during the violent struggles of the 60's.

His editorials made many think of him as a crusader -- a term he disavows.

Dr. Knight went to the Home Mission Board in 1959 well prepared for demands of a convention-wide publication.

HIS FATHER, managing editor of his hometown's morning and evening papers, gave Dr. Knight his first writing job, during his senior year in high school.

Bouts with alcoholism kept his father constantly in trouble with the paper's management. In 1942, overwhelmed with his sickness and responsibilities, his father simply disappeared.

Oldest of nine children, young Walker became his mother's mainstay, taking on financial responsibility for the family.

In 1943 he joined the Army Air Corps. Radio school took him to Texas where he made two major decisions.

He met Nell Moseley at a Baptist Training Union social and married her. And he decided to attend Baylor University to prepare for the pastorate.

While in service he wrestled with his call to a full-time Christian vocation and his love for journalism. He resolved the problem by taking a double major in journalism and Bible.

AFTER GRADUATION from Baylor and a stint at editing a small town weekly, Dr. Knight became associate editor of *The Baptist Standard*, state paper for Texas Baptist Convention.

In 1959 the Home Mission Board made him director of its Editorial Department where his policies on race soon put him in conflict with administration.

But he had the reporter's drive to uncover the truth. "If it's the truth of the Bible or the truth of an event or the truth within society, it (truth) must be ac-curately and truthfully presented."

In order to do this, he withstood pressure from within and without the board, but he never took the reader's criticism personally.

"I DON'T think reactions I got from people out in the convention ever really got to me. We all have brothers and relatives struggling with these kinds of questions, and you don't cut off communication just because they have a different view than you do," Dr. Knight stated.

It was this kind of attitude that kept Dr. Knight open to truth wherever he found it.

It is this same outlook that pushes him into a new venture after 23 years as *Home Missions* award-winning editor.

Amid anguished cries of his co-workers, he announced his decision to become editor of a new magazine.

SBC TODAY will be a continuation of Dr. Knight's editorial policy, a publication which will inform readers on current issues and give them a chance to express themselves.

He feels that one of the greatest dangers we have now is that people have little respect for each other's ideas.

He sees *SBC Today* as a "vehi-

DR. AND MRS. Knight look over the premier issue of *SBC Today* with board chairman David Sapp (r), pastor of Chamblee First church.

The Christian Index, May 5, 1983

an editorial assistant, clerk, and volunteers. It was like going back twenty-four years to my first days at the Home Mission Board.

Another challenge was to meet the needs and expectations of enough subscribers and donors for the publication to stand on its own. We needed to demonstrate that we could live past the controversy within the SBC and produce a lasting publication. Our one advantage: We had the mailing list of more than 30,000, which we used all through the first year.

A third challenge was to satisfy those who had helped us at the beginning. Clearly, the moderate political group wanted us to be more combative. We lost some of their funding, but I would not publish articles I could not document, and I have never been one to rant and rave.

In their disappointment the moderates started other publications, including issues of *The Call*. They were single subject publications, and I knew they would not be sustainable because readers by instinct could sense what the content would be. Also, they were not subscription based. I did not feel they were competition, and I shared the subscription list with *The Call* and wished them well.

The twenty-eight-page first issue of *SBC Today* presented a national and international scope in its news reports, including a firsthand report of the annual SBC Christian Life Commission meeting. Susan did most of the reporting and was shocked when one of the officials warned her of dire consequences if she did not treat the Commission well.

We also published a report of the first meeting of what would later become the controversial Southern Baptist Women in Ministry. Elaine Furlow had volunteered as our Washington editor, and her first report dealt with the strength of the New Right. Reporter John Long of Louisville provided an update on an Arkansas fundamentalist's accusation that Professor Dale Moody of Southern Seminary was teaching apostasy.

Other items in that first issue included a story on Baptist involvement with the Shroud of Turin, a fight against pornography by Paul McCommon, extensive foreign reports, a survey of readers asking if they thought the SBC would split, a photographic feature on building a home for a widow, a sermon by John Nichol of Decatur, Ga., reviews of books and movies, the first of a series of humor columns by journalist Roddy Simpson, an editorial cartoon, and the first of a three-part historical look at the glue that holds Baptists together by historian Walter Shurden of Mercer University.

The issue also included a feature unique to Baptist publications, "Politics and Corridor Talk," that dealt with the political process at work in the SBC, with reports of rumors and behind-the-scenes activities, all clearly labeled for what they were.

My first editorial, "Why *SBC Today?*" presented the publication's reason for being. I outlined my experience as a journalist and my thirty-four years with Southern Baptists. I wrote that I was not breaking my relationship with the denomination.

I affirmed the publication's support for missions and my belief in the autonomy of the local church, a regenerate church membership, and "the individual's ability and right to go to the Scriptures without a creedal straitjacket." (The latter was directed at the fundamentalists' rigid view of Scripture.)

I also wrote, "We believe the Scriptures have as much to say on the many justice issues . . . as on the equally important subjects of evangelism, worship, education, and missions." I contended that religious liberty and the separation of church and state followed from these other principles and would be championed.

Reaction crossed the spectrum from elation to despair, to charges of liberalism, slanted news, and a counterpoint to the fundamentalist-sponsored *Southern Baptist Journal.* Nevertheless, the following issues of *SBC Today* did not vary greatly from the categories in the first issue, and before too many months had passed we had secured 4,000 subscribers and significant advertising, as well as additional gifts and pledges.

Susan was still working on a modest salary, and in 1985 she resigned to begin work on her doctorate in economics. Michael Tutterow took her place on a part-time basis. He was a student at Emory's Candler School of Theology and a comrade who had worked in the news section of the HMB editorial department. Others were employed part-time as needed.

In the fall of 1984 a committee of moderate leaders, all dear friends, visited me to ask that I take a stronger position attacking fundamentalists. I told the group I would have difficulty making attacks on individuals without facts, but that I would be willing to publish articles written by moderates as long as accusations could be documented. I told them that I saw my role as primarily that of a journalist and I felt the controversy would be lengthy, which meant that the publication had to meet more extensive needs than just the political battle in order to survive.

In November 1986 Nancy Sehested, the associate minister of youth and missions at Oakhurst, and I joined a group of twenty-two Baptists meeting at the Providence Baptist Church in Charlotte, N.C. They were from various states but had in common a desire to move beyond politics to preserve Baptist "principles, freedoms, and traditions."

The 1986 Southern Baptist Convention had proved to be a watershed defeat for moderates, and now various options were surfacing. Those of us gathered in Charlotte decided to form the Southern Baptist Alliance (SBA), operating within the convention, but "dedicated to the preservation of historic Baptist principles, freedoms and traditions, and the continuance of ministry and mission within the Southern Baptist Convention." The Alliance adopted a covenant stressing seven principles:

1. the freedom of individuals to read and interpret the Scriptures
2. the autonomy of churches
3. cooperation with the larger Christian body
4. the servant role of leadership
5. theological education characterized by open inquiry and responsible scholarship
6. evangelism and social and economic justice
7. a free church in a free state.

The Alliance decided to make simultaneous announcements on February 12, 1987 in Atlanta, Charlotte, and Raleigh. One Atlanta TV station interviewed me about the emergence of the new group with Fred Powell, associate pastor of Atlanta's First Baptist Church, defending the Southern Baptist Convention shift. Pastor Jim Strickland of Heritage Baptist Church in Cartersville, Georgia, announced and explained the formation of the Alliance on another Atlanta station.

Local newspapers reported the news about the Alliance, and *SBC Today* gave it front-page space. We also offered a reduced subscription rate to Alliance members for the first year and provided space for articles written by leaders of the organization.

Oakhurst gained some notoriety when we returned on Wednesday night from the Charlotte meeting to find the church in business session. We explained what had happened in Charlotte and then moved that Oakhurst become the first church to officially join the Southern Baptist Alliance. The motion was approved. We did not know it at the time, but there would always be a strong tie between the two institutions.

SBC Today during my remaining years would continue to reflect that first issue and continue its relationship with what became known as the Alliance of Baptists. On occasion we would publish in book form or find a publisher for one of the series of articles from the paper.

However, in February 1989 I would become sixty-five, and in the fall of 1987 I told the board I would like to retire at that time. I felt this would allow them the time to secure another editor. With a volunteer board of directors, I sensed the time would be needed.

However, one board member recommended Jack Harwell, editor of the *Christian Index* of Georgia, for consideration. Jack had served as a member of our board for a three-year term and had been a strong ally over the years. He was under pressure by fundamentalists to resign, even though he had earned a reputation as an outstanding journalist.

Our board asked if I would contact Jack to discover his interest. He was interested. Jumping ahead of us, the Georgia Baptist Convention Executive Committee, by a narrow vote of 57 to 54 had fired him. Our paper's board acted quickly, and the 1987 March issue of *SBC Today* carried the news of Harwell's acceptance of the editorship, including the announcement that I would retire the next February.

The board also named me publisher. For the rest of the year Jack and I worked together, and then I shifted gears to work one week a month during my sixty-fifth year. I felt I was leaving the publication in capable hands and that it would endure.

NOTE: A 30-year history of *Baptists Today* by Bruce T. Gourley provides additional information. *Baptists Today at 30: Enabling, Recording and Shaping a Baptist Movement* is available at nurturingfaith.info.

Chapter 14

SACRAMENTO

On June 22, 1999, the week the Knights were holding their family reunion in Henderson, Kentucky, my daughter, Nelda Coats of Stone Mountain, Georgia, read an article in *Investor's Business Daily* on "Getting in Touch with Your Roots Online." She immediately went to her computer and entered at www.ancestry.com the name of Cooksey Knight.

To her surprise, up popped one match from the Social Security Death Index for Cooksey Knight, "born 5 June 1902, died May 1975, residence: Sacramento, CA; SSN 403-01-5261 Issued in Kentucky before 1951."

She immediately called me in Tyler, Texas, where we were visiting my wife's mother. I was stunned by the news, for it was the first time we had learned of my father's death, and it came thirty-four years after his leaving on Labor Day weekend of 1942.

I quickly contacted the family in Kentucky, and June Knight, the wife of William Griffin, called the county records office in Sacramento. She learned that Daddy had died May 2, 1975, a pauper. No one claimed the body, and he was buried by the county as a homeless person.

June called the county coroner's office in Sacramento for a copy of the death certificate. From that we learned Daddy had "jumped from the fifth floor of the Ramona Hotel fire escape to the sidewalk below."

The Ramona Hotel in
Sacramento, California

He had lived at the hotel for some time. The certificate stated that he had been a resident of Sacramento for fifteen years and was buried at Camellia Memorial Lawn Cemetery on May 12.

The family discussed bringing the body to be placed in the cemetery where Daddy's parents are buried, but the consensus was not to move the body for a variety of reasons.

Oakhurst Baptist Church in Decatur, Georgia, of which I am a member, had more than 100 families linked by e-mail at the time, and I quickly communicated the news to them. I had shared my story in many small groups over the nearly half century that we had been members.

I had told them and had written how I had often looked for Daddy on the streets of every city I would visit in the United States, with special attention to San Francisco. Mother had received the first year after his leaving a report from the government of his annual earnings in San Francisco.

Once in the 1970s, while keeping a journal, I had used a technique of dialoguing, and I chose to compose a conversation with Daddy. In the process I came to realize I had never cried for him, probably because of anger. I still held anger over his leaving. I had a period of venting the grief I had. I wept for Daddy and for all of us.

Church members and family have been very supportive and informative during the grief process. My present pastor, Lanny Peters, who has also worked through a lot of issues around his father, said, "It's been worth all the struggle. I think that the light of God's love can shine on any dark secret and bring healing. Hope that happens for you and your family in all this. It may not happen quickly, though."

A former pastor and a close friend, John Nichol, on learning of the news wrote of a day of weeping for his father, not realizing the depth of unexpressed emotion. He wrote, "I want to believe that your father's experiences of unrealized aspirations and uncontrolled cravings may have made him one of those especially conscious of and open to the experience of God's relentless pursuing grace. If I never met him and yet feel this great flood of love for him, does it not follow that he was greatly loved and generously cared for by our Heavenly Father?"

On Sunday, August 15, 1999, we arrived at Sacramento after 5 p.m., having driven from San Jose after flying from Atlanta in the morning hours. Joining us for this last leg of the trip were Walker Jr. and his partner Jud McDonald. They drove Nell and me in their '86 Mercury, a grand old car with only 70,000 miles on it. We checked into the Radisson

Hotel near the outskirts of downtown, and, since we had ample daylight remaining, decided to visit the cemetery where Daddy was buried. We drove through residential, industrial, and even barren strips of countryside before reaching the cemetery at 10221 Jackson Road, about twelve miles from downtown.

Its frontage was a five-foot-high heavy metal fence, with two openings through wrought iron gates, bordered by brown stonework. One gate was closed, but the other was open. We took the small paved road that circled through the less than fifty acres of trees and shrubs into a well-kept cemetery.

Beside the gate, like a real estate sign, we were informed that there was a "pre-need office" located in a trailer at the left back corner. More substantial offices were located to its right amid well-landscaped shrubbery and trees, fronted by a five-tiered fountain with water actively spilling over the sides.

To our immediate left was a mausoleum of permanent though modest construction of stone, with the names of the deceased clearly shown on the outside. A larger mausoleum guarded the right back corner, and there was evidence of new graves and the opening of new sections. The entire cemetery was graced by scattered trees, most of which appeared to be about twenty-five years old. We were to find that the cemetery had opened in the late 1960s.

The cemetery listed itself on a plaque at the stone entrance as an endowed facility, evidently meaning perpetual care was assured. All of the markers on the graves were ground-level metal slabs (mostly brass) of modest sizes, ranging from 6x12 inches to 2x4 feet, and the cemetery appeared to have certain sections for veterans and other groups such as Asians.

We searched over most of the area looking for Daddy's marker, but we were to find that the indigents were buried without markers. We took pictures as the light was fading and decided to drive back into town to see if we could find the location of the Ramona Hotel where Daddy had jumped to his death.

The death certificate listed the address as 1007 Sixth Street. We thought it unlikely that the building would still be standing after twenty-four years, but wanted to check it out anyway.

We quickly made our way downtown. The core city has numbered streets running east and west and lettered streets going north and south, with many of the streets designated as one way.

We followed a lettered street that stopped at Sixth Street, and I immediately saw a five-story, white stucco building diagonally to our left with a lighted sign hanging nearly from top to below the second floor spelling out "The Ramona."

A shudder went over my body. Only two of the letters on the sign were burning. A bail bond office occupied the frontage on Sixth Street, with three brightly lighted signs saying basically the same thing: announcing the owners' willingness to go one's bail. We were later to see a number of such bail offices, as we were near the police department and other government structures.

As we glanced around the area, we noticed that most of the other buildings were of recent origin, clear evidence that the downtown had undergone a renaissance. We saw no lights in the upper floors, and a lone worker was on the phone in the bail office. After all, it was Sunday night.

We took photographs from every angle, noting a Korean restaurant inside was closed, and doors at the sides were locked, but we could see a fountain with running water, a tiled floor, and mailboxes. The building was in use.

We paid close attention to the back alley. Metal balconies attached at each of the east corner windows appeared to have been made from what once had been a fire escape. We saw the fifth floor balcony from where Daddy had jumped at 11 a.m. on a Friday.

Monday morning we stopped at the *Sacramento Bee* to check if a news item had been published about Daddy's suicide. A quick look by a very polite researcher revealed no report, and we paid her the required $10.78. She later sent me a letter that she had found nothing else.

We then returned to the cemetery, after calling to make sure it would be worthwhile, and a young African-American clerk looked up the record of where Daddy was buried. Another person was ahead of us, and we were told that as soon as the workman had taken her to find the plot she sought, he would assist us.

When he did not return in about ten minutes, the clerk told us we might go ahead and look ourselves, explaining how the coordinates worked. The grave was Lot 99, Row 27, Section A. We commented to her that it must be in one of the first areas to be used, and she said it was. We surmised that when it was opened the owners were eager to get the city's business at this rather isolated spot.

We walked up row 27 to the fence at the road and found only one plaque there. By this time the workman arrived, carrying a large, black registration book, looking much like a bookkeeper's ledger. He said we were at the correct location, and he placed the book on the ground and opened it to the page where Daddy's name was listed. The word "indigent" had been written slantwise in one square. We also noted that a second person had been buried in the same grave about six months later, a common practice.

This 2000 clipping, used in the Knight family's annual news report, was taken in 1999 and pictures Walker's search and discovery of the gravesite of his daddy in Sacramento. Later, the families placed a marker at the site listing his full name and the dates of his birth and death: 1902-1975. Shown are Walker Jr., Walker, Nell, and Jud McDonald, Walker Jr.'s partner.

There were no markers at the grave or at three other plots along row 27 adjacent to Daddy's grave. After photographing the grave, the registration book, and the cemetery from that angle, we returned to the office to learn what the procedure was for placing markers on graves.

The worker at the newspaper had told us that all back issues were on microfilm at the Central Library downtown. We decided to go there and do some research. For more than three hours we checked issues of the *Bee* and the *Daily Union*, but we found no notice of Daddy's death.

We did check the files on The Ramona and found articles revealing that in late 1978 the hotel was used to house the elderly and indigent until the city government had found it to be in an extremely filthy condition and then condemned and closed it. In 1986 it was refurbished as an office building and serves that purpose today.

We found no record of Daddy in the city directory, and the telephone books were not available to us back to his time in Sacramento because that section of the library was closed. We also went to the nearby police department and discovered that all of its records are purged after ten years.

forgiving our fathers
By Dick Lourie

maybe in a dream: he's in your power
you twist his arm but you're not sure it was
he that stole your money you feel calmer
and you decide to let him go free

or he's the one (as in a dream of mine)
I must pull from the water but I never
knew it or wouldn't have done it until
I saw the street-theater play so close up
I was moved to actions I'd never before taken

maybe for leaving us too often or
forever when we were little maybe
for scaring us with unexpected rage
or making us nervous because there seemed
never to be any rage there at all

for marrying or not marrying our mothers
for divorcing or not divorcing our mothers
and shall we forgive them for their excesses
of warmth or coldness shall we forgive them

for pushing or leaning for shutting doors
for speaking only through layers of cloth
or never speaking or never being silent

in our age or in theirs or in their deaths
saying it to them or not saying it –
if we forgive our fathers what is left

(Excerpt reprinted from "Ghost Radio" © by Dick Lourie by permission of
Hanging Loose Press)

Chapter 15

REDEMPTION

Leaving Sacramento, my heart was heavy with grief. The thought of my daddy in such a blinding state of despair that he deliberately stepped off that fifth floor landing to his death was almost more than I could bear.

The sorrow was heightened by my realization of all that he had missed since deserting his family at the age of forty-one. He never saw a child of his grow into adulthood.

. . . Never laid eyes on his youngest, Jimmy, born after he disappeared.

. . . Never touched the cheek of his first grandchild, carried by Bettye at the time of his leaving.

. . . Never saw my Nell's big smile or met my sons and daughters or knew that he had led me to my life's vocation.

. . . Never came to realize that his love affair with his high school sweetheart had resulted in a large, healthy, happy, industrious clan of individuals who would love to have known him.

I came to believe that his intentions were as good as our mother's to have a strong family life. I ache to think of the shame he must have felt, unable to conquer alcoholism, and I wonder often how much more could have been done for him with proper treatment, given all that's been learned about addiction.

I think, too, that his desires and expectations for me must have been great, and I wonder how much like him I have become.

One of my clearest memories of Daddy pictures him sitting at his old Underwood typewriter, coat off, shirtsleeves rolled partially up, tie pulled open, and chewing on a cigar. He is wearing a headset and speaking into a telephone attached to an accordion-like extension. His task each day at the *Gleaner* was to type the Associated Press news as dictated to him by an AP staffer in Louisville. He could work hard and fast.

My first job had been to sell on the streets of Henderson the newspapers he had created. Later, Daddy hired me to answer the phone following sports events when the curious called to learn the scores, and in my idle times I typed on the big Underwoods or searched out the comics for the approaching month. I loved the trips to the back shop to watch the night shift prepare the morning editions.

Then came the thrill of my life, when he suggested I finish high school by studying at night and working as a cub reporter. True, the experience was not pleasant for either of us. He expected more from me than I could deliver quickly and accurately. And I was almost brought to tears by his criticism, which I'm sure in his mind was simply instruction.

In our trips to work he would tell me of things they did not publish because of the control gamblers held over the county. Over the years I came to believe that he wanted me to follow him as a journalist, that he truly loved it, and that he took me to work with him in my preteen years for that purpose.

I think Daddy hoped that eventually I would experience what he had experienced: the long hours and grueling work and responsibility of producing a newspaper, but more important, the romance of it—the smell of newsprint and ink; the heating of lead until it flowed like water, then quickly hardened into letters, words, and sentences; the grind of the presses—the whole clanking, mechanical miracle of getting out the word.

My first years in military service, traveling from state to state, I continued to scan faces hoping, maybe even expecting, to spot him, almost to the point of obsession. This faded as my life quickly changed.

I am now certain that my love of journalism—my calling—came from my daddy. I think of it as his legacy, and I believe he would have been proud. At times I even think my drive to see things done with integrity, even at the risk of my employment, was a trait of his passed on to me—that he had a stubborn sense of right and wrong when he was sober and working.

I am greatly comforted, still, by the words of my friend and former pastor, John Nichol, when he heard that our family had finally learned the news of Daddy's suicide: "I want to believe that your father's experiences of unrealized aspirations and uncontrolled cravings may have made him one of those especially conscious of, and open to, the experience of God's relentless pursuing grace. If I never met him and yet feel this great flood of love for him, does it not follow that he was greatly loved and generously cared for by our Heavenly Father?"

Amen. It is both a relief and a joy to remember Daddy with love and affection, and even admiration, just as I do Mother.

Over the years we have all marveled at Mother's restraint when talking about Daddy, never berating him and often saying, "If Bennett returned he would expect me to take him back today."

And she never said she wouldn't. Other than when he was drunk, they were very affectionate with each other and with the children. I cannot separate memories of Daddy from memories of Mother.

While corresponding with Mother during military service, I came to see that she had given me more than my physical life. She had freed me to be myself. She had not imposed upon me her expectations. Her love had never demanded, had never smothered, but had set me free.

From the distance of hundreds of miles, sitting in a faded resort hotel hallway, I had a clearer view of our relationship. I now could see that I alone had made the decision to volunteer for the Air Corps, as I had earlier made the decision for a Christian vocation.

If Mother had said anything to me with her silence and the lack of pressure, it was, "Be yourself. Make your own decisions, for you are the one who will have to live with them throughout your life."

She gave me the freedom to fail without rushing to hold me up or to burden me down. As I write this, I realize I might not have been able at nineteen or twenty to verbalize it, but I do remember feeling it and being grateful to her. How she could accomplish all that she did in the midst of her great needs, I shall never know.

Looking back, it is ironic that our dear mother died in 1976, one year after Daddy's suicide and five years after the death of our stepfather, Roy Crenshaw. She died at age seventy-one, without the knowledge of Daddy's death. I am grateful she did not have to share that knowledge and grief.

THE PEACEMAKER

Republishing "The Peacemaker" is long overdue; it is, sadly, as timely, and, God knows, as prophetic today as it was in the Vietnam era.

Our world, in the nearly four decades since Walker first envisioned "peace, like war, is waged," seems to have moved little toward understanding or adopting Christ's message of nonviolent but active resistance to evil.

Thus "The Peacemaker" remains as fresh, as moving, and as insightful today as when first written in 1972 as five opening devotionals for a Florida Woman's Missionary Union annual meeting.

President Jimmy Carter recognized its beauty, wisdom, and truth by quoting a section at the signing of the Israeli-Egyptian peace treaty in March 1979.

Over the years the Baptist Peace Fellowship of North America has kept its core concept—"Peace must be waged"—alive in numerous ways, including as a large poster, a bookmark, and as a small refrigerator magnet. A friend visiting Israel found one in a house there.

"The Peacemaker" has also been used as a litany for worship. Reprinting it here reminds us that Walker's vision continues to live with its message of grace, hope, and shalom as vital and as needed as when first published in the now-sepia pages of the December 1972 *Home Missions* magazine.

—Everett Hullum
Long-time friend and colleague
Retired editor, *Home Missions*

"The Peacemaker" was written in 1972 when I followed the custom of that day in referring to God as masculine, but I have changed the language for this edition to be more inclusive. Also, I have changed the title in the first section from "Shalom . . . a feeling of peace" to "Shalom . . . a psalm of peace," and edited a few words throughout for greater clarity.

—Walker L. Knight

The Weather

Today cloudy, high near 50, low near 36. The chance of rain is near zero through tonight. Wednesday, sunny, high in the 60s. Yesterday—2 p.m. Air quality: 38. Temperature range: 49-36. Details, C2.

The Washington Post

FINAL
22 Pages—4 Sections

Amusements	B16	Financial	D 9	
Classified	C 6	Metro	C 1	
Comics	B15	Obituaries	C 4	
Crossword	B15	Sports	D 1	
Editorials	A20	Style	B 1	
Fed. Diary	C 2	TV-Radio	B14	

102nd Year — No. 112   TUESDAY, MARCH 27, 1979   15c

Sadat and Begin Sign Treaty; Carter Pledges to 'Wage Peace'

30 Years of Strife Officially Ended

By Edward Walsh and Jim Hoagland
Washington Post Staff Writers

The leaders of Israel and Egypt finally concluded a treaty of peace yesterday as President Carter pledged to join them in protecting the agreement against those who oppose it.

President Sadat, President Carter and Prime Minister Begin clasp hands on north lawn of the White House as they complete the signing of a peace treaty between Egypt and Israel.

'It Will Make Him Look Presidential'

By Myra MacPherson
Washington Post Staff Writer

Israelis flock to celebrate signing.   Page A12.
Egyptians show joy and indifference.   Page A12.
Thousands crowd into Lafayette Park.   Page A12.
Treaty text, accompanying documents.   Page A11.

Judge Forbids Magazine To Print H-Bomb Article

By Morton Mintz
Washington Post Staff Writer

See PROGRESSIVE, A8, Col. 1

Michigan State Wins National Basketball Title

Michigan State captured the NCAA basketball championship with a 75-64 victory over Indiana.

Details on Page D1

Johnson Reenacts Slaying

Thought Officer 'Was Going to Kill Me,' Youth Says

By John Feinstein
Washington Post Staff Writer

Terrence Johnson testifies yesterday.

See JOHNSON, A1, Col. 6

Califano Acts to Cut N.C. University Aid Over Bias

By Spencer Rich
Washington Post Staff Writer

See CALIFANO, A2, Col. 1

The Peacemaker

(A Psalm of Peace)
By Walker L. Knight

Shalom . . . a psalm of peace

Terror, raw, unmasked fear twisted their faces
into grotesque shapes,
The fear was so open you could touch it.
You could smell it.
They were frozen by it,
    impotent,
           immobile.
Kneeling, they raised their hands
in prayer-like gestures of mercy. Pleading—
Not for the straw hut so quickly fired.
Not for the few possessions snatched from poverty.
But for life itself, these villagers pled.
And the American stood there tall in his green fatigues
girded with the accouterments of war
casually holding the death machine
now no more than an extension of himself,
playing God with their lives . . .
Or was it with his own life that he played God?
In anguish I cried, "My God, give us peace!"

Shut your stupid mouth," she shouted,
reddening in her anger,
and he moved threateningly closer
while the children cowered in the corner
whimpering, frightened
the adults in their world,
the security of their lives at war
and their world was cracking at the seams.
The meal simmered on the stove;
a faint curl of smoke escaped the neglected food.
As he moved, he staggered,
knocking a cup from the half-set table.

Over the odor of singed food came the whiff of alcohol,
his doorway to another world,
separated from failure beyond shattered dreams
past expectations unrealized.
Frustrations boiled. He struck her in the face.
"My God," in anguish I cried. "Give us peace!"

She held the crying child in listless embrace.
Her strength nearly gone,
and she squatted still in her accustomed way.
The dry stench of hunger was stirred by the wind,
but her face was without emotion.
Too weak for the luxury of hate,
too drained for the appearance of passion,
she simply stared ahead into the African sky.
And the child cried, and cried, and cried,
while his bloated stomach
appeared to beat to an endless plodding time.
His eyes loomed out from sunken sockets
and his skin pulled tight against the bone.
Humankind's wanton rape of land and sea
had birthed an illegitimacy—famine.
In anguish I cried, "My God, give us peace!"

Pig!" she snarled,
and her lips curled to twist the youthful face in hate,
as others joined her in the war of protest.
Her weapon was the word
and she hurled it with the force of passion long denied.
"Pig!" she yelled into the forest of raised clubs.
"Pig!" she screamed into the iron faces.
Firsthand she knew the power of words,
how they could cut and maim,
how they could be driven into the heart all askew,
nearly impossible to remove.
Words were the tools by which her parents had raised her.
Too civilized for switch or club
they had beaten her with the lashing tongue
    a barrier to their love.

She had learned her lessons well.
In her turn she jeered, "PIG-PIG-PIG"
and the young, white helmeted men
struck back with their weapons.
Blood splattered across the trampled sign,
and one could barely discern its message: PEACE NOW.
In anguish, I cried, "My God, give us peace!"

Peace?
What is peace? Is it life prolonged,
calm amid storms,
terror removed,
the absence of pain,
health amid sickness,
silence in an angry room,
an undelivered blow,
directions to nowhere?

Peace?
What is peace? Where shall I look for peace?
History knows but little of the word—
humankind tells its story by recording its wars:
we humans have few words for peace.
In all the fifty centuries of recorded time,
the brief intervals of peace,
all the days and years together,
human beings have known but 300 years of peace—
for only 300 of our 5,000 recorded years
have the battlefields been silent.

Even that record is deceptive,
like smiles that cloak anger, like gifts given to deceive.
What we so easily call peace has been no peace at all.
We were fools to believe such peace could ever endure—
erected as it was upon the backs of slaves,
it was a house built on sand.
Such peace stopped the fighting by men subduing men.
If the record of those years is closely read,
one quickly finds the pages filled with quiet wars,

little undeclared wars, plans for war,
humans waiting for the right moment to start the new war.

Again in my anguish I cried, "God, today, give us peace!"

In angry tones I heard God ask,
"Can my world have peace as long as men and women fight?
Can there be world peace as long as men and women kill
in Vietnam, or Cambodia, or Ireland
[in Iraq or Afghanistan] or
in the United States?"
"Can there be peace in the United States
        if there is no peace in your state?
"Can there be peace in your state
        if there is no peace in your city?
"Can there be peace in your city
        if there is no peace in your house?
"Can there be peace in your house
        if there is no peace in you?"

Wait just a minute, I cried.
You've put the whole world on my back,
and Lord, that's too much of a load. That's unfair.
Peace is needed out there—
out there's where the killing bloodies the ground
out there's where violence destroys life
out there's where the widows cry
        the children go hungry
        the land is ravaged
out there's where men and women anger at each other.
That's where peace must come, Lord.
So I pray, bring us Peace.
Why withhold peace, Lord, why?

No answer came and in the quietness
I slowly began to understand,
just a little, as the meaning soaked in.
Peace does not wait on God,
Peace waits on me.

God does not withhold peace, I do.
Peace—it's internal;
    nothing outside
        not words
        not writings
        not even deeds.
God does not deny peace.
Peace waits on me.
Peace—it's an attitude
    a way of life
    a point of view
    an ordering of existence.
Peace is not knowing how to act,
Peace is how to be.
Peace is existence. My existence.
Peace is being. My being.
Peace is essence. My essence.
Peace is life. My life.

Peace is of me.

"The waters of peace come up like the dew from the ground where even the grains of sand are individual." —Carlyle Marney

Peace does not wait on God.
Peace waits on me.

So into the stormy silence of eternity I changed my cry,
"God, give me me me, give me Peace."
And even more silence filled the room:
    I felt it,
        feared it,
            welcomed it.
In the quietness would reside the truth, I thought.
I listened for the silence, strained to hear the nothing.
At first it came in little snatches,
fighting with the tiny sounds of the night
that chipped away as at a granite wall.

The noises finally faded, and the silence crept in
chasing the shadows of my thoughts
until only the silence seemed there.
But other vibrations filled the void, and I was trapped.
This time the sounds arose from within,
stronger than the others, more threatening.
In the silence I had dropped the veil,
tore it asunder and exposed myself . . . to myself.

My God, my God, have mercy.
Blot out my sins for they obsess me.
They are always before me.
I have always known sin. I was shaped in sin.
Cleanse me, Lord.
Make me to hear joy and gladness.
Blot out my sins.
My spirit dies, my heart is defiled,
and I feel separated from you.
Create in me a clean heart,
renew a right spirit within me.
I am at war within myself—at war, God.
I weep bitter tears for peace   —Psalm 51

There is no peace in silence, I know.
There is no such thing as silence.

"My God, My God, give me peace!"
Into the silent din came a new sound—
    Shalom
            Shalom
                    Shalom!
And in expectancy,
aquiver with the joy of new discovery, I waited.
Like a puppy for its master
Like a bee for spring's first flower
Like a traveler for the oasis
Like a lover for one's beloved, I waited
    and peace flooded my soul.

Joy returned. My spirit soared.
Shalom was mine.

Where once I was far away from God,
now I have been brought very near.
Christ is my way of peace.
He has made peace between me and myself
    between me and God
    between me and my enemies.
We are one family. Walls between us have crumbled.
Christ ended the anger, annulled the dividing lines.
He took us—me and my enemies—
and he made us part of himself.
He fused us to become one, we are new persons.
At last, there is peace—Shalom!
Parts of the same body—our anger has disappeared.
We are friends, friends of God, Sons and Daughters of God.
The feud ended at the cross.
Christ brought the Good News—the news of Shalom.
It came to me though I was far away,
to my enemies, though they were nearer.
Now we all have come to God, our Creator,
with the Spirit's help, because of Christ.

No longer a stranger, no more a foreigner,
I am a member of God's family.
I am a citizen of God's land.
I am a child of God's house.
It is a house of peace and the cornerstone is Christ.
We are joined with him,
parts of a beautiful, growing temple of God.

SHALOM is of me. SHALOM is mine.

I am a maker of peace.
"Blessed are the peacemakers,
for they shall be called the sons of God."
In Christ, God has given me peace,
Christ has given me God's nature,

Christ makes me like himself.
Now I know Christ as the God of peace,
the prince of Peace,
the Christ, my Peace.

There's freedom in that knowledge, my friend,
lilting, unshackled freedom;
soaring, unburdened freedom.
There's assurance in that freedom, my friend,
knowing that the rock will hold,
feeling that it bears my weight.
There's strength in that assurance, my friend,
being garrisoned from within.
No longer at war within myself,
there is calmness in my soul.
The reed blows not in the wind,
the leaf tosses not with the gale,
"My anchor holds." I am at peace within myself.
Contented, strengthened, I stand
prepared for the work Christ gives me.
I am at peace, ready for peace making.
But I must confess,
I'm not too sure what it all means,
this making peace, this Shalom.
I hear it sounded, I feel its comfort.
I need its power—
but I must learn this peace, this Shalom.

One thing I sense intuitively—
It's not just loving peace, wanting peace
    while sitting back and waiting for peace to come.
It's not just hating war, despising war
    while sitting back and waiting for war to end.

Peace has one thing in common with its enemy,
    with the fiend it battles, with war.
Peace is active, not passive
Peace is doing, not waiting
Peace is aggressive—attacking.

Peace plans its strategy and encircles the enemy.
Peace marshals its forces and storms the gates.
Peace gathers its weapons and pierces the defense.

Peace, like war, is waged.

But Christ has turned it all around:
the weapons of peace
    are love, joy, goodness, long-suffering
the arms of peace
    are justice, truth, patience, prayer,
the strategy of peace
    brings safety, well-being, happiness,
the forces of peace
    are the children of God.
Yes, Christ has turned it all around:
I am to love my enemy.
I am to do good to those who despise me
I am to turn the other cheek.

The peacemaker intrudes—
The peacemaker is salt, attacking to save.
The peacemaker is leaven, penetrating to quicken.
The peacemaker is light, shining to illumine.
"Jesus called it striking with the other cheek,
capturing a person in the trap of the second mile." —J.P. Allen

That is waging peace, that is making peace.

"God's plan of making peace doesn't just bring
outward settlement between evil people.
God creates persons of good will." —Clarence Jordan

God makes peacemakers.

"We peacemakers are agents of the Kingdom,
enlisting the kingdoms of this world
into the Kingdom of our Lord. —Revelation 11:15

Away then with violence,
    Christ's kingdom is one of peace.
Away then with force,
    God's children endure injustice.
Away then with arrogance,
    peacemakers suffer quietly.
Away then with hate,
Christ's sisters and brothers never break fellowship.
As peacemakers we seek to overcome evil with good.
We meet the wicked and in our agony at their accusations,
    in our pain at their hands,
we lift the tree upon which peace was nailed.
As peacemakers we carry this word:
Through what God's son did,
God cleared a path for everything to come to God.
Christ's death on the cross made peace with the Divine.
This, stunningly, included our enemies,
separated by evil, now brought back as friends.

"Christ brought us into the presence of God,
and we stand before God with nothing against us.
Only one condition, we fully believe the Truth,
standing in it steadfast and firm, strong in the Lord,
convinced of the Good News that Jesus died for us.
Never shifting from trusting him to save us.
This is the news of the peace we wage over the world,
that Christ in our hearts is our only hope of glory.
So everywhere we go we talk about Christ
to all who will listen, warning them and teaching them
as well as we know how. We want to be able to present each one to
God, perfect because of what Christ has done for each of us.
This is our work, and we can do it only because
Christ's mighty energy is at work within us."
    —Paraphrase of Colossians 1:20-29

We are reconcilers. We are peacemakers.

At peace with others

I am black man,
born in slavery, nurtured in neglect.
I am 50 years old and still called "boy."
I am "granny" when I have no grandchildren.
I am "darky" when my back is turned.
"Mean" … "Lowdown" … "Evil" … "Lazy"
These words bite into me.
Your children point at me and call me "him."
Your wife calls me "that one."
You call me "nigger."
And I wonder who I am.
I am 20 million from 20
who came first to this land 350 years ago.
I braved Jamestown winters and Plymouth snows
with Christians who believed
no other Christian should be held in bondage.
But such ideals proved fragile
beneath the weight of cotton blossoms,
and I became worth more as a slave
than as an object of Christian brotherhood.
The legacy and prejudice of my slavehood live on.
I am black man—*searching for peace.*

I am brown man,
American because I was born here,
Texan because I was born in Texas, and
Mexican—because no one will let me forget it.
Anglos tell me how they love
Mexican food. Tequila. Bull fights.
Me, I like professional football.
In Texas, I'm Mexican
In Miami, I'm Cuban
In New York, I'm Puerto Rican.
But everywhere, I'm uneducated "Pedro"—
victimized by segregation, harassed by placards shouting
"Be American: Speak English."

I'm often low man on the ladder of life,
unappreciated, overlooked, even unknown.
In the West I gave America its cowboy: spurs, boots, chaps and hat
are mine. The lore of the cattle country is mine.
Words like rodeo and lariat and adobe are mine.
But I am cheap labor—
the migrant trucked across the land,
the maid, the garbage collector, the yardman.
I am brown man—*searching for peace.*

I am red man—
still the government's ward,
squeezed in a vise between the cultures,
lured by promises of plenty into empty self denial.
I am red man—
red for blood spilled in greed,
red for the blush of the broken deed
red for the anger bottled inside
red for the debt that left no pride.
I am red man—You call me
savage, squaw man, firewater thief,
stoic, placid. But never Chief.
Bought off with trinkets; driven off with guns
Force marched and herded like cattle in runs.
I am red man—*and I search for peace.*

I am woman.
I live in a male-dominated world—
Black man, red man, brown man, indeed!
You were speaking of woman, too.
How do you think we will plead?
I am woman, always a lady, never a person.
My role is fixed, and I am fitted into the mold
by the time I'm six.
Boys won't like you if—
    if you're too smart
    if you're too strong
    if you're too ambitious
if you want to be anything other than wife or mother.

I am woman, a sex object, a centerfold,
a non-person without an identity of my own.
I'm known by the men in my life,
I've even lost my name.
I'm paid less, passed over more, given jobs as helpers—
I am nurse to doctors, secretary to bosses, assistant to all.
Without husband or children I'm pitied
"Old maid"—"unfulfilled."
I am woman—*much in need of peace.*

Wait a minute! Where does that leave me?
I'm neither black nor brown—neither red nor female.
I'm white, man, and I've got problems, too,
not the least of which are you.
I've paid the price of sweat and toil for all I've got—
and now I'd like to have a little PEACE—
A little of that "at-ease-in-Zion"
give me some of that "Shalom"
        you throw about so easily;
Shalom to you, Buddy—
After I've put in my eight hours, fought that traffic,
listened to the latest about the kids, fixed the leaking faucet,
I've just about had it.
You still want me to take another look at Peace?
You think I've missed Shalom altogether.
What did you expect me to find?
Love?
I should think about love first . . . ?
It is hard for me not to think the old ways of love.
Love has always been an emotion,
a feeling, a fondness for someone known.
Now you ask me to believe God's love embraces all?
Including, God forbid, the ugly, the corrupt, the cruel?
Haters and murderers? The Lost?
And God commands me to include them too?
To love even my enemy?
But love of my enemy cannot be emotion or feeling,
for commands do not suddenly, mesmerically,
change hate to love.

Ah, here's the insight: The clue to understanding
God's love, the breakthrough I need comes
in personification of God's Word.
The Lord God spoke.
Worlds were created.
Light splashed over darkness.
And the stillness was broken by the breath of life.

God's Word.
Not letters strung together.
God's Word
    IS
Jesus Christ.
And God's love, revealed in Christ's life,
was not emotion. But stooping, heedless self-giving,
aimed straight at benefiting me.

God's love—I can now understand—
seeks until it finds entrance,
    mends what is broken,
    purifies what is corrupt,
    releases what is bound,
    redeems what is lost.
God's love shows itself in action.

Likewise my love must become a design
chiseled in the mind to produce a pattern of response,
a way of giving myself.
Love shows itself as I serve another.
This is the new, fulfilled meaning of agape: God's love.
Like a gem sparkling in the light
Shalom now captures my attention,
and invites closer inspection—
for this is no simple greeting of peace,
no quick, automatic word for friends,
no carelessly dropped salutation.

Shalom—I had missed its meaning, too,
for I had thought too long in easy, simple ways.
I had missed its depth,
    for it is as deep as the nature of God.
I had missed its breath,
    for it is as wide as the nature of humankind.
I had missed its length,
    for it is as long as the span of Divine time.
Shalom, my friend,
    conveys my desire for your good health.
Shalom, my friend,
    conveys my desire for your sound strength.
Shalom, my friend,
    conveys my desire for your well being.
Within this word, my friend, is my desire
for your happiness.
In Shalom I wish for you the best, and more—
I commit my love to you, the agape of my soul.

Peace is none other than an offspring of love,
engendered by God and nurtured in God's bosom.
Peace is the issue of God.
Peace, like true love, like the gift of God that it is,
reaches beyond friends, beyond family . . .
peace reaches out, out,
to embrace the enemy herself, himself, ourselves.
What God does in me, and for me,
is done so that God might do things through me
    for others.

At peace with God, secure in God's concern,
I am free to wage peace,
I am a complete person, no longer at war within myself.
In the wholeness of Christ
I can do what peace demands.
No matter if you are black or brown,
red or yellow, male or female
I can now love you, my brother, you, my sister.
Shalom, my friend.

At peace with creation

I saw my world from outside,
a view of the spinning spaceship
rolling like a milky bowling ball
down the black alley of space.

Jarring white-capped peaks broke the silence
and called to me in loneliness.
They spoke of creation's agony and pain.
I heard the speech of gutted valleys
when the drip of days filled such cups to overflowing and
flooded out these ways.
I heard the whisper of hanging shroud
a softly told tale of stranger vapors,
of liquid rock, freezing into these tortured vales.
I heard the jagged rock and eaten stone
make their fierce witness of the years.
They cried in misery at divinity's toss
of forming sphere into cooling midnight bier.
I read the centuries' storied history—
how hotter inner fires in convulsions
pressed this stone toward the heights
and finally left these whitened spires exposed.

I saw the cooling volcanoes burst,
these bubbles of the sphere.
They spilled out and spewed,
raced hot and raw, burned slow and black
as they built the land, running to the sea,
filling in the cracks, burning down the slopes,
nothing to hold them back.
I saw the tree and heavy fruit,
the sea and swimming fish.
I saw the bees and soaring birds
the animals and the land.

And then God said, Let us make man
and woman in our image, after our likeness:
and let my people have dominion over . . . all the earth.
So God created man and woman and God blessed them,
and God said, "Be fruitful and multiply
replenish the earth and subdue it."
God saw everything . . . *and behold it was very good.*

And in it all, over it all—I saw God's images.
The spark was struck, the flame was lit,
the fire danced in their eyes: Power was in their grasp.
As the cold crept closer the flame was warmth,
As the darkness pressed in the flame was light,
As the hunger gnawed away the flame was cooking fire.
Around the fire's flickering fingers,
around its heat and light, the family gathered.
In its white heat, its yellow flames, its blue darting shadows,
even in its ashen coals, I glimpsed the future—
    the city was foretold.
I saw the day when the pendulum would swing,
when time itself would serve these humans,
when this huddled band of threatened men and women,
so awed by fire and rain,
would one day in their billions live throughout the land
and threaten earth herself.

Spring, unfolded: I looked into the treasury of God.
I entered the awakening woods, led by a yellow butterfly.
and we flitted carelessly, hungrily, insatiatingly
from sight to sound to smell.
Brilliant purple petals opened to the sun.
Antenna sepals embraced floating pollen.
Fading dogwood blooms surrendered to tender leaves.

Cascading melody showered down in harmony.
And the musty pine touched the memory of another spring.
But we stopped at the rotting log where busy vermin fed—
some feasted on the wood; others on a lifeless 'possum.
The circle of the woods was complete.
The beginning and the end did meet,
Alpha and Omega now intertwined.
Amid this hopeful bursting scene,
I looked on death, and knew the cycle of life.

"A pebble, a drop of water, and a blade of grass
these are the magic ingredients.
These are all the tools we have;
to destroy them, abuse them,
to interrupt their function, is to destroy ourselves.
Not all the decisions of business,
not all the laws of politics, not all the money of banks,
not all the power of armies can change this fact.
Yet we act as if they could.
The laws of man take priority over the laws of nature;
Wealth is more precious than life.
A pebble, a waterdrop, a blade of grass are not 'things.'
They are phases in a process
that moves as waves of energy through time and space,
We are at best poor voyagers upon this tide." —Don Fabun

I see the land.
I measure its boundaries and define its limits only—
so many yards, so many miles.
But what of us, Lord; where are our limits?
How many of us can one mile hold
and how many come before we explode in war?
Before there is blood upon the land?
Before there is peace for every one?
How many, Lord, how many?

I see the air, I test its heights.
and define its limits only—
so many cubes, so many pounds.

But what of us Lord, where are our limits?
How many of us can one cubic sustain
and how many days before we restrain
our greed? Before there is death
in the air? Before there is health
and care? Before there is peace?
How many, Lord, how many?

I see the sea, I plumb its depths,
and define its limits only—
so many waves, so many fathoms.
But what of man, of woman, Lord, where are our limits?
How many of us can these fish feed,
and how many Lake Erie's will we need
to see before there is famine upon
the land? Before there is peace for every one?
How many, Lord, how many?

I hear Isaiah's cry—
"The earth mourns and withers
the world languishes and withers:
the heavens languish together with the earth.
The earth lies polluted under its inhabitants;
for they have transgressed the laws, violated the statutes,
broken the everlasting covenant.
Therefore a curse devours the earth,
and its inhabitants suffer for their guilt."

You made it, Lord, and called it "good."
You gave it beauty, Lord,
in its strength, in its plenty, in its perfection.
We are subduing it, Lord,
and the garden becomes a desert,
the fig gives way to thistle,
the land lies buried beneath the road—
in blindness we war with your creation.
We are subduing it, Lord, but you call it "greed."

Give us a new vision, Lord,
renew your covenant with us.
All life is yours, all things are blessed by you.
Teach us to bear our burdens,
to respect life, to guard the land,
to clean the air, to purify the sea.
O Creator, renew in us the right spirit,
the strength to resist greed,
the insight into your glory, the ability to share.
We are part of your creation. Keep us from becoming
the cancer that would destroy all life.

"May we be reconciled in Christ, not only to you, Lord,
but to all that you and he have made.
He is Creator, who made heaven and earth,
all were made by Christ for his use and glory.
He was before all else began,
and it is his power that holds all together." —Colossians 2

Give us a new vision, Lord, let us see the new humanity
in Christ, the center of his new creation.
We cry for a new heaven and a new earth,
help us to renew the one you have given us
that all things may become complete in Christ.
"As the rain and snow come down from heaven,
as they stay upon the ground to water the earth,
as they cause the grain to grow and produce the seed
as the seed makes bread for the hungry,
so also is your Word. You send it out,
and it always produces fruit . . .
"We will live in joy and peace.
The mountains and hills, the trees of the field—
all the world around us—will rejoice.
Where once were thorns, fir trees will grow;
where briars grew, the myrtle trees will sprout up.
Your name is ever great, and this miracle
will be an everlasting sign. We will live in peace
with you and with all creation. —Isaiah

At peace with the nations

They marched us off to war, boys,
They marched us off to war.
We sang our songs of war, boys
We sang our songs of war.
We fought the men of war, boys,
We fought the men of war.
We slew the men of war, boys,
We slew the men of war.
We bombed the house in war, boys,
We bombed the house in war.
We dropped the napalm down, boys,
We dropped the napalm down.
We met the child of war, boys,
We met the child of war.
His father died in war, boys,
His father died in war.
We did grow old in war, boys,
We did grow old in war.
We knew not why the war, boys
We knew not why the war.
Why the war, boys?
Why the war?

The news from the war was skimpy—
"Light casualties" the headline said,
"Light?" I said, *"Light? When our son died?"*

It was here we cried—
right here in this old room that the tears came.
They came flowing free for some and salty hot,
for others there was only a trickle.
It wasn't they didn't feel, they just weren't used to crying

We cried those tears
for a life cut off in early bloom
for one who lived well, lived zestfully,
and never gave anyone but his due,
those tears, they hallowed this old room.

We cried those tears
for the ache of birthing pains,
for first steps and first grade,
for early smart and late dumb,
for baseball, track, and football, too,
Those tears, they hallowed this old room.

We cried those tears
for the college years of law and Grace
for the love he found and the place
she found in all our hearts
for plans and hopes never to be.

Those tears, they hallowed this old room
and we aren't through crying yet.

The fire of ours, that tiny flame
that fought with darkness for its life,
grows now beyond our control.
There is swelling of the fire—a pressure from within.
The inner flame heats the shell
until the force begins to build and grow and swell
again and build and heat the outer skin
and still it grows, this swelling cloud of fire
until it threatens all our lives.
How like a dangling sword it hangs about our world
until all of us turn to watch its turn
    immobilized
        transfixed
impaled upon this blade of fear and dread.
It is the weakness of our strength.
It is failure at its peak.

Beneath the dangling sword
the nations rage and snarl and starve
while inept men and women debate the means of peace.
The nations swell and build another pressure from within
as babies cry, wrenched too quickly into a bitter fate
of little food, heavy filth and serious hate.
There's where the killing bloodies the ground.
There's where the violence destroys life,
There's where the widows cry
the children go hungry—the land ravaged.
There's where we anger at each other.

Those bitter cries, that mounting fire,
the coming stench like vapors from the deep
assail the nations, transcend their borders
and rise to debase the nostrils of our God.
God abhors our wars,
     our hate,
             our violence.
God calls us to climb the violent stairs,
to ascend the heights from which comes that summons.

Ahead of us the answer lay
as we climbed those violent stairs.
We walked that way in our infancy,
as the steps led through the jungle path.
There we huddled in our fear, and in our rage,
all were slain when one of them did sin.

Ahead of us the answer lay
as we climbed those violent stairs,
We walked that way in our early years,
as the steps led through the country side.
There we gathered in our hope,
and in our justice life paid life and eye paid eye
when one of them did sin.

Ahead of us the answer lay
as we climbed those violent stairs.
We walked that way in our maturity,
as the steps led through the village square.
There we gathered to forgive our friend,
and in our selfishness
our love was freely given, but only to him.

Ahead of us the answer lay
as we climbed those violent stairs.
We walked that way in our later years.
as the steps led through the city streets.
There we celebrated our joy,
and in Christ there was love enough to forgive
our friends and enemies alike.

Like a gem sparkling in the light
Shalom captures our attention
for this is no simple greeting of peace,
no quick word for friends,
no carelessly dropped salutation.
Shalom, my friend,
    conveys my desire for your good health.
Shalom, my friend,
    conveys my desire for your sound strength.
Shalom, my friend,
    conveys my desire for your well being.
Within this word, my friend,
    is my desire for your happiness.
In Shalom I wish for you the best and more—
I commit my love to you, the agape of my soul.
It's not just hating war:
    despising war,
    sitting back and waiting for war to end.
It's not just loving peace,
    wanting peace,
    sitting back and waiting for peace to come.
Peace, like war, is waged.

Peace plans its strategy and encircles the enemy.
Peace marshals its forces and storms the gates.
Peace gathers its weapons and pierces the defense.
The weapons of peace
　　are love, joy, goodness, long-suffering.
The arms of peace
　　are truth, honesty, patience, prayer.
The strategy of peace
　　brings safety, welfare, happiness.
The forces of peace
　　are the children of God.

Now Christ has turned it around:
I am to love my enemy.
　　. . . do good to those who hate me.
　　. . . turn the other cheek.
I am salt, so I attack to save.
I am leaven, so I penetrate to quicken.
I am light, so I shine to illumine.

I serve the Prince of Peace.
His ever expanding, peaceful government will never end.
He will rule with perfect fairness and justice
from the throne of his father David.
He will bring true justice and peace
to all the nations of the world.
He has made me a Peacemaker,
and he has given me the ministry of reconciliation.

Shalom, my friend.
Because I love you.

CPSIA information can be obtained
at www.ICGtesting.com
Printed in the USA
EDOW031047270313
1019ED